More Than Movement:

An Introduction to Physical Education

More Than Movement:

An Introduction to Physical Education

JAN FELSHIN, Ed.D.
East Stroudsburg State College
East Stroudsburg, Pennsylvania

Lea & Febiger
Philadelphia
1972

Health Education,
Physical Education, and
Recreation Series

DR. RUTH ABERNATHY, *Ph.D., Editorial Adviser*
Director, School of Physical and Health Education
University of Washington
Seattle, Washington

ISBN 0-8121-0403-X

Library of Congress Catalog Card Number 72-79346

PRINTED IN THE UNITED STATES OF AMERICA

PREFACE

The term "physical education" is an encompassing one. We use it to refer to school programs, to children at play, to joggers in the park, and to the Ohio State-Michigan football game. The literature of physical education ranges from advice about swinging a golf club to information about how viewing a wrestling match increases either the heartbeat or aggressions. The physical educator may actually be a teacher or a coach, a researcher or a scholar, or a physiologist, a psychologist, or a sociologist.

The profession of physical education is characterized by the diversity of its members. There are a multitude of professional organizations, interests, goals, and conceptions of what this field is and should be. Even in educational settings, one finds physical education in administrative alliance with a variety of other disciplines or, sometimes, as an entity that defies categorization, and which stands apart from the logical organization of the institution. Departments of physical education may be organized on the basis of the sex of students and faculty, or as units responsible for different program areas, or according to various perspectives of content.

Somehow, both students entering physical education and long-term members of the profession must find a way to "make sense" out of the realities that exist in this field. The prevailing diversity must be analyzed and understood in such a way that the individual physical educator can understand his relationship to his field. Constructive effort, planning, and decision making depend on this understanding; the alternative is continual "hit-or-miss" progress toward vaguely defined goals.

This book is the outgrowth of an intense commitment to physical education that my colleagues and I share. As we grappled with the problems of professional preparation, curriculum, policy decisions, and programs in physical education and athletics, the need for a cohesive framework for action for ourselves and our students was clear. We developed a common course experience for physical education majors that seeks to explicate a theoretical view of the concerns of this field. Our purpose was to enable all of our students, with their diverse interests and goals, to understand the conceptual relationships that express physical education with reference to both its content and its programs. Hopefully, this process also helps faculty and students to clarify their commitments and assume responsibility for their own continued learning and growth as well as to contribute to the profession.

In accepting the central role of organizing and presenting the content of this course, I assumed the most serious professional obligation of my career. The real success of our effort, however, is least mine; for it is the excellence of the actual "teachers" in translating this theoretical framework into learning experiences that has made this an exciting and significant enterprise. Richard DeSchriver, Barry Green, Betty Lou Murphy, Arne Olson, William J. Penny, Maryanne Schumm, and Barbara Wilke are the men and women who have worked with this course; all possess the finest professional qualifications and commitment. In our structure, I lecture to all the students in the course; the following hour and an additional hour during the week students meet in small groups with their discussion leaders. The faculty involved meet frequently to discuss and clarify concerns with both content and learning, and to share insight into teaching techniques and tools. The final chapter of this book written by Maryanne Schumm deals with the actual learning experiences designed and used with students in our setting.

In order to fulfill the potential contribution of this book to knowledge and understanding, several outstanding individuals were asked to write in areas of their expertise. They are introduced more fully on the following pages, but I would like to acknowledge both my indebtedness and my gratefulness to them. Edrie Ferdun, as always, supported my efforts and provided excellent material as well as continuing insights and critical reading that I have come to depend upon and do not always document. Ellen W. Gerber is a good friend, and I am grateful for her willingness to add her unique historical perspectives to this work. Arne L. Olson graciously found time to compensate for my limitations in the areas he understands so well. Maryanne Schumm frequently shares her creative teaching ideas with us, and I wish there had been sufficient space to include them all. In spite of the demands of his doctoral work and a full teaching schedule, Stephen E. Stone contributed a most illuminating treatment of the coach.

In addition to the contributions prepared specifically for this book, others were very kind to permit me to include their work here. The only previously published materials used are "The Code of Ethics of the Education Profession" and the article "A Personal Philosophy of Physical Education" (*JOHPER*, June, 1970), to which Anthony A. Annarino, Edward H. Kozloff, Betty Lou Murphy, Charles Schmidt, M. Evelyn Triplett, and Paul R. Varnes contributed statements. Both of these have proved to be so useful to our students that I am very grateful to be able to reprint them.

Eleanor Metheny indicated that she was pleased that I had found her historical chart useful in my teaching for so many years, and permitted me to include my modified version of it. Virginia Caruso, Lynne Fitzgerald, Claudia Geyer, Suzanne Hoffman, Henry Kearns, and Lorraine Schwinger were all full-time graduate students in 1971 enrolled in a course that I taught, *Professional Perspectives for Physical Education,* as part of their master's degree program. When the PEPI project solicited the development of concepts of physical education, these students responded as part of their work for that course, and since these have not been disseminated elsewhere, I am delighted to be able to present them here. In addition to some of the sample materials, Maryanne Schumm also permitted me to use a short paper she developed some years ago for use in her classes.

I am grateful to EAPECW for allowing me to use material that Ellen W. Gerber and I originally presented at the 1970 Fall Conference, and which does appear in those *Proceedings*. There is also material here that was prepared and is in use in the Department of Professional Physical Education at East Stroudsburg State College and in dance at Temple University, and I am pleased to be able to use it to amplify the content and framework of this book.

Many individuals contributed to the technical preparation of the manuscript. I appreciated the contribution of Lorraine Schwinger to the bibliographies. Lois Payne was exceedingly patient about the process of hurried typing and retyping, and Frances Ross was continually accommodating in fulfilling heavy typing chores at my convenience.

The fact that this book was to be published by Lea & Febiger was an especially pleasant aspect of its preparation. Edward H. Wickland, Jr., as editor, was extremely conscientious and helpful. Lea & Febiger and I are privileged to have Ruth Abernathy serve as Editorial Adviser. A decade and a half ago, Ruth Abernathy was my doctoral adviser as well, and I have both good "vibrations" and high esteem for her.

This book is, of course, my responsibility. Essentially, I have written it to enhance the process of understanding and developing knowledge about physical education as I have been able to contribute to the refinement of that process at this time. This approach has proved to be an eminently practical and important one for us in our situation as members of the profession and as teachers in a large and effective professional program. In my view, there is no more important task for anyone in physical education than the development and understanding of a cohesive framework of ideas about knowledge and its applications in this field. This book, the discussion statements, the selected bibliographies, the sample teaching materials, and the amplifying readings are offered to you as a source of help in the quest for understanding physical education.

East Stroudsburg, Pennsylvania   JAN FELSHIN

CONTRIBUTORS

Edrie Ferdun is a native Californian who earned degrees at the University of California, Berkeley; UCLA; and the University of Southern California. As Associate Professor and Chairman of the Dance Faculty at Temple University in Philadelphia, she is engaged in the broad demands of dance in a program with a dance major at the baccalaureate, master's and doctoral levels. She dances with *Zero Moving Company,* and is a member of the Executive Committee of the Dance Division of AAHPER. Edrie Ferdun is a talented athlete and gymnast as well as a dancer, and is both interested and well qualified in physical education; it is interesting to note her contributions to both of the AAHPER statements, "This is Physical Education" (1965) and "Designs for Dance" (1968).

Ellen W. Gerber is an outstanding historian in physical education. In addition to articles in JOHPER, *The Physical Educator,* and *Quest,* her book *Innovators and Institutions in Physical Education* (1971) is recognized as a significant contribution to the literature. As an Associate Professor at the University of Massachusetts, Amherst, she is responsible for courses that emphasize the intellectual history of physical education and the conceptual development of the profession. Within a focus on sport, Ellen W. Gerber has edited an important work, *Sport and the Body: A Philosophical Symposium* (1972), and is pursuing specialized study of women in sport.

ARNE L. OLSON is Professor of Professional Physical Education and Dean of the School of Health Sciences and Physical Education at East Stroudsburg State College in Pennsylvania. He is noted for his own research and publications, has served as Research Consultant for AAHPER, and has been responsible for Research Laboratories at Temple University and the University of Oregon. In addition to fulfilling broad administrative and consultant roles, Arne L. Olson finds time to teach both undergraduate and graduate classes, and to defend his unofficial badminton title within his institution.

MARYANNE M. SCHUMM is a noted teacher and coach of archery who serves as a staff member of the National Archery Camp, Teela-Wooket, and whose teams are consistently within the top ten in intercollegiate competition. At East Stroudsburg State College, she is an Assistant Professor and Coordinator of Women's Intercollegiate Athletics, and in addition to activity classes she has taught Introduction to Physical Education for the past six years.

STEPHEN E. STONE is an Instructor of Physical Education at Texas A & M University, College Station, Texas, where he is completing a Ph.D. and specializing in the history and philosophy of sport. Stephen E. Stone coached both football and wrestling for many years in Wilmington, Delaware, and Hazleton, Pennsylvania, and has pursued study of the personal dimensions of the coach-athlete relationship.

CONTENTS

Chapter I

INTRODUCING CONCEPTS AND RELATIONSHIPS

Part of the confusion about what physical education is has resulted from the practice of defining the field according to its functions. In that sense, physical education *is* its programs in schools or colleges; or its activities, such as archery, badminton, and basketball; or the ways it contributes to better health, fitness, socialization, and so on. If function is the organizing basis for a definition of the field, then knowledge and ideas are relevant only when they serve whatever aspect of application is being considered. Ultimately, because physical educators are involved in so many diverse applications, communication about the field is difficult and somewhat unproductive.

The problem seems to be to develop a model of physical education that tells us what the field includes and how its various concerns relate to one another. If we can clarify the focus of physical education and distinguish between content and applications, we should be able to order knowledge so that we can develop insight into the field and our own relationship to it. It is a complex task, however, because applying rational processes is difficult and because we are sometimes impatient with "theorizing" and eager to deal with "useful" information.

The contention here is that knowledge and understanding are the most useful aspects of any field. No matter how dedicated and concerned they may be, the practitioners in a field are severely restricted from making significant contributions if their understanding of what they are trying to do and why it is important is limited. The history of physical education is testimony to the neglect of its own rationality. Questions about what it is, whether it is of any value, and whether or not it ought to be in schools or colleges are continually raised. Each physical educator is confronted with questions like this with reference to his own areas of interest and the field as a whole, and somehow each must learn to understand and be able to discuss the nature of his commitment to physical education.

There are several concepts that express the process of clarifying physical education and serve as assumptions for the development of a theoretical framework. The focus of this chapter is the exposition of the pervasive concepts that are developed throughout the remainder of the book, and the structure of relationships within which these concepts are used and understood. Ultimately, each physical educator develops his own understanding and commitment and is led to a personal framework of theory that he can express, refine, and act upon. It is crucial, however, that this task reflect the finest consideration and judgment if it is to lead to a point of view that is useful as a basis for action and can also accommodate change.

FIELD OF STUDY

The concept of an identified field of study for physical education is still an unfamiliar notion. The profession endured a long time without recognizing the cognitive dissonance in the fact that almost all the other fields represented in colleges and universities were defined easily as "the study of . . ." some specific body of knowledge, and physical education always seemed to be defined with disparate lists of activities or benefits. In fact, in some ways there has been a "conceptual revolution" in physical education.

Physical education emerged in the United States primarily as an effort to serve the health of children in schools, and the assumption of teaching and learning as its characteristic concepts is not surprising. The limitations of this as a theoretical base are obvious; for if physical education is presumed to be the teaching or the learning of activities or skills, or the development of fitness or good human relations as the result of such learning, then it is not a *subject* at all. In other words, if physical education describes only a school process, then it is a *medium* of education. The unfortunate implications of this position are that (1) substantive knowledge is neglected in the effort to study and refine the process, and (2) any medium is only important in relation to the "real" purposes, and in some cases these could be better reached by avenues other than physical education. In that sense, the very defense we provide contains the argument for our elimination in programs.

The field of study as a basic concept for physical education serves to root the concerns of the field in knowledge, and to do so firmly and without reference to the ultimate applications of such knowledge in programs. The field of study defines the focus of physical education in terms of the knowledge with which it is properly concerned, and implies that this focus is unique and worthy of pursuing.

"Field of study" and "body of knowledge" are terms that can be used interchangeably. Sometimes, "academic discipline" is also used to mean the same thing, but others suggest that the term has connotations of clarity of focus, ordering of knowledge, and refinements of modes of inquiry not yet identifiable in physical education. It seems more appropriate in view of this to refer to the field of study or knowledge, but if an academic discipline is thought to imply a scholarly focus on knowl-

edge only then it, too, is an acceptable term. The name "physical education" is not compatible with the whole notion of a discipline since it
implies a professional focus. This has been a continuing problem to
the field, but no adequate resolution has been found. Since "physical
education" refers to both academic majors and activity programs, the
conceptual issue has varying degrees of importance to different groups
of physical educators. Some departments in colleges and universities are
presently distinguishing, at least, between their professional programs,
called "physical education," and their field of study, called such things
as "kinesiology," "human movement," "ergonomics," "sport science," or
"sport theory." Whether or not departmental names are changed, distinctions are also evident between academic majors that reflect an emphasis on the substantive content of the field of study and professional
preparation. These academic majors may reflect diverse assumptions
about the nature of the field of study related to physical education.

At State University College at Brockport, New York, two different
conceptions of the field of study of physical education serve as bases for
academic major programs. Students there can pursue a program of
studies with a focus on "the significance for man of experiences in
selected forms of physical activity" (Jensen, *JOPHER*, September, 1970),
or they can major in "Sport Science" with a focus on "man as he develops
and participates in the social institutions that supply his varied needs and
wants for competitive physio-cognitive behavior" (Whited, *JOPHER*,
May, 1971). In the current outline of graduate curricula of the School
of Physical Education of West Virginia University, Morgantown, the
statement is made that "the portion of reality assumed by physical educators is sport and the scientific analytical study of this phenomenon
provides a body of knowledge (content or subject matter about) which
is indigenous to and uniquely within the domain of physical education."

These examples suggest that the real conceptual revolution has already
occurred; that is, most colleges and universities have accepted that there
is disciplinary content in physical education and that the idea of major
curricula in physical education based only on educational concerns and
processes is untenable. So far, it has been a fairly quiet "revolution,"
and it is surprising to find how extensively it is manifest in contemporary programs of professional preparation whether or not teacher education is separated from an academic major in physical education. We
have come a long way since the statements developed at the University
of California, Los Angeles, in 1957 suggested that there was a body of
knowledge underlying physical education concerned with "the art and
science of human movement."

It is also apparent, however, that if the profession is fairly well agreed
that identifying a body of knowledge is desirable, there are dichotomous
points of view about *what* focus of knowledge is appropriate. Franklin

Henry's statement "Physical Education: An Academic Discipline," that served to clarify the issues less than a decade ago, seems naive today. Definitions are important. Is the "proper focus" of the field of study of physical education "human movement" or is it "sport"? Is dance properly physical education or is it not? Are the criticisms of "human movement theory" as vague, illogical, and abstract well-taken, or is the choice of a focus on "sport theory" simply pretentious and arbitrary? These questions are beginning to divide the profession of physical education today just as the "battle of the systems" of formal gymnastics once did.

The problem is compounded by the fact that the demands of a disciplinary focus for the generation of theoretical models and new knowledge have occupied the attention of many scholars in physical education during the past decade. Even professional activity has centered around the unprecedented growth of associations and conferences devoted to sport sociology, sport psychology, sport history and philosophy, perceptual-motor development, kinesiology, and the like. While the attention of scholars has been diverted to the clarification and expansion of knowledge, the teacher has had to deal with the implications of all this for programs and teaching. This has resulted in a great deal of confusion, and though the notion of a field of study has had an impact on school programs, it has not always been a positive one.

It is not likely that the question of what *the* appropriate focus for knowledge in physical education is will be resolved in the foreseeable future. The Physical Education Division of the American Association for Health, Physical Education and Recreation has prepared a "theoretical perspective" statement, but without truly clear and cohesive insights as well as implied priorities and guidelines for programs, it will probably not solve the problem.

The controversy about the nature of the field of study is a source of excitement and challenge. Our undergraduate and graduate students can truly be our colleagues as we all seek to develop rational perspectives and define both our field and the phenomena with which it is concerned. If dogmatism can be contained and final judgments withheld, conceptual clarification is an exciting enterprise.

On the other hand, we do need definitions in order to approach our task of developing a framework. It must be understood that there are simply some arbitrary aspects presently involved in deciding what is or is not an appropriate focus for the field of study of physical education. At the same time, our use of terminology is necessarily somewhat imprecise. The definition of the focus used here is "the study of man as he engages in gross movement and its forms for their own sake or his own enhancement." This implies the importance of the movement forms of sport, dance, and exercise, but includes movement itself as a process and a generic term as well. This view may not prove to be an enduring one, but it seems premature to accept a restrictive focus, and this view does provide for the possibilities of selective conclusions as a result of broad study.

Perspectives of Knowledge

It is important to develop some ways of ordering the facts and understandings of the field of study. One way to do this is to establish some perspectives of knowledge; that is, ways of dealing with all that is known and identifying those areas in which knowledge is limited.

Movement Can Be Described. In this perspective, movement is considered as a biomechanical and sociocultural phenomenon. The knowledge involved in considering the biomechanical aspects is concerned with such things as how movement occurs in the context of mechanical and physical principles; how movement is produced; how the body is affected and modified by movement and exercise, and what the capacities and limitations of man are in relation to movement. The study of sociocultural aspects would involve understanding the cultural connotations and the social uses of movement and its forms; the values and attitudes that determine our movement, our participation, and our reactions to it; and the role of movement in culture.

Movement Forms Can Be Studied.   Dance and sport and exercise are forms that man has created and finds significant. These forms have persisted and endured throughout recorded history, and there is a great deal to be understood about how they have functioned and been both persistent and dynamic. Sport, dance, and exercise as symbolic forms need to be studied with reference to their own essence, which is not explicated by describing movement only. These forms have sources in play and art and ritual, and these must also be studied and understood.

Experiencing movement forms is a unique perspective of knowledge. The meanings and motivations of man as he pursues sport, dance, and exercise are important aspects of understanding. Why have these forms persisted as a significant aspect of man's activity beyond his survival needs? What is inherent in the experience of forms that explains its significance, and what variables enhance or restrict that meaningfulness?

SCHOOL PROGRAM

If physical education is to transcend its image as a medium of education whose worth lies in its potential enhancement of all and any purposes of the school, the concept of physical education as a school program based on the field of study must be developed. In this view, the field of study is used as the basis for developing purposes for the school program of physical education. The key and crucial concepts of the field of study become the basis for physical education in schools.

At the same time, the concept of the school program of physical education is developed with reference to the nature of the school and based on an analysis of the educational context. The school is a unique social institution, and the variables that define its role are found in sources of knowledge and understanding of society, the functions of education, and how individuals develop and learn.

The school program of physical education, then, depends first on the field of study as a source for deriving purposes, but the selection of purposes depends upon the educational context. Ultimately, the school program and especially statements of purpose express an integrated view of the significance of physical education and its potential contribution to youth.

Actual programs are designed to fulfill the purpose of physical education by providing experiences in movement and its forms that are most likely to help students achieve the selected goals.

PROFESSION

The concept of the teacher in relation to a profession is a basic view. A profession is characterized by its body of technical knowledge, educational requirements, and ethical commitments. The physical education teacher is a person who fulfills ideal roles in relation to students, culture and community, the school, and his own field of study. All of these depend upon his insight into his field of study, the educational context, and into himself as he personally expresses his values, beliefs, and attitudes.

The teacher fulfills his roles as he perceives them. The beliefs and values that a teacher holds, especially those that relate to behavior, learning, personality goals and effects, and the area of knowledge of physical education will determine the method and content of teaching, the image that is projected to all concerned, and the quality of professional contributions.

The teacher, coach, or anyone else who assumes responsibility for affecting others in institutionalized ways must not act in unconscious and unexamined ways. The commitment implied by a profession means that the individual engaged in it has developed and refined his knowledge and understanding and has made the finest effort to apply a cohesive framework in what he does so that potential contributions to human welfare are fulfilled.

APPROACH AND SUMMARY

The pervasive purpose for considering the concepts of a field of study, school program, and profession of physical education is to provide understanding of the domain of study and its applications in teaching and learning. The key processes involved are identifying and clarifying concepts and seeking insight into their logical relationships. Developing an orientation toward a field implies that there is a perspective within which the field is viewed so that, in fact, it does "make sense" and is not just a collection of disparate ideas and concepts. Whenever a frame of reference is established, concepts are identified and analyzed, and relationships among concepts are developed, the general approach must be considered "theoretical." Actual theory-building, however, depends upon sets of propositions that have truth-value that is fixed and are themselves logical constants. In this sense, our present capability is probably limited to the identification and analysis of concepts and the propositions that represent the relationships among them. We can, however, refer to our beliefs as "theories" insofar as they do represent some of the relevant processes.

Because we are seeking to understand physical education and to be able to deal with information, ideas, and orientations to it, a convenient approach might be called a "method of intelligence." Our "data" are all that is known and believed to be true about our concerns. Some of these data are the results of scientific investigation and empirical findings, and some are the results of conjecture and the critical analysis of beliefs and ideas. We must be able to discriminate between the kinds of knowledge with which we deal. To do this, we analyze the sources of our data; that is, we ask where this knowledge came from, why and how it is "known" and documented, and we judge the degree of "truthfulness" that it seems to represent. All data are subject to critical analysis, and insight depends on the accuracy with which it is applied. Our frameworks need to be flexible enough to provide for new knowledge and understanding.

The task of dealing with the varieties of concepts that are the concern of our frame of reference depends on dealing with diverse sources of knowledge. The method of intelligence is used in various ways for our purposes. For convenience, the concepts that we are concerned with might be called "assumptions." Then, no matter whether we are talking about the field of study, programs, or teaching, it is clear that our data are really beliefs that seem acceptable and logical and consistent at the time that they are being expressed. Because "assumption" implies a basic aspect of belief, it is also helpful in encouraging critical insight into the bases of ideas rather than only their actual expression which is sometimes misleading. The identification of assumptions becomes a critical process of examining ideas, statements, and beliefs, whether our own or someone else's. As we seek to identify those assumptions that are crucial or important, they are also subject to evaluation, and their validity depends on where they came from and why they are accepted.

In general, the use of the assumptions we derive and accept is two-fold: (1) we gather and classify assumptions that serve to *explain* phenomena, and (2) we seek to relate assumptions that enable us to make "educated guesses" or to *hypothesize* about future or unknown events. Explaining and predicting events are crucial processes in perceiving, understanding, and behaving. In other words, each person acts on the basis of what he believes to be true and important, and how he perceives the consequences of his behavior. To understand physical education is to be cognizant of all the connotations it has, and to develop a framework of beliefs about what it is, why it is important, and how it should function. Effectiveness in physical education implies another dimension: that of the actual knowledge and the data and their sources.

Although the method of intelligence is a logical process, there are some pervasive approaches involved in our consideration that are not subject to validation. In other words, understanding and frameworks of beliefs and even theories have "starting points" that might be called philosophical. In the physical and natural sciences, empirical knowledge can ultimately become dependable enough to serve as the basis for axiomatic deductive approaches and the development of theory. Philosophy and the humanities, however, depend upon consistent and logical formulations and sets of assumptions that are not always subject to empirical validation. Physical education is a humanistic field in that its focus is clearly on man, and the scope of its concern with man and his movement behavior includes both philosophical orientation and empirical and documented knowledge.

The actual existence and history of physical education influence our point of view about it. In spite of the fact that this name for the field implies an untenable hypothesis, namely that the "physical" can be "educated," it persists. Within the profession of physical education the dissonant concepts of the unitary nature of the human being and the goal of helping people to become "physically educated" are found together. Furthermore, in its obvious emphasis on education, the title of the field serves to foster a conception of its concerns as solely educative. Efforts to change the name of this field have simply not succeeded. At the present time, the most logical usage would indicate that "physical education" be used to refer to the school program. In suggesting such an approach, Brown and Cassidy (1963) contributed to the clarification of the concerns of the field.

The field of study underlying physical education includes knowledge about human movement and its forms when these are pursued by man for their own sake or his enhancement. Traditionally, physical education has been primarily concerned with the movement forms of sport, dance, and exercise, and these are a logical focus of study. The inclusion of dance as part of the field of study does not negate its functions in art, but is based on the recognition of the use of movement as its primary mode and part of its basis as form. Neither sport nor dance is explained by an analysis of the movement behavior involved, and even exercise, which is more directly an outgrowth of movement, cannot be wholly understood on that basis alone. The study of movement forms is extremely important to physical education both conceptually and in relation to programs. It is possible that such study is a crucial element in understanding our existing programs.

Partially because concerns with the body and with play have had historical connotations of "triviality," physical education has consistently had to fight to maintain its position in school programs. Understandably, it sought to justify its existence through rationally documented contributions to education and individuals. Movement experiences do, in fact, contribute to better functioning and effectiveness in many ways, and because these effects *are* more rational than those fostered by participation in sport and dance, they have been emphasized as the basis and nature of physical education. It is not the intent of this book to negate the importance of the rationalized contributions of movement to the human organism; rather, it is to provide a framework within which these and other concerns of physical education can be understood. Knowledge about the field of study should provide a broad base for understanding physical education that simplifies the process of planning programs.

The content of this book is not intended to be definitive; it does, however, provide sufficient insight into relevant knowledge to be useful in both understanding and applying the concepts involved. The framework for dealing with the content is suggested by a model of conceptual relationships. Ultimately, each of us—whether as student, scholar, researcher, teacher, or coach—is responsible for both understanding and cohesive action. Knowledge, beliefs, and frameworks are modified and changed as a result of increased awareness and understanding. Every exposure or relationship to content and theory is an opportunity to refine and develop that knowledge. The following model suggests an orientation and a starting point for that process.

DISCUSSION

Examples of statements which might be used for the purpose of applying the process of identifying assumptions and providing for discussion. Statements here might be used in conjunction with (1) the concept of theory, and (2) the concept of a field of study.

Theory and Critical Evaluation

1. Some things are O.K. in theory, but just don't work that way; if you really want to find out about something, ask the person who's *experienced* it.
2. Being able to "make things work" is great, but what good is it if you don't understand why they work?
3. "My mind is made up—don't confuse me with facts" is said as a joke but it's also true sometimes; that is, if I want to know about something, I just

MORE THAN MOVEMENT: *An Outline of Conceptual Relationships in Physical Education*

Physical education exists as a FIELD OF STUDY, PROGRAMS IN SCHOOLS AND COLLEGES, and a PROFESSION. Knowledge within the field of study is centered around the study of man as he pursues and engages in movement or its forms, either for their own sake or for his own enhancement. Curricula in physical education are programs developed on the basis of the field of study but within the context of education; that is, programs designed in light of knowledge about how education functions in our society and how individuals develop and learn. Presently, the profession of physical education is most concerned with teaching and learning, and is focused on the teacher and coach in their relationships to the field and its contexts.

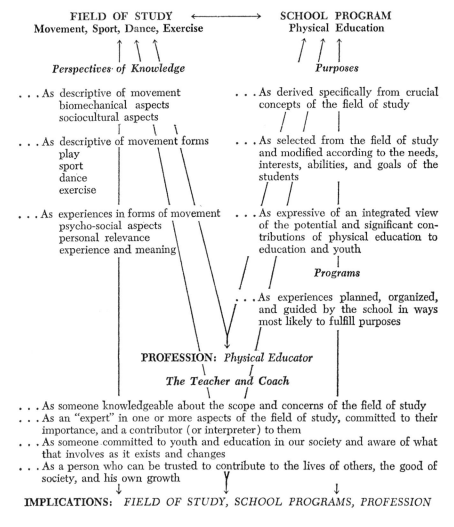

FIELD OF STUDY ⟵⟶ SCHOOL PROGRAM
Movement, Sport, Dance, Exercise — Physical Education

Perspectives of Knowledge — *Purposes*

. . . As descriptive of movement
biomechanical aspects
sociocultural aspects

. . . As derived specifically from crucial concepts of the field of study

. . . As descriptive of movement forms
play
sport
dance
exercise

. . . As selected from the field of study and modified according to the needs, interests, abilities, and goals of the students

. . . As experiences in forms of movement
psycho-social aspects
personal relevance
experience and meaning

. . . As expressive of an integrated view of the potential and significant contributions of physical education to education and youth

Programs

. . . As experiences planned, organized, and guided by the school in ways most likely to fulfill purposes

PROFESSION: *Physical Educator*
The Teacher and Coach

. . . As someone knowledgeable about the scope and concerns of the field of study
. . . As an "expert" in one or more aspects of the field of study, committed to their importance, and a contributor (or interpreter) to them
. . . As someone committed to youth and education in our society and aware of what that involves as it exists and changes
. . . As a person who can be trusted to contribute to the lives of others, the good of society, and his own growth

IMPLICATIONS: *FIELD OF STUDY, SCHOOL PROGRAMS, PROFESSION*

want to be *told* what I need to know—not confused with a lot of other information.

4. What is "theory" anyway—it seems to me that if people can come to different conclusions, then theory is the same as opinion, and there's no way to evaluate it.

5. If two people who are *supposed* to know can disagree, how can I decide whom to believe? I think everyone dealing with the same thing should present the same point of view about it.

6. There are a lot of things I don't agree with, but I don't know how to "prove" something is wrong; I don't even know when things can be argued with facts—usually I just *know*, and that's good enough for me.

7. I don't think anything should be discussed in college or a profession except the *truth*; if it's just a "theory," it shouldn't be presented until its proved.

8. Lots of the people get along without knowing a lot of theory; I think it's a waste of time, and we should spend our time learning how to do things.

9. I don't mind learning things as long as I know what it is I'm supposed to know, but a lot of emphasis on relationships and putting knowledge together isn't necessary and takes a lot of time.

10. Why do we have to spend time talking about what "physical education" is? We already know that or we wouldn't be here.

Field of Study (Body of Knowledge; Academic Discipline)

1. Physical education cannot be considered an academic discipline although it is accepted that the body of knowledge has been defined; it's possible that someday it will be ordered into an academic discipline.

2. People who want to be physical education teachers should be taught about teaching; for instance, in major activity classes, they should learn how to teach and be graded on how well they teach; if there is a field of study, it should be about how skill is developed.

3. If physical education is concerned with human movement, then it's appropriate to study all the ways in which people move, including chewing, digging ditches, and anything else.

4. There really isn't a field of study called "physical education"; it's just psychology, physiology, and bits of other fields.

5. The body of knowledge of physical education centers around the study of human movement in activities which are designed either as "play" or for the purpose of enhancing the organism.

6. The body of knowledge of physical education centers around the study of sport and should involve knowledge relevant to sports and athletic performance.

7. The proper concern of physical education is how the organism can function most effectively; it should include the study of mechanical and physiological effects, how fitness is developed, and the best training methods.

8. Physical education as a field of study is very important and might contribute a great deal of important knowledge to mankind; it should be studied for its own sake, and it would be desirable to have some people who did study it, pursued research, and developed theories.

9. Physical education as a field of study isn't very important—it's mostly concerned with play and other frivolous pastimes and doesn't deserve much attention.

10. The idea that there is any point in studying physical education "for its own sake" is silly; how you use it to earn a living is the important consideration, and I shouldn't have to learn anything that isn't going to be useful to me.

SELECTED BIBLIOGRAPHY

Abernathy, Ruth, and Waltz, Maryann. "Toward a Discipline: First Steps First." *Quest II.* April, 1964, 1-7.
Presents a view of human movement as the approach to identifying the field of inquiry of physical education.

Brown, Camille. "The Structure of Knowledge of Physical Education." *Quest IX.* December, 1967, 53-67.
Discusses areas of study within the body of knowledge; identifies a structure of instruction for human movement based on this knowledge.

————— and Cassidy, Rosalind. *Theory in Physical Education: A Guide to Program Change.* Philadelphia: Lea & Febiger, 1963.
Presents a theoretical framework based on the art and science of human movement with implications for the school program of physical education.

Fraleigh, Warren P. "A Prologue to the Study of Theory Building in Physical Education." *Quest XII.* May, 1969, 26-33.
Discusses the purpose of a theory of physical education and several approaches to theory building.

Henry, Franklin M. "Physical Education: An Academic Discipline." *Anthology of Contemporary Readings: An Introduction to Physical Education.* 2nd ed. Edited by Howard S. Slusher and Aileene S. Lockhart. Dubuque, Iowa: Wm. C. Brown Company, 1970, 277-281.
Compares physical education to other fields of study, outlines appropriate knowledge distinctions, and suggests the development of an academic discipline.

Howell, Maxwell L. "Toward a History of Sport." *Journal of Health, Physical Education and Recreation.* March, 1969, 77.
Discusses the role of the sport historian and the various disciplines which are of concern to him.

Jensen, Judy. "Perspectives Unlimited: A New Undergraduate Physical Education Major." *Journal of Health, Physical Education and Recreation.* September, 1970, 83-84.
Focuses on the study of the significance of movement activities for man.

Kenyon, Gerald S. "On the Conceptualization of Sub-Disciplines Within An Academic Discipline Dealing with Human Movement." *Anthology of Contemporary Readings: An Introduction to Physical Education.* 2nd ed. Edited by Howard S. Slusher and Aileene S. Lockhart. Dubuque, Iowa: Wm. C. Brown Company, 1970, 285-300.
Proposes several sub-disciplines of the study of human movement as a result of an analysis of the field of study in relation to the criteria for a discipline.

Metheny, Eleanor. "Physical Education As an Area of Study and Research." *Quest IX.* December, 1967, 73-78.
Identifies the scope and structure of physical education as an area of study, and deals with an operational definition of physical education.

Nixon, John E. "The Criteria of a Discipline." *Quest IX.* December, 1967, 42-48.
Presents views of various scholars with reference to the criteria of a discipline.

Phenix, Philip H. "The Architectonics of Knowledge." *Quest IX.* December, 1967, 28-41.
Discusses the significance of categorizing knowledge and deciding upon an appropriate classification.

Rarick, G. Lawrence. "The Domain of Physical Education As a Discipline." *Quest IX.* December, 1967, 49-52.
Gives attention to the development of disciplines and the need for a synthesis of knowledge. Defends human movement as a field of study for physical education; identifies the domain of physical education; and suggests a framework for structuring a body of knowledge.

Schwab, Joseph J. "Problems, Topics, and Issues." *Quest IX.* December, 1967, 2-27.
Points out problems in determining the membership and organization of disciplines, identifying the different disciplines, and locating their relationship to one another.

Sheehan, Thomas J. "Sport: The Focal Point of Physical Education." *Quest X.* May, 1968, 59-67.
Advocates the necessity for physical education to justify its existence by using sport as the proper focus for study.

Smith, Nancy W. *Focus On Dance IV: Dance As A Discipline.* Washington, D.C.: American Association for Health, Physical Education and Recreation, 1967.
Expresses a theoretical foundation and body of knowledge revolving around dance as creative movement used for experiencing and expressing.

————. "Movement as an Academic Discipline." *Journal of Health, Physical Education and Recreation.* November-December, 1964, 63-65.
Defends movement as a body of knowledge and stresses the importance of sensorimotor activity in contributing to intellectual development.

Steinhaus, Arthur H. "The Disciplines Underlying a Profession." *Quest IX.* December, 1967, 69-72.
Distinguishes a discipline from a profession and suggests the need for a more diverse body of knowledge to serve the profession.

Ulrich, Celeste and Nixon, John E. *Tones of Theory: A Theoretical Structure for Physical Education—A Tentative Perspective.* Washington, D.C.: American Association for Health, Physical Education, and Recreation, 1972.
Explicates a theoretical perspective for all the concerns of physical education with a central focus on human movement phenomena.

VanderZwagg, Harold. "Sports Concepts." *Journal of Health, Physical Education and Recreation.* March, 1970, 35-36.
Suggests several concepts which should be subjected to philosophical analysis as part of a disciplinary approach to sport.

Whited, Clark V. "Sport Science: The Modern Disciplinary Concept for Physical Education." *Journal of Health, Physical Education and Recreation.* May, 1971, 21-25.
Describes the concept of sport science and a new college physical education program based on this concept.

Chapter II

DESCRIBING MOVEMENT

Any approach to the field of study underlying physical education is somehow concerned with the study of man in motion. "Motion" refers to the action or process of changing position of the body or its parts, and there is a wealth of knowledge about such action that is descriptive in nature. "Movement," however, can be described as both a process and a product. Descriptions based on visual data are usually concerned with the products of motion; that is to say, whenever we talk about movement as it occurs and is perceived in space, we are describing it as an observable phenomenon without reference to time or force. "Angles of release," "positions of the body," "relationships of body segments," and a host of other phrases are descriptive of movement as a result of actions or processes.

Motion as a process is more difficult to describe. Since it is concerned with how movements occur, it depends upon describing phenomena that are not available for direct observation. Insofar as movement is produced by the body, it can be understood only in relation to knowledge about the body as a biomechanical system. Descriptions of movement as process, then, derive from understanding of the human body in relation to how body positions are changed in time and space by the applications of varying degrees of force.

It is through his movement that man primarily copes with the environment. Man's movement is inextricably related to both his structural and functional capacities and limitations, and beyond these, it is affected by the environment. There are laws of physics and mechanics that provide an inviolable context within which movement occurs and can be described. Movement is basic to all of man's functioning, and it is his ability to move that is central to most of his other abilities and achievements. Movement, in turn, affects man.

Because physical education is concerned with the study of man in motion, another appropriate focus for describing movement has to do with the ways in which it is used by man. Movement has discrete existence as both process and product, and it has connotations, or suggestive or associative implications, as well. Because these have developed in the context of communal and human living, they can be termed "socio-cultural" in their orientation.

It is, of course, only particular individuals who move, and movement, therefore, is always personal. A focus on describing movement, however, is based on generalizations about it and is concerned with an abstraction that is the result of separating the qualities of movement from the actual act of moving. For convenience and clarity, the scope of study of movement can be divided into descriptions of its biomechanical and sociocultural aspects.

BIOMECHANICAL ASPECTS OF HUMAN MOVEMENT*

Arne L. Olson

For convenience, the biomechanical aspects of human movement can be divided into separate (but related) areas generally labeled the structural, functional, and mechanical aspects of human movement. This section is divided into brief introductions of these areas with descriptions of the framework of knowledge and some illustrations of how these aspects of human movement are studied. This major breakdown is followed by a section which outlines the limitations and/or advantages of such things as body compositions, somatotype, strength per pound of body weight, and experience as they affect human movement. The specific intent is to focus on *how* movement is described biomechanically as well as to outline the range and framework for the content within this area of study.

STRUCTURE AND FUNCTION

The human body is made up of some 206-plus distinctly identified bones, and some 639-plus muscles interconnected and activated by miles of an intricately designed nervous system. Although each of these systems can be identified by its distinct structure and purpose, the systems interact with the nervous system activating the muscular system, which in turn activates the skeletal system. The actual process for the muscle-nerve interaction is an electrical-chemical phenomenon.

Joints

At the point of contact between two or more bones are joints. There are three types of joints in the human body; the immovable, slightly movable, and freely movable. Examples of the different types of joints include the immovable sutures of the skull, the slightly movable joints between the vertebrae, and the freely movable ball-and-socket joints at the shoulder and at the hip.

The structure of the bones and the type of joint limit the motion or specialize the functions of the various parts of the body. For example, the hinge joint at the elbow makes it convenient to raise food and drinks to the mouth but it requires a complex movement at the shoulder joint in order to throw a ball.

The different parts of the skeleton are held together at the joints by ligaments. Ligaments, which are composed of tough but flexible con-

* Some of this material appeared originally in two mimeographed compilations, *Basic Concepts of Physical Education,* Temple University Bookstore, 1967, and *Physiological Foundations of Physical Activity* (a revised version), Temple University Bookstore, © 1970.

nective tissue, take the form of long strands, encircling bands, or wide sheets. Ligaments generally have poor blood circulation and therefore are very slow to heal when they are injured.

Muscles

Muscles are attached to the bones of the body and cause the bones to move by pulling on them. In addition to the muscles of this system, there are smooth muscles and cardiac muscles that can also exert force. Smooth muscle tissue is most frequently found in the walls of the digestive tract and blood vessels and gives the walls an elastic quality which helps them retain their shape and tone. This type of muscle is not contracted willfully but is controlled automatically by the autonomic nervous system. The cardiac muscle is the muscle of the heart, and its "squeezing" contraction is responsible for propelling the blood through the circulatory system. The skeletal and cardiac muscles are the ones which are most affected by exercise.

Movement in the body takes place as a result of the skeletal muscles shortening (or contracting) when stimulated by the nervous system. It is important to understand that muscles develop force by shortening and pulling—they cannot push on bones. Muscles generally span a joint and are attached at their ends or edges to two bones so that when they shorten, there is movement at the joint. By knowing the general location and attachments of the muscles, you can determine what movement will occur when they shorten. For example, if the fibers of the biceps brachii, in front of the upper arm, are stimulated by the nervous system, the forearm will move closer to the upper arm by bending at the elbow joint. From a similar analysis, you can also determine which muscle needs to be strengthened in order to increase the force of certain movements.

If the muscle shortens, and movement occurs, this is called a *concentric* isotonic contraction or movement. If, however, the muscle does not or cannot contract enough to overcome the resistance against which it is working, and no movement takes place at the joint, it is known as an *isometric* contraction. This type of contraction is illustrated if you strain in an attempt to open a door that is stuck; there is contraction but no movement. A third type of contraction takes place when a muscle lengthens slowly when a resistance is applied. This action is called an *eccentric* contraction.

Examples of these three types of contractions occur when you execute a pull-up on a chinning bar. In the pull upward to raise the chin above the bar, the biceps brachii contract concentrically. While the chin is momentarily held above the bar, the biceps are contracting isometrically, and little or no joint movement occurs. As the body is lowered back to the starting or hanging position, an eccentric contraction of the biceps brachii muscle takes place. Actually, gravity is providing the movement force, while the muscles on the front of the arm are resisting this force as the body is lowered.

A skeletal muscle consists of thousands of long, thin muscle fibers bound together by connective tissue. These fibers shorten when stimulated and a consequent bulge develops in the belly of the muscle. Each fiber contains a large number of myofibrils. These fibrils are divided into a number of microscopic segments called sarcomeres. Under a low-power microscope, these sarcomeres cause skeletal muscle to appear striated or striped. The dark sections of these striations have been identified as the protein myosin and the light sections (which disappear when the muscle contracts) as another protein, actin. These contrasting protein filaments exist inside the sarcomeres. The actin filaments are attached to the Z-lines at the end of each of these units. When the muscle shortens, the sarcomeres contract as units with the Z-lines coming closer together.

The mechanics of muscular contraction have been described by several different theories. Currently the most widely accepted theory is the Huxley sliding filament theory. Under the recently developed ultra-powerful electron microscope, small "cross-bridges" have been found on the myosin filaments. Upon stimulation (either electrical or chemical), they become very active and grab, pull, and re-grab on the actin filaments causing them to slide over one another. This happens many times in the briefest instant. Since the actin filaments are connected to the Z-lines, this pulling action brings the two ends of the sarcomere closer together. As this shortening occurs in many units of the muscle fibers, force is exerted on the tendons at each end of the muscle. This usually results in movement of a bone at one end of the muscle while the bone at the other end is frequently stabilized by an isometric contraction of other muscles.

The strength of a muscular contraction depends upon the number of muscle fibers which are active at one time, the mechanical advantage of the muscle at the particular position, and the arrangement of the muscle fibers. For example, when lifting a book, fewer muscle fibers are called upon to contract than when lifting a box of books. It is easier to bend the arms and carry the box of books closer to the body than to hold them straight out in front because of the gain in mechanical advantage afforded by shortening the lever involved.

There are several different arrangements of muscle fibers which affect the strength of a contraction. If the fibers lie parallel to the long axis of the muscle, as they do in the biceps brachii on the front of the upper arm, the muscle is able to shorten a great distance but is not particularly strong. On the other hand, if the muscle fibers are short and fan out from the center as they do in the gastrocnemius (calf) muscle, the muscle is very strong, but the movement permitted is small (raising on toes). In between these two extremes is the arrangement of the hamstring muscles located in the back of the leg above the knee. These muscles are able to shorten a relatively long distance yet still exert a reasonable degree of force.

The stimulus that triggers a muscular contraction is a nerve impulse. For a voluntary muscular movement, this impulse originates in the motor area of the cerebral cortex of the brain. It travels down the spinal cord, out the motor nerve to the junction of the muscle and nerve, called the motor end-plate. When the nerve impulse arrives at the motor end-plate, it stimulates the production of a chemical, acetylcholine. This chemical substance transmits the impulse across the short gap between the nerve ending and the muscle. It is then received by the muscle membrane (sarcolemma) and conducted through the membrane to the contractile substance (the myosin protein) within the cells, stimulating the cross-bridges to grasp and pull on the actin filaments, which brings the Z-lines closer together and consequently shortens the muscle fiber.

A single muscle fiber will contract maximally in response to any stimulus that is strong enough to excite it. This is known as the "all-or-none" law. The strength of the contraction of an entire muscle depends on the number of fibers contracting at any given time. Therefore, if a large number of fibers are stimulated at any time, the contraction will be stronger than if only a few are activated.

Kinesthetic Sense Impulses

In addition to the impulses that come from the brain, there are impulses that originate within the muscles themselves. These impulses are called "kinesthetic sense impulses." They allow an individual to have a feeling of position and movement. In stroking a tennis ball, for example, a person can tell the location of his hands and feet without looking to see the position of these body parts. Within the muscle itself, there is an organ called a "muscle spindle" that lies parallel to the muscle fiber. When the muscle is at normal length, it discharges nerve impulses of a certain frequency. If the muscle is stretched, the frequency of discharges increases proportionately to the amount of the stretch. The frequency with which these impulses are sent to the brain is interpreted as a "feeling of position." Another kinesthetic sense organ that is used by the brain to determine the position of the body is the Golgi tendon organ. This organ is located at the junction of the muscle fibers and the tendon at either end of the muscle in line with the muscle fibers. These organs are stretched both when the muscle is shortened and when it is lengthened. This stretching of the Golgi tendon organs causes them to discharge nerve impulses. A third receptor is located within the joints themselves and is sensitive to the position and rate of movement of the joint. The brain is thus able to determine the relative position of body parts by interpreting the frequency of impulses sent by the muscle spindles, the Golgi tendon organs, and joint receptors of the muscles involved.

A fourth kinesthetic sense organ that is used by the brain to determine the relative position of the body is the pacinian corpuscle. This organ transmits impulses when it is compressed or deformed. The pacinian corpuscles are particularly prevalent in the sole of the foot and are therefore used to help one "feel" when he is leaning toward one side or the other because of the increase in pressure on the pacinian corpuscle.

In sports, you try to involve the kinesthetic sense organs so that you will be able to make the right movement reflexly without having to "think about" it. The brain is not involved in the stimulus-response action. However, if you think back over a movement (for example, a missed shot or a bad throw), sometimes you are able to determine what you did wrong and make a conscious effort to correct it. The reflex movement is exhibited by a skilled performer who has conditioned his reflexes so that his muscles will respond correctly to a specific stimulus.

In addition to the kinesthetic sense organs, the brain makes use of the more common known senses of sight, touch, and balance (the inner ear) to interpret the position and movements of the body.

The Contraction Process

When a muscle is voluntarily contracted, several changes occur inside of it. In order for the physical action of the cross-bridges and the consequent sliding of the filaments during contraction, certain chemical reactions take place which provide energy for the muscular contraction. The chemistry involved in a muscular contraction is very complex. However, it is summarized here in order that you may have a general understanding of the chemical processes which occur during muscular contraction.

Energy is a prerequisite to a contraction; it is obtained from one of two general classes of compounds stored in the muscle. The two sources of energy are organic phosphates and glycogen, which is the form in which carbohydrates are stored.

The first reaction to occur when a muscle fiber contracts is a breakdown of the organic phosphates which release some simple compounds (inorganic phosphates) and energy. This energy is used for the muscular contraction.

During a period of heavy muscular activity, the supply of organic phosphate is quickly depleted. Therefore, another reaction must occur to provide energy. This second reaction involves glycogen, which is stored in the muscle fiber. This compound breaks down releasing pyruvic acid and energy. This energy is used to rebuild the inorganic phosphates back into organic phosphates. It would appear that this process is rather complete; that is, the organic phosphates are continually rebuilt as a result of the three chemical reactions. The store of glycogen is continually being used up; however, pyruvic acid is converted to lactic acid, a waste product which retards contractions, if sufficient oxygen is not available. The equilibrium of this reaction, therefore, is not maintained. If this were the complete process, a person could continue heavy muscular activity only for approximately 30 seconds because of the build-up of waste products and the depletion of glycogen. It should be noted so far that no oxygen was required in this process. The reactions, which can occur without oxygen, are known as "anaerobic reactions."

In order for muscular activity to continue, oxygen must be carried to the muscles by the hemoglobin in the red blood cells. Sufficient oxygen allows two further chemical reactions to occur. First, the pyruvic acid which resulted from the breakdown of glycogen interacts with the oxygen (O_2) to produce carbon dioxide (CO_2), water (H_2O), and energy in a series of steps commonly called the "Krebs' cycle." The carbon dioxide and the water are removed by the circulatory system.

(1) Organic phosphates $\longrightarrow$ Inorganic phosphates $+$ Energy
   (This energy is available for muscular contraction.)

   Anaerobic

(2) Glycogen $\longrightarrow$ Pyruvic Acid $+$ Energy
   (This energy is used in reaction 3.)

(3) Inorganic phosphates $+$ Energy $\longrightarrow$ Organic phosphates

(4) Pyruvic acid $+$ O_2 $\longrightarrow$ $CO_2 + H_2O +$ Energy   Aerobic

This set of reactions is theoretically perfect and when the muscular work is not intense, the oxygen supply is adequate to permit the complete breakdown of glycogen and the waste products (CO_2 and H_2O) to be removed. Work of this type can be continued for long periods of time. This is called "aerobic exercise" which implies that air, or really oxygen, is required.

When the exercise is more intense and the oxygen supply is not sufficient and pyruvic acid is converted to lactic acid, a different situation exists. The lactic acid begins to build up in the muscle. The presence of more than a few tenths of one per cent of lactic acid in the muscle fluids results in muscular pain and the cessation of muscular contraction. This may be recognized as one of the symptoms of fatigue. This type of fatigue is the type most commonly experienced, and is a result of the direct action of the lactic acid on the muscle rather than the depletion of the energy-supplying substance. This occurs when the exercise is so intense that the oxygen supply is not able to keep up (although some "oxygen debt" is possible) due to either a lack of breathing or restricted

2

circulation. You can experience this type of fatigue by running as fast as you can as far as you can. The body makes an attempt to remedy this type of fatigue by bringing more oxygen to the affected areas and by carrying away the waste products faster. Evidence of this attempt is the automatic increase in the rate and depth of breathing and the increase in circulation, as indicated by the elevated heart rate. Lactic acid produced in anaerobic work diffuses out of the cells and is carried in the blood stream to the liver, where it is oxidized and reconverted to glycogen after exercise is stopped and the oxygen is adequate.

Sometimes continued isometric contractions or constriction caused by adhesive tape or garters may restrict the circulation to such a degree that fatigue pains in the restricted area force the individual to stop work. For example, most of us have carried a heavy object so long that local pain develops. The isometric contraction of the muscles restricted the circulation in the arms, causing this.

Although the chemical process has been simplified to make it easier to understand, it illustrates the importance of the circulatory system in supplying oxygen and glycogen to the muscle and removing the waste products resulting from contraction to enable the muscle to continue exercising.

The major part of the body's energy is supplied by glucose, which is produced in the digestion of carbohydrates. Glucose is stored in muscles as glycogen. In addition to carbohydrate, fat is utilized as a source of energy. Fat molecules are split up into glycerol and fatty acids before they are absorbed from the intestinal tract. Glycerol can be oxidized readily to supply energy for contraction, while fatty acids are oxidized in the same way that glycogen is utilized as a source of energy. Only a very small amount of the energy for muscular work comes from protein metabolism.

The major function of the circulatory system is to transport glucose and oxygen to the cells and to remove the waste products of metabolism. The circulatory system has two major components: the vascular system and the blood. The vascular system includes the heart, which provides the force to pump the blood, and the vascular bed (arteries, veins, and capillaries).

All body cells metabolize; that is, carry on life processes. In order to do this they need the raw materials of food and oxygen. In the metabolic process, the cells produce waste products which must be removed from the area of the cells. The circulatory system fulfills the transportation needs, but the actual chemical reactions involved are the function of the respiratory system, since the prerequisite for most of these reactions is oxygen.

The main function of the circulatory system is to supply the active cells with oxygen and remove the waste products of metabolism, particularly carbon dioxide. The degree to which the circulatory system, in conjunction with the respiratory system, is able to fulfill this function during exercise is called circulatory-respiratory endurance. Stress on the circulatory and respiratory system is caused by general body activity, such as swimming and running, as opposed to localized muscular effort, such as sawing wood or lifting weights.

There are many factors that influence the amount of oxygen required to perform an activity; the quantity of the activity (walking a mile requires more oxygen than walking a half-mile); the speed at which the activity is performed (running a half-mile requires more oxygen than walking it); and the load carried (walking a half-mile with a 30-pound pack on your back as opposed to just walking it without a pack). These factors are, in turn, influenced by other factors such as body weight (heavy people carry a greater load), skill (a skillful performer makes few wasted movements and therefore performs less activity), and other similar factors. The greater the metabolic activity of a muscle, the greater will be the demand for oxygen. If the oxygen requirement for a certain activity can be decreased (e.g., through improved skill, weight reduction, etc.) then the individual will be able to sustain the activity for a longer period of time.

When the oxygen requirement for an activity exceeds the ability of the circulatory-respiratory system to keep up, a deficit develops. Some of the metabolic processes of muscular activity are anaerobic (can take place without oxygen), and a considerable amount of work can be done before sufficient waste products (CO_2 and lactic acid) build up to halt the activity. This buildup is called "oxygen debt." You have experienced the symptoms of oxygen debt, better known as "physical fatigue," during heavy exercise (breathlessness, muscular pain, dizziness, etc.). After the exercise is stopped, sufficient oxygen must be taken in to enable these waste products to be eliminated. This is why your respiratory and heart rates remain high for a period of time after the activity has been completed. As a result of certain types of endurance-training activities, one's tolerance for oxygen debt is increased, and the ability to perform more activity is likewise increased.

Study Procedures

It is possible to study the structure of the human body by photographic processes. The static structure can be described by still pictures and a structure in motion can be studied and/or observed by moving pictures or sequence cameras. In addition to the possibility of making objective measurements from the photographic records, it is possible to describe the structure of an individual or a culture of individuals objectively by taking a series of anthropometric measurements of the various lengths, breadths, and widths of the body. Although there is some disagreement (varying techniques) in relation to actual measurement procedures, most externally observed structures can be measured with calipers, tapes, and scales. The only accurate way we have at present of observing internal structures in a living person is through radiographic techniques which allow us to observe the shadows of the varying densities of materials found in the body. These shadows can be described and measured accurately by investigators who are experienced in this work. For health reasons, medical doctors occasionally inject substances into portions of the body to allow them to study the suspected damaged area in some detail. Sound waves have been used to study the body composition of an individual as they reflect at different levels according to the density of the materials of the body. Some radioactive counting techniques have also been developed which react to the concentration of some minerals naturally found to be present in varying types of body tissues in predictable quantities. An example would be the potassium level normally found in lean muscle tissue. These observational techniques occasionally are important to an individual who has become injured in play, dance, or sport or is not able to perform at top levels for some unknown reason.

Individual Differences

Although the structures of an individual are usually similar to others of his culture, extremes of sizes and shapes are also found with many of the characteristics distributed like a "normal curve." The reasons for the individual as well as cultural differences are both hereditary and environmental in nature. Such things as nutrition and exercise have an effect on the structure and development of the body. Occasionally injuries will affect specific structures such as the ligaments of the knee or the tendons of a muscle insertion. Severe damages frequently have to be repaired surgically but following most injuries the body adapts by rehabilitating itself. Some individuals are born with some aspect of their structure distinctly different than that of others. Examples are those people who have missing limbs but many other more subtle differences are found, such as a missing palm muscle which the individual learns to compensate for by grasping with other muscles. In many movements, several different muscles can contract to provide the desirable action. Certainly, many different fibers within a muscle structure can contract to result in similar action. Because of the fact that the electrochemical state of the connecting sections of nerves and muscles can allow different muscle fibers to react to the same stimulus, it is extremely difficult for a beginner to reproduce distinct, fine moves. As one repeats and learns a skill, it seems as though the paths become more like "ruts in a road" and with use, the actions (within limits) become more repeatable. Most insertions of muscles vary not only in the proportion of the length of the limb upon which they insert but also with the surface in which the muscles insert and attach to the bones. This provides for advantages in some kinds of motion for some individuals and disadvantages for others in similar motions or actions. This combined with the development of the muscle tissue, the length of the limb, and the experience of the individual accounts for the wide range in quality of movement exhibited by performers in the various forms of human movement.

LIMITATIONS AND ADVANTAGES

When an individual moves or performs, he has not only quantity but also quality of movement. Some types of movement require quantity such as strength, endurance, or distance. Other types of activities require certain qualities with specific skills involved. The quality of a performance can range from that of a rank beginner to that of a skilled professional; but throughout the range of performances, both the quantity and quality have certain factors which provide an individual with limitations and/or advantages. Some of these factors are body composition, somatotype, training level, strength per pound of body weight, endurance or fatigue level, handicaps (such as physical, mental, or emotional), as well as the experience level of the individual.

Body Composition

The body organs (heart, lungs, spleen, eyes, brain, and so forth) are involved importantly in human movement, but the role is primarily that of a support function. Some of these organs are affected by certain human movement routines; the heart and lungs, for instance, increase efficiency with endurance training. In general, however, the body organs have specialized functions which do not relate to body composition.

In relation to human movement, the body composition of an individual is considered to be made up of primarily bone, muscle, and fat. Bones and muscles put together in particular quantities and qualities may provide advantages or disadvantages for an individual. Fat is usually considered a limitation to performance, particularly if fat is found intramuscularly or deposited as excess weight. The body composition of an individual is somewhat determined by heredity, but in addition it is affected by the general metabolism and functioning of an individual which is his norm. It is also possible for other environmental conditions to change the body composition, particularly as it relates to the work and recreation activities of an individual. These changes are particularly noticeable when the activities are intense and extended periods are spent in participation. In today's society, most people realize that if they take in more food than they utilize due to their physical activity, most of the excess is deposited as fat rather than excreted as waste as it might be ideally. This means that a person will increase fat deposits if his activity level is low and his intake level is high. Fat deposits locate generally throughout the body with a typical patterning according to the body type and according to the typical regular physical activity of an individual. For example, if a person works very hard with his legs but does not exercise the upper part of his body, the upper part of his body is likely to be composed of considerably more adipose tissue than the lower portion although generally fat deposits throughout the body in most individuals unless the activity level is extremely divergent. Adipose tissue deposited intramuscularly reduces the efficiency of the muscle, as the fibers are mechanically less efficient due to the resistances against which they can pull and due to the probable increased circulation in nonfunctioning tissue (adipose tissue is frequently full of small capillaries). This shunting of red blood cells to adipose tissue reduces the availability of oxygen as well as energy-producing substances for the muscle fibers.

When an individual has excess body weight, it is clear that he needs to do more physical work in order to accomplish the same task if he has to move his body in the process. It is possible to have a great proportion of body weight in inactive adipose tissue, but an important point is that how much a person actually weighs in pounds is not the critical issue; it is what proportion of his body weight is lean muscle tissue and what is bone and what is fat. It should be mentioned that muscle weighs more than adipose tissue and frequently when a person exercises with certain types of strength-building exercises, his muscles increase in size (because of growth of individual fibers and consequently of the muscle belly), and this resulting increase in body weight may actually be functional and beneficial. This makes exercising as a way of losing body weight sometimes very discouraging. A typical experience will be that considerable weight loss occurs at the beginning of an exercise program (primarily water loss) followed by a stabilizing and perhaps even an increase in weight as a person returns close to his former body weight. It is very discouraging to a person who does not realize that weight alone is not the only factor in "what he should weigh," as all aspects of body composition need to be considered.

If an individual has exceptionally large bones, he will probably be taller than another individual as well as have broader shoulders and/or hips, and frequently he will weigh more than a person with small bones. This part of his body composition is labeled as his "skeletal structure." The bones form a framework upon which the body can be developed or be left undeveloped. Some individuals seem to have certain natural tendencies towards having good musculature, and others have the opposite tendencies. It should be made clear that although these tendencies do exist, the effort and activity levels of individuals with various musculature must be observed. Usually it can be shown clearly that the muscular tissue of an individual is affected by his activity level, and that this effect results in a change in body composition.

A person can determine his body composition by measuring the lengths of the long bones or other bone structure estimates as well as the widths of the hips and shoulders. This can give a general indication of the shape of the body as well as the proportions to be found in the lower and upper halves of the body. The muscle estimations in a living person are usually made with a tape measure around the girth of muscles in the flexed-tensed state as well as in the relaxed condition, although these girths also include any adipose tissue that is located under the skin or within the muscle itself. Fat estimates are usually made with "pinch calipers," which measure a double skinfold of fat where the fat lies superficially under the skin. Superficial skinfold measurements are good estimates of the total fat found in most individuals. Standard measurements are taken below the scapula on the back, juxta (close to) the nipple on the chest area, above the crest of the ilium on the hip area, at the umbilicus area in front of the body, and in the front and rear of the upper leg as well as on the rear of the upper arm. Occasionally specific skinfold measurements are made for a particular reason in other regions of the body such as under the chin or on the cheeks.

Another technique to determine the body composition of an individual is to weigh him under water to obtain the density of the body. Since bone, muscle, and fat have different densities, the proportions of each can be predicted. The techniques used are to have a person expel most of his air and then, by attaching a specific amount of weight to his waist, submerge in a body of water, and just as he goes completely under, expel all of the air that he can so that his underwater weight can be determined. Correction factors are made for such things as residual volume of air and gastrointestinal air which would be influential in the floating (weighing) characteristics. The specific formulas that can be used are as follows:

$$\text{Estimated body density (from skinfolds alone)} = 1.08012 - .007123X_1 - .004834X_2 - .00513X_4$$

Where X_1, X_2, and X_4 = skinfold thicknesses (in cm) taken respectively at the chest in the midaxillary line at the level of the xiphoid, at the chest in the juxta nipple position, and on the dorsum of the arm at the midpoint between the tip of the acromion and the tip of the olecranon. (R = .85) and SE = 0.0065 body density unit.

$$\text{Estimated body density (with underwater weighing)} =$$

$$\frac{\text{Body weight (kg)} \times \text{density of water at water temperature}}{\text{Body weight} - [\text{underwater weight} + (G)]}$$

Where G = kg of water displaced by residual lung volume

Somatotype

The constitutional makeup (shape of) an individual also affects his ability to perform various human movements. A person is typically classified as a wedge type—a mesomorph (narrow at the hips and wide at the shoulders), or an inverted wedge (pear type)—an endomorph (wide at the hips and narrow at the shoulders). An individual with a third type of body build is an ectomorph (thin and linear throughout his general body composition). Most people have some aspects of endomorphy, mesomorphy, and ectomorphy and are therefore not "pure types." In Sheldon's system of describing body build, each person is rated for each of the three components on a 7-point scale. A 4-4-4 would be a mid-type in all components, a 5-6-2 would be a 5 in endomorphy, a 6 in mesomorphy and a 2 in ectomorphy. Many professional football tackles would be somatotyped similar to a 5-6-2. Performers in particular sports frequently fall into similar somatotype categories, and activities requiring performance skills as agility, strength, and endurance favor various body builds. Good athletes generally are at least a 5 in mesomorphy. Most of us can visualize a body type which would be typical of the wrestler (short with long arms and/or legs and usually a general wedge shape), or of a long-distance swimmer, a football tackle or a football end or halfback, or a field hockey fullback or forward wing. It is fairly easy to somatotype people who would earn A's in physical education activity classes and those who will have difficulty learning many activities.

Many people believe that the shape can only be slightly modified with exercise, nutrition, and/or maturation. The probable range of modification (in Sheldon's 7-point system) is a point or a little more in mesomorphy and only a half-point or a little more in endomorphy or ectomorphy. It should be pointed out that fatness or thinness (or other aspects of body composition) probably affect the somatotype or general constitutional outline of an individual very little.

It has been found that some characteristics not necessarily related to human movement are also related to the body type of an individual. Delinquents, for example, are frequently found to be of mesomorphic body type whereas a person who has great personal drive is frequently found to have very mesomorphically rated legs. Sheldon has written a series of observations on "constitutional psychology" which imply that many characteristics of individuals are related to the way that they are "physically put together." It is difficult to establish a cause-and-effect relationship, but trends are observed with many exceptions as well because of the complexities of human behavior. Although it is easy to see how many of these characteristics can come about due to the interactions of individuals in human movement (such as those who can and those who cannot), other social interactions are the result of the first impression or the follow-up impressions one gets by looking at the shape of a person.

Specific limitations on human movement can be predicted with a moderately high degree of certainty according to the shape of an individual. A person who has a pear shape, for example, will find it very difficult to develop an upper-body strength that will allow him to handle his body in such events as the high bar and body support activities on other gymnastics equipment. In contrast, however, he frequently can easily stay afloat in the water because of his low density and sometimes makes a good long-distance swimmer if he is interested in training and developing the skills that are necessary to be a good swimmer. Champions will have a high rating in mesomorphy as well.

Training Level

The training level or physical fitness level of an individual provides him with certain limitations and/or advantages in motor performance. A person who is "out of shape" or who has not participated in a physical activity for some time will find that his skill level, his performance itself, and his ability to repeat a performance are very much reduced from his previous capabilities. A person who has learned a skill well, however, will probably be able to repeat that skill with a little practice provided age deterioration is not too great. Skill is usually regained most rapidly, but strength, flexibility, and endurance require a progressive and rather extensive program. The types of events which require considerable strength or endurance, however, frequently require hard training before the level of performance can approach a previous high level if a person has allowed himself to get really "out of shape." This is particularly true of an endurance event, although it is somewhat true of a strength or power event as well. If you have been there before, however, it is usually easier to get there again than it was the first time, if age or other factors are reasonably similar. Age affects the potential for training as progress is usually slower as one passes the early twenties. It is clear that older people can develop skills they had not developed as youths, but the physiological and anatomical characteristics usually slow the process. Motivation can more than make up for these limitations in some instances, however.

When an individual is close to his peak of training, he still may not be capable of performing as well as another individual who is not near the peak of his training. This phenomenon presents a great deal of confusion for the individual who is trying to improve. It has been clearly shown that a maximum capacity for most individuals can be identified and categorized roughly; if a person is near this maximum, of course, he will not improve very much with a training program, whereas an individual who is a long distance away from his maximum capacities will improve greatly with little effort as he or she undertakes a training program.

Some physical feats of athletes have recently been shown to be improved by chemically stimulating changes in the body, such as using steroids to put on body weight or increase muscle mass. Some drugs have been used to increase the physical performance of an individual, but the long-term effect frequently presents an individual with rather serious unpredictable problems. Sexual impotency and voice change are two of the identifiable problems of persons who have used certain types of chemicals. In addition to these possible problems, some performers react differently and may "lose their timing." Others become unrealistic about their performances and think they are doing well when, in comparison with their normal play, they may be considerably below par. The ethics of using drugs has been seriously questioned by the over-30 group, but many people believe that it is the performance that counts and that a person should be allowed to "do his own thing" to achieve this performance. It is an important philosophical question.

Strength per Pound of Body Weight

Many performances are limited by the ability of a person to handle his body. The direct relationship of strength per pound of body weight has been found to be a good indicator of a person's general ability to handle his body. This is particularly evident in events like gymnastics where a participant must make certain movements in complicated positions while he must support all or portions of his body in a balanced, controlled move. If an individual has great strength per pound of body weight, he is potentially able to perform extremely well on gymnastics apparatus where a person with a low strength ratio finds it difficult to control his body even in normal daily activities. This is one of the better measures of general sport performance, although it does not take into consideration such factors as agility and coordination, skill and experience which are, of course, important in most kinds of sport movement.

Endurance—Fatigue Level

If a person is in good physical condition from a cardiorespiratory or muscular endurance standpoint, he probably will be able to work for long periods of time and still be able to give a quality performance. In contrast, a person whose cardiovascular system is in poor condition will probably fatigue quickly and not be able to perform efficiently under these conditions. Cardiorespiratory endurance is affected not only by the oxygen-carbon dioxide exchange function of the lungs but also by internal respiration (ability to get oxygen to the cells and remove carbon dioxide) and the carrying capacity and efficiency of the circulatory system. The heart is a key organ in regard to endurance performance and must be able to operate efficiently and powerfully enough to transport the blood to the parts of the body as needed. We speak of the aerobic capacity of an individual as that capacity which does not involve an oxygen debt, and when the pulmonary and circulatory systems can "keep up" with the oxygen requirements of the activity. When a person begins to operate without sufficient oxygen (anaerobic capacity), he begins to build a lactic acid debt due to the build-up of lactate waste product in his blood; the oxygen-carrying capacity of the red blood cells is then reduced. When a person reaches his maximum in oxygen debt, he is usually near an unbearable fatigue level, and he must stop his performance. Sometimes this can be a local fatigue problem, such as long-term intensive working with the hands or fingers in a specific activity, but it can also become a total body problem as in a distance swimming or running event.

Generally a person's body adapts to the stresses that are placed on it; and if one works progressively by overloading the body requirements compared with normal requirements, a person will improve his endurance capacities so that he is able to perform and move for much longer periods of time. Again the trainability factor comes in, and improvement rates are reflected not only in the quality and quantity of the training but also in terms of the individual's present state as a percentage of his maximum training capacity.

Handicaps

A person can have several types of physical, mental, or emotional handicaps. Physical handicaps are those of a temporary or permanent nature due to limited function of the nervous, skeletal, or muscular systems. Most people who work with the physically handicapped are amazed by handicapped persons' ability to adapt their performances as well as their total capacities. If a handicapped individual is allowed to progress by using overload and progression principles of training, he is usually able to make his unaffected body parts operate very efficiently (at least as efficiently as a non-handicapped person—and frequently better because of motivation or some other factors). Some of the handicaps of an individual are of a temporary nature, and a simple adjustment for a brief period of time is all that is necessary. Occasionally these brief adjustments may cause more damage than the original injury if adjustments such as walking with a limp because of a sprained ankle become habits; the person may then get a dislocated back or sore hip because of the limp. An individual needs to understand the structure and function of his body so that such problems are not developed unnecessarily.

Mental handicaps are usually found to be related to permanent damage or hereditary conditions. These conditions may provide an individual with limitations which set his maximums for performance at a lower level than a person who is not so handicapped. Evidence of experiences with individuals who develop a desire to do certain human movements indicate that limits are very high in most circumstances. Limitations, depending upon the complexity of the performance and the amount of time spent learning the specific movement, interact with the severity of the handicaps, but surprises are frequent. Those with emotional handicaps find limitations in their own performances difficult to accept. Many kinds of problems are misunderstood by the performer himself, and as a result of his confusion, he frequently makes matters worse for himself. He may decide to quit a team or interact poorly with a teammate, for example. An individual with an emotional handicap frequently has unpredictable reactions to stimuli, and he may react very favorably under one condition and very unfavorably under an apparently similar condition. These limitations are frustrating to the individual involved as he gets a chance to reflect upon them, but he frequently does not realize or understand what is occurring to his performance or to his interactions with others.

Experience

One of the most critical factors in human performance is experience. When a person simply experiences a movement or a series of drills related to a movement a number of times, he is frequently able to learn to perform that movement provided he uses mechanical and physiological principles advantageously. An individual who has not handled a lacrosse stick will find it difficult to cradle the ball, but a person who has worked with this experience on some occasions will normally be able to recall it and repeat it during most of his lifetime. The quantity and quality of prior experience influence the limitations and/or advantages that one may find relating to the performance. A person who has had a great quantity of successful experience in a particular area will usually have an advantage over an individual who has had a limited quantity of experience, even though the qualities of both may be equal. If the quality of performance of an individual is not first rate, he will, of course, in all probability not be able to perform a first-rate movement consistently at a later time unless he proceeds through usual developmental stages. The motor performance ability of an individual is probably most related to the experience of that person (especially recent experience) although the previously outlined factors may restrict him or provide him with advantages depending upon the qualities of his performance.

Recording Movement

Human movement is recorded for several reasons, among which are: (1) to study the movement so that improvements or changes can be made or so that it can be repeated, (2) to record the aesthetic form so that it can be viewed and enjoyed again, or (3) to establish records of movement performance. Still and motion pictures are among the most commonly used records of human movement. High-speed cameras which can take up to 12 thousand pictures per second are available to record the minute details of rapidly moving objects. Stroboscopic units are also available to record the sequential paths of movement on a single picture. Rapid-sequence still cameras have also been developed primarily to record sport movement.

Other devices have recently been developed and/or modified to record what occurs in human movement; such techniques as recording the action potentials (muscle activity) involved in selected muscles during specific movements have become common in laboratory settings. This type of equipment allows an investigator to determine when muscles are actively contracting and when they are not. The technique is also used to monitor muscular relaxation, and it can be used with telemetering equipment so that wire connections between the performer and the recorder are not required.

Films can be analyzed to study gross movements such as the rise and fall of the center of gravity of a subject during a run or the reaction of one part of the body during a twisting dive. It is possible to do a frame-by-frame analysis of movie film to plot the sequential movements of various joint angle changes or direction of movement of specific parts of the body during rapid movements. For example, if you were to plot the elbow as the center of the angle and a spot on the shoulder and the wrist as the two sides of an angle, you could plot the change in elbow flexion or extension during a throwing movement. It is also possible to mark an adhesive bracelet placed around a body part with letters or designs so that the amount of rotation during a specific period of time (one frame to the next, for example) can be observed. Rotating movements as well as angle changes can be recorded with electronic goniometers which react parallel with the angular change or rotation of joints.

Force platforms have been developed which allow an investigator to plot forces in three planes simultaneously. They allow an investigator to study the horizontal and vertical forces as well as the lateral forces in a performer's track start, for example. If the runner lifts his head too quickly, much of the force will be projected upward, and therefore the force that is available to be applied in the horizontal direction (toward the finish line) is reduced. Force platforms can also be used to study the beneficial effects of such movements as arm action in a broad or vertical jumping move or the efficiency of a right- versus a left-foot or even a two-foot takeoff for a specific event.

The physiological functioning of the human body during movement can be studied biochemically in such specific assays as determining the acid-base balance following exercise, the level of free fatty acids in the blood following intakes of high-fat meals and various types of exercise, or such blood analyses as total volume, hemoglobin, hematocrit, or specific cell counts.

The response of the body to exercise, sport, dance, or other movement forms can be described by recording the heart rate or the changes in the configuration of the phonocardiogram, electrocardiogram, or ballistocardiogram. Measuring the amount of oxygen consumed by the body during specific exercise, as well as measuring other dynamic pulmonary functions can contribute to the evaluation of the functioning of the oxygen delivery systems. Superficial or internal temperature reactions can be monitored with present techniques readily available to the physical educator. Linear distance measurements or timing techniques are often also used in analyzing performances. Such recording techniques as timing a 40-yard dash or mile run, and measuring a stride, a javelin throw, or a shotput distance are frequently used in recording human movement. Recording such sporting phenomena as the length of the field goal kicked and long jump shots in basketball is of interest from the spectator's or sport enthusiast's point of view.

Several notation systems have been developed to record movement in such areas as dance and exercise. Stick figures are frequently used in exercise descriptions and a type of "shorthand" has been developed to record a sequence of dance movements.

THE MECHANICS OF HUMAN MOVEMENT

For convenience, the mechanics of human movement can be divided into applied anatomy principles as well as mechanical principles. Actually there is much overlapping of these two aspects of kinesiology (science of motion), and all principles can be generalized under improving the efficiency of human movement. The prerequisites to efficient movement have been identified and the relationships shown in the following chart prepared by Kraus.[1]

The basic mechanical principles can be grouped into the following categories: gravity and buoyancy, equilibrium, motion, leverage, force, angle of rebound and spin, projectiles, and friction. Depending upon the particular movement, each of the above may assume a magnitude of importance ranging from little to great. If one is to be consistently efficient in movement, he should know the various applications of these basic principles and use them to best advantage. The remainder of this section will be used to illustrate some principles and their applications in each of the basic areas. Although they are treated separately, it should be emphasized that they do not apply separately.

---

[1] Kraus, Hans. "Therapeutic Exercises in Pediatrics." *Medical Clinic of North America.* 31:629, May, 1947. Cited by Broer, Marion R. *Efficiency of Human Movement.* Philadelphia: W. B. Saunders Company, 1960, 17.

Gravity and Buoyancy

The center of gravity of an individual has been described as the point about which the weight of an individual balances. If you were to lie on the floor, your center of gravity would be found just above your hip area and about in the midline of your body approximately 3 inches off the floor. The location, of course, would vary with the structure of the individual and would change toward the head if the person put his hands behind his head. The center of gravity is important in many sport movements, such as rotating dives, because the body will revolve around the center of gravity. If the center of gravity moves outside of the base of support, it becomes difficult to maintain one's balance. Therefore, in sports like wrestling, one attempts to get his opponent in such a position that his center of gravity is near the edge of his support; it is then easier to make the person "lose his balance."

When an object falls through the air (disregarding air resistance), gravity is the force that makes all bodies fall uniformly and with the same acceleration. To project an object upwards, one must overcome gravity with other forces. Gravity acts only in a straight line towards the center of the earth, and therefore if the object does not go straight up and straight down, other forces must be operating: wind, spin, direction of original propelling forces, and so forth.

Buoyancy is important primarily in aquatic events. A primary principle is that identified by Archimedes (Archimedes' principle) which states that a fluid will "buoy up" an object by a force equal to the weight of the fluid the body has displaced. Therefore, if someone is well muscled (frequently heavy in relation to size), he will usually find it difficult to float high out of the water. Perhaps some people would learn to swim more easily if they started by becoming accustomed to floating on their backs. Can you describe the type of person who might fall into this category?

Equilibrium

When the center of gravity is over the base of support, the person is in a state of balance. Would he become more stable if he raised or lowered his center of gravity? Can you explain why, based on this reasoning? (Draw a picture if you need to.) When one changes the size or the shape of the base, balance is affected in several possible ways. Can you describe them? Discuss their importance in sports or dance movements with which you are familiar. When an object is taken in one's hands, the center of gravity is changed according to the weight and distance of the center of gravity of the object from the center of gravity of the individual as well as his weight. Can you diagram this phenomenon?

Organization of Prerequisites and Controls Involved in Efficient Movement

(Courtesy of Marion R. Broer: *Efficiency of Human Movement*. 3rd ed., Philadelphia, W. B. Saunders, Co. In Press.)

Prerequisites to Efficient Movement

A. PHYSICAL

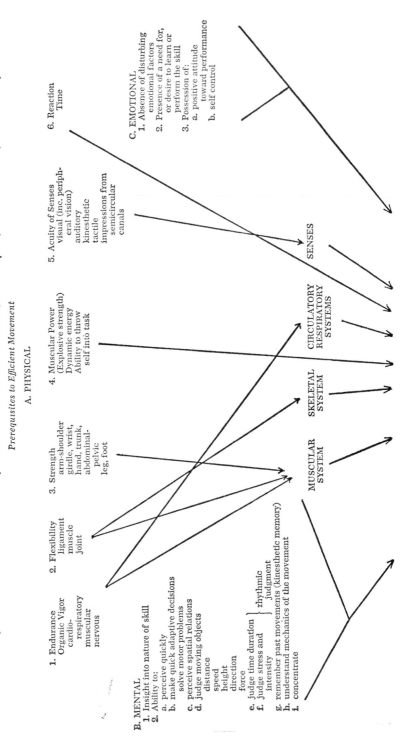

1. Endurance
   Organic Vigor
     cardio-
       respiratory
     muscular
     nervous

2. Flexibility
   ligament
   muscle
   joint

3. Strength
   arm-shoulder
     girdle, wrist,
     hand, trunk,
     abdominal-
       pelvic
     leg, foot

4. Muscular Power
   (Explosive strength)
   Dynamic energy
   Ability to throw
     self into task

5. Acuity of Senses
   visual (inc. periph-
     eral vision)
   auditory
   kinesthetic
   tactile
   impressions from
     semicircular
     canals

6. Reaction
   Time

B. MENTAL

1. Insight into nature of skill
2. Ability to:
   a. perceive quickly
   b. make quick adaptive decisions
     solve motor problems
   c. perceive spatial relations
   d. judge moving objects
     distance
     speed
     height
     direction
     force
   e. judge time duration ⎫ rhythmic
   f. judge stress and   ⎬ judgment
     intensity   ⎭
   g. remember past movements (kinesthetic memory)
   h. understand mechanics of the movement
   i. concentrate

C. EMOTIONAL

1. Absence of disturbing
     emotional factors
2. Presence of a need for,
     or desire to learn or
     perform the skill
3. Possession of:
   a. positive attitude
       toward performance
   b. self control

MUSCULAR
SYSTEM

SKELETAL
SYSTEM

CIRCULATORY
RESPIRATORY
SYSTEMS

SENSES

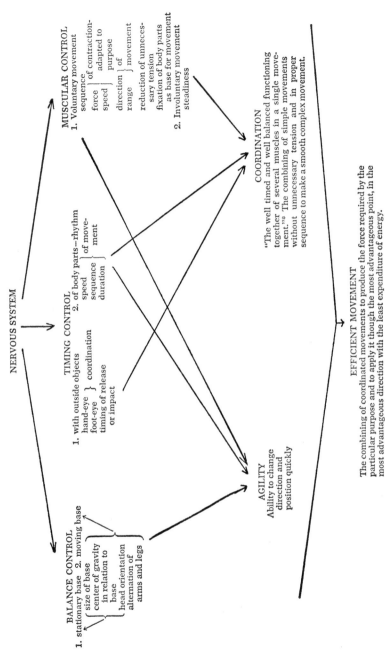

NERVOUS SYSTEM

MUSCULAR CONTROL
1. Voluntary movement
   sequence
   force } of contraction-
   speed } adapted to purpose
   direction } of
   range } movement
   speed
   reduction of unnecessary tension
   fixation of body parts as base for movement
2. Involuntary movement
   steadiness

TIMING CONTROL
1. with outside objects
   hand-eye } coordination
   foot-eye }
   timing of release or impact
2. of body parts—rhythm of movement
   speed
   sequence
   duration

BALANCE CONTROL
1. stationary base   2. moving base
   size of base
   center of gravity in relation to base
   head orientation
   alternation of arms and legs

COORDINATION
"The well timed and well balanced functioning together of several muscles in a single movement."* The combining of simple movements without unnecessary tension and in proper sequence to make a smooth complex movement.

AGILITY
Ability to change direction and position quickly

EFFICIENT MOVEMENT
The combining of coordinated movements to produce the force required by the particular purpose and to apply it though the most advantageous point, in the most advantageous direction with the least expenditure of energy.

*Kraus, Hans: Therapeutic Exercises in Pediatrics. *Medical Clinics of North America,* 31:629, May, 1947.

In addition to the many physical principles involved in equilibrium, many sensory organs within the body also contribute to the maintenance of static or dynamic balance. The semicircular canals of the middle ear, one's eyes, the organs of touch, and the stretch organs in tendons and muscles and joints all help one to know his status in regard to balance. When you close your eyes and stand on one foot, not only do you discover the importance of vision but you also react to the pressure sensors of touch in the bottom of your feet. Dynamic balance, such as is required in keeping your footing on slippery turf, is very complex, but it is very important to the student of human movement or the performer.

Motion

Linear, curvilinear, and rotary motion occur in human movement. These types of motion are affected by Newton's three laws.

1. An object at rest or in motion will tend to stay at rest or continue its motion at the same speed unless it is acted upon by a force.
2. When a body is acted upon by a force, its resulting acceleration or deceleration is proportional to the force and inversely proportional to the mass.
3. With every action force, there is an equal and opposite reaction force.

Can you describe a sport situation illustrating the importance of each of Newton's three principles? Have you ever played a game which made use of any of these principles?

Leverage

A lever is a rigid bar which revolves around a fixed point called a "fulcrum." Depending upon the relationship of the *fulcrum*, the *resistance*, and the *effort* applied, the lever is classified as a first-, second-, or third-class lever. $F^1R^2E^3$: when the fulcrum is in the middle it is a first-class lever; when the resistance is in the middle, second-class; when the effort is in the middle, third-class. The important consideration is this: by applying a lever properly, one can gain either force or speed. A first-class lever can gain either force or speed depending upon the location of the fulcrum and, of course, the direction of the force out is opposite to that applied. A second-class lever (wheelbarrow) always gains force since its effort arm must be longer than its resistance arm. The human body contains few second-class levers. Most of the levers in the human body, usually muscles attached to the skeleton, are third-class levers; this class favors speed and range of motion. After studying the following sketch, can you tell why?

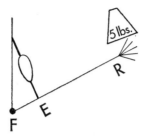

The reaction of a lever is in proportion to the length of its effort and resistance arms, which are defined as the distance of the effort and of the resistance from the fulcrum. Could you make use of the following formula—the "principle of levers"?

$$E \cdot EA = R \cdot RA$$

Levers in the human body rarely, if ever, perform alone; instead, several levers acting in concert produce the movement.

Force

Both the magnitude and the direction of the force applications are important in regard to producing motion or obtaining lever action. In addition, the point of application of the force is also important. For example, if the force is applied on the surface of an object and through the center of gravity, linear motion will result. If, however, the force is not applied in the direction of the center of gravity, rotation or spin will develop. The result of two or more forces can be described by drawing vectors (which have both magnitude and direction) as shown below.

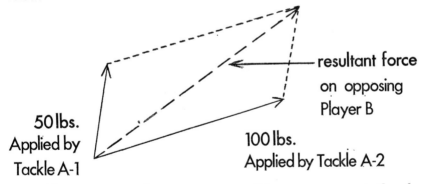

resultant force on opposing Player B

50 lbs. Applied by Tackle A-1

100 lbs. Applied by Tackle A-2

In addition to its application to sports of human movement, the absorption of force also becomes important in such actions as falling or catching a moving object. The direction, magnitude, and location of the contact again are important. The general principle is to absorb the force over as much distance and area as is in keeping with the required outcomes. If you fall on your elbow and the surface does not give, injury is probable if the distance and force involved are great. If you fall on soft tissues and spread out the contact area, the probability of injury is much less. Apply these principles to the act of catching a fast hard ball. What kind of glove and action would you like?

Angle of Rebound and Spin

When a moving body contacts a surface, it will rebound at an angle which is approximately equal to that at which it approached the surface. When spin is applied to an object such as a ball, this angle will be modified according to the amount of spin, the flattening of the ball (caused by velocity as well as coefficient of restitution), and the interaction of the surfaces. The modification of the angle of rebound is predictable and is taken into consideration by the skilled or knowledgeable performer.

When a ball spins, it tends to build up greater air resistance on the side that is moving against the air and this pressure may push the ball in the other direction—a "curve ball." If a baseball has no spin at all, it may move irregularly as flows produce a "drag" on its seams. This turbulence also occurs with balls which are relatively light, such as volleyballs, when they move fast with little or no spin. Spin can also affect the roll of a ball when it moves against a solid surface.

Projectiles

When an object is "projected" through the air it is affected by the release velocities (the vertical and the horizontal components), the air resistance, the force of gravity, and other external forces. The distance a projectile will travel depends upon the initial speed of the object as well as the angle at which it is projected. The angle of release is dependent upon the relative vertical and horizontal velocities. If such things as wind and air resistance are neglected, a projected object will follow the path of a parabola. If it lands at a lower level than that from which it was projected, the "range" is longer depending upon the difference in level. The best angle to project an object depends upon the purpose. If speed is the important factor, the object should be projected as near as possible to the horizontal; but it must have enough velocity to carry the distance. Can you think of circumstances when speed is not the most important factor?

Friction

In addition to air resistance (sometimes considered a type of friction) and water resistance, an object (person or other) may take advantage of or be hindered by the friction developed with supporting surfaces. The "coefficient of friction" is affected by the area of the surfaces in contact, the force being applied by the objects in opposition to each other, and the types of surfaces involved. In addition, the type of friction changes the amount of resistance. Sliding friction, for example, is much greater than rolling friction. The surface can directly affect the amount of resistance to motion; as an example, think about rolling a wheelbarrow on deep sand or over a sidewalk. Some sport playing surfaces are slippery while others are "good surfaces" upon which one can change directions easily. What does this have to do with friction?

SOCIOCULTURAL ASPECTS OF MOVEMENT

Moving is overt behavior, and as such is the product of an elaborate process of perceptual organization and selection. The social and cultural setting is a significant aspect underlying the organization and selection of perceptions related to why and how people move and to the meanings that movement suggests both to the mover and to the observer. The focus of study of the sociocultural aspects of movement is the cultural connotations of movement and the ways in which movement is understood in society and social units.

There are several definitions of culture relevant to our study, and it is important to distinguish among them. In biology, "culture" is used to refer to a nutrient medium, and the first definition that is useful to us is closest to that concept. In its broadest meaning, culture is all the socially transmitted behavior patterns that exist; such patterns include beliefs, institutions, the products of human effort or thought, and the characteristic modes of relating to both the environment and other people of any group or society. In another sense, culture refers to particular products or modes of expression, usually artistic or intellectual, that are considered "higher" forms peculiar to a society or class.

CULTURAL CONNOTATIONS OF MOVEMENT

When culture is used to describe the totality of nonbiological human heritage of a society, the implication that it depends upon learned behavior is clear. Every member of a human or national society must become "encultured" in order to survive and be effective beyond biological levels. The man-culture relationship is interactive; that is, "culture" is human products and understandings, and the human, in turn, internalizes the modes of behaving, thinking, and feeling that constitute his existing culture, and he acts in ways that shape culture. Even seemingly innate dispositions and needs are more cultural than genetic or biological since the means to their fulfillment are learned. The satisfaction of hunger, for instance, depends upon a biological need, but the kinds of food that are chosen and the way it is eaten emanate from processes of enculturation.

The capacities for movement behavior are biologically and structurally inherent in the human being. It is the ways in which man uses movement and the meanings that he ascribes to his own movement and to that of others that are sociocultural. Culture even shapes our physical bodies and expression. Western man finds squatting for long periods of time uncomfortable and even impossible; yet in other cultures, it is a characteristic position of resting or listening. When we enter a lecture hall and immediately choose an available seat, we are expressing the ways in which we have been shaped by our culture. Other societies or selected groups gathering for a similar purpose might squat, or sit on the floor cross-legged, or even stand on one leg resting the other foot on the knee. It is interesting that when Japanese restaurants became popular in the United States, *tatami* rooms were included with the idea that one could best experience that culture by sitting as the Japanese sit, preparing food at the table as they do, and so on. Americans, however, found that sitting cross-legged throughout a meal was too uncomfortable to endure, and where these rooms still exist, a deep well has been provided under the table, so that the sitting position characteristic of Western culture can be maintained. Even so, the lack of a backrest is a problem for adults, and they marvel at the Japanese woman who prepares the food and serves from a position of either kneeling or sitting on her heels.

Movement behavior, then, like all behavior, represents perceptions that have been enculturated, and one of the ways to study movement is to try to identify the generalized connotations of movement that obtain within a culture. Perhaps this is most easily understood with reference to "gesture." Movement behavior is nonverbal, but anything that has identifiable connotations or suggestive meanings may be said to be communicative. Gestures that are culturally understood may be thought of as a system of "shorthand"; that is, they communicate in both denotational and connotational ways that are generally recognizable by most members of the society. Some gestures are largely denotational in that they directly represent a fairly discrete act or idea. Babies are taught to "wave bye-bye" and at the same time actually use the words "bye-bye." The gesture of waving goodbye is useful because it can be perceived over greater distances than can the sound of the words. The "peace sign" or previously agreed-upon "V" signal has connotations beyond the word for which it stands. A whole host of attitudes and ideas is expressed by the use of it, and assumptions are made about the people who characteristically or even occasionally use that gesture.

The popularized concept of "body language" is based on the idea that the body expresses feelings, whether these are conscious or not. It has been defined as "movement of a part or all of the body, used by a person to communicate an emotional message to the outside world" (Fast, 1970, p. 2). Actually, it would be more correct to suggest that the communicational aspect of the movement is inferred by the observer rather than consciously intended by the mover. "Kinesics," the science of body motion communication, is a developing field of study. One of its primary assumptions is that "while body motion behavior is based on physiological structure, the communicative aspects of this behavior are patterned by social and cultural experience" (Birdwhistell, 1970, p. 173). The kinesicist, employing many of the techniques of linguistics, analyzes the communicative aspects of the body and focuses on interactive behavior. Structural units of body communication called "kinemes," have been isolated and identified, but their analysis depends upon the contexts within which they occur.

The cultural connotations of movement relevant to our field of study are those that affect our understanding and interpretation of man's behavior as he engages in activity for purposes of his own enhancement or because of his involvement in the symbolic forms of sport, dance, and exercise. The patterns of any culture contain a host of prescriptions for what is to be understood as acceptable or appropriate behavior in general as well as for specialized groups. In a sense, certain contexts may be considered subcultures, in that other prescriptions for behavior derive from them. In the United States today, for instance, the expression of aggression is not generally acceptable although it is increasingly common. Men, however, are "allowed" by the culture to behave more aggressively than are women. And in the specialized subculture of football, aggression is encouraged and rewarded. Any individual, of course, internalizes the negative connotations of displayed aggression from the culture, but the intensity of his own internalization depends upon his particular cultural experience. If he then plays football, he must be enculturated into that sport; sometimes, displaying aggression and hostility arouse cultural guilt to such an extent that this is impossible.

The transmission of culture is a subtle process of apprehending and internalizing the symbols that communicate. The symbolic systems of culture are inseparable from the experiencing of reality. Man's image of himself and his roles, as well as his values, depends on language and other symbols that shape his perception, understanding, and expression. That which we call "male" and "female" refers only superficially to the biological differences that define the sexes. In the process of growing up, one learns what it means to be a "girl" or "boy," "man" or "woman," and one develops concepts of masculinity and femininity that contain a host of assumptions about roles and values. There are many implications of this particular concept for movement behavior and activities. The importance and appropriateness of involvement in movement activities are not viewed in the same ways for both sexes in our society. The expectations for movement abilities and the development of movement skills differ for men and women, and the opportunities and rewards for the actualization of skill are divergent. Even movement behavior itself is sometimes said to be "masculine" or "feminine," and there are people who help boys and girls change their movement patterns so that they will be more appropriate to their sex.

The cultural connotations of movement have to do with the culturally agreed-upon meanings associated with it; the study of these may derive from a focus on either cultural patterns or on the ways in which movement is understood and used in the culture. "Society" refers both to a group of human beings that participate in a common culture and to the totality of their social relationships. Sometimes, "culture" and "society" are used almost interchangeably in referring to their impact on behavior. A focus on social values and interactions and the processes upon which these depend may help to explicate the sociocultural aspects of movement.

SOCIALIZATION AND MOVEMENT BEHAVIOR

The transmission and absorption of culture are ultimately understood and studied in relation to how individuals are socialized. Modes of perception and behavior are learned in social settings, and personality is thought to be as much a social construct as a psychological one. Movement activities are one of the principal means for children to learn those attitudes and behaviors valued by society, and are, therefore, socializing experiences. This is not to imply that there is any reason to believe that movement experiences are necessarily positive in their effect on socialization, although many researchers have tried to establish that they are.

Beyond the pervasive valuing of skill and excellence in the society of the United States, participation in movement activities itself is considered valuable. Because the society is graded according to age and sex (that is, persons apply varying standards of appropriateness to behavior depending upon those factors), the degree of approval granted movement participation varies. Children, for instance, are generally expected to be "active"; to play games and sports, to dance, and to devote a great deal of their time to movement-centered activities. At any age, boys are presumed to be more interested in action than girls, but this becomes especially true for the adolescent. Even the forms of movement have gender connotations in that sport is considered masculine, dance somewhat feminized, and it is considered desirable for men to exercise in the pursuit of strength and vitality while women's exercise aspirations have to do with developing more attractive bodies.

Immersion in movement activities is not quite so acceptable for adults as it is for children. Remnants of the Puritan ethic that dichotomized work and play and attached negative and dangerous connotations to play obtain in the society to some extent. Movement activities still represent aspects of living that are somehow less important and worthy of serious engagement than other pursuits, and many individuals are socialized to perceive their movement participation as temporary and trivial.

Movement behavior, however, is crucial to all behavior, and movement forms are generally widespread and important as social expression in the United States. In that sense, the use of movement must be considered a crucial aspect of both personal and social definition. The individual learns about himself, his capabilities, and his environment through his movement and the attitudes toward it expressed by the society. The capacity to move describes the power to shape self and environment, and the personal manipulations of time, space, and force in movement behavior express that relationship. The individual learns to evaluate movement as "graceful" or "awkward" or in terms of its efficiency and effectiveness. In so doing, he develops a sense of his own abilities and their worth. At the same time, his movement behavior is socialized to enhance the processes of sharing and communication requisite to social interaction. Perhaps this idea can be clarified by thinking of "body mechanics" as an area of movement description that derives its focus from knowledge about efficiency as a mechanical concern related to the functioning of the body. At the same time, our notion of what constitutes good posture or mechanics is influenced by socialized attitudes about what "looks good" as well as simply mechanical analysis.

The socialization of movement behavior is understood most easily with reference to the movement forms that are social forms as well. Sport, for instance, is a social institution in the United States as well as the expressive phenomenon observed in most cultures. Sport itself is socialized to the extent that it represents the values and realities of society, and participation in sport is socializing insofar as the individual absorbs the modes of relating and behaving common to both sport and society. The study of the socialization of sport is a fascinating one, and addresses itself to such questions as why it is important and valued in a society, what social attitudes and interactions are fostered and approved in sport, what the roles and statuses of both players and those related to sport, in other ways are, and so on. To be a successful football player in the United States implies a host of roles and values that represent socialized attitudes and have connotations way beyond the actual playing of the game.

Sports themselves have social connotations according to how desirable they are considered to be. In part, this is determined by availability; that is, because the United States is a mass society, status is sometimes attached to those things not generally available to all. If participation in a sport is expensive or exclusive, it tends to hold social status. Some sports are desirable because their origins had aristocratic connotations; golf, for instance, was played by the aristocracy, hence "the sport of kings" actually was.

In general, sport itself represents opportunities for the actualization and documentation of important social values of success and achievement. The truly outstanding athlete gains social approval almost without qualification in the case of men. The Olympics, as an example, represent a highly valued excellence, and participation in them is socially applauded.

The social connotations of participation in dance are more varied than those that apply to sport. Dance is manifest in many different ways within societies and has different socialization effects. The prevailing social forms of dance are most like sport in that they express certain attitudes about role and social interaction. The study of the ways in which individuals relate, touch, or act independently in dance forms is very interesting and yields insight into diverse social attitudes. Dance, too, preserves cultural approaches among its forms, and folk dance, ethnic dance, and square dance are examples of this.

At the same time, dance in the United States and other cultures derives from aesthetic as well as social expression. In this sense, certain forms, primarily of performance dance, represent specialized social views, usually somehow associated with notions of culture as aesthetic expression. When this is so, dance can still be understood as a socializing experience, but in ways that are less representative of society as it exists and more representative of "higher" values.

The use of exercise in the United States has always reflected confused and unclear attitudes toward the body and its improvement. "Fitness" is valued and considered worthy, and efforts to attain it are surrounded by social attitudes that express slightly unpleasant and therefore "virtuous" connotations. Because it is the form of movement considered most like "work" and least like "play," exercise is socializing in its enhancement of attitudes of obligation and responsibility toward the body. The routinization of exercise programs expresses these attitudes, and exercise approaches gain social currency and then decline in popularity. "Jogging" as a form of exercise is socially widespread and seems likely to retain its appeal because it can be participated in by anyone and provides for individuals pursuing it in their own ways.

The field of study in its concern with movement behavior is peripherally concerned with attitudes toward the body. Standards of attractiveness of the body are socially derived and frequently influence the degree of interest in movement participation, and the social and psychological freedom with which movement activities can be pursued. Behavioral expectations, which we know influence the individual, are often the results of assumptions made on the basis of appearance and incipient movement style. To describe the social and cultural aspects of movement is to study all of the ways that movement behavior and attitudes about movement derive from the society. It is a vast area of study, and one which has only been defined recently enough so that the evidence of cohesive study is not available.

DISCUSSION

Examples of statements which might be used for the purpose of applying the process of identifying assumptions, clarifying theory, and discussion. The three aspects of theory that are involved are (1) identifying the scope of knowledge in the area and classifying it; (2) exploring related concepts and the relationships between and among them; and (3) understanding the implied applications of knowledge for building theory and for application as use (but not in programming movement experiences for others).

Describing Movement (Biomechanical Aspects)

1. The definition of movement "as the change of position of the body or body segments in space and time through the application of varying degrees of force" does not really explain the complexities of the subject.

2. That "movement is basic to life" is probably true, but breathing is also basic to life; somehow, "moving" and "breathing" are not parallel functions in terms of their relationships to other functions.

3. Movement is both a process and a product, and both of these aspects contribute to understanding it as a phenomenon.

4. Man copes with his environment through movement, but movement takes place in a context of physical (mechanical) laws and principles, and these cannot be "violated" insofar as they are *laws*.

5. In general, man's capacity for movement is inextricably related to human structure and is universal, but there are many individualized capacities and limitations even in biomechanical contexts.

6. Although descriptions of movement mostly depend on what is *seen*, such descriptions imply understanding of a host of crucial events and relationships that cannot be observed.

7. Movement is at once an expression of the capacities of the organism and an important modifier of the organism.

8. Complete understanding of an individual's movement would rest on knowledge about that individual from birth to death; understanding at any point in time is, therefore, incomplete, but we seek data which permit hypothesizing about that which we cannot know.

9. The notion of "training" derives from a complex body of knowledge about both the human being and the phenomenon of movement, and theories of training differ and change.

10. Studying "movement" can involve using such diverse techniques as electrocardiograms, measurement, algebra, geometry, urinalysis, electrical impulses, reflex testing, and so forth.

Describing Movement (Sociocultural Aspects)

1. Although knowledge about structure, functioning, and the physical environment is important in explaining and describing movement, such knowledge alone fails to explain the movement behavior of man.

2. The notion of movement as communication or "language" implies some kinds of "universal" understandings of movement, and these are cultural, though many aspects of nonverbal communication may transcend specific societies; on the other hand, it is possible to "misread" body position, gesture, or facial expression.

3. Movement patterns within a culture can be used to describe the culture in terms of its value orientations, which implies that movement expresses culture.

4. Culture "prescribes" acceptable movement patterns through a process of implicit expectancies; within these, the individual learns what is "appropriate" according to his age, sex, social background, and so forth.

5. Man pursues those activities which are valued by his culture; in the United States, all boys are likely to feel encouraged to become skilled athletes, develop movement abilities, and behave in vigorous and courageous ways toward movement challenges and demands.

6. Movement is understood to express feelings, sensibilities, and predilections; in this sense, movement can be assumed to be "masculine" or "feminine"—even "youthful."

7. The society in the United States is so heterogeneous that it is difficult to talk about things being *true* of this culture; on the other hand, we do talk about cultural values and trends and attitudes toward movement.

8. The relationship between body type and personality may or may not be inherent, but, at least, its truth in cultural terms is easily documented.

9. Cultural attitudes toward movement are not static—there are a thousand examples of the changes going on around us today.

10. Sociocultural contexts of movement are crucial considerations of understanding movement and movement behavior; theory which is centered only in biomechanical concerns is simply based on inadequate assumptions.

SELECTED BIBLIOGRAPHY

Describing Movement (Biomechanical Aspects)

Alley, Louis E. "Utilization of Mechanics in Physical Education and Athletics." *Journal of Health, Physical Education and Recreation.* March, 1966, 67-70.
    Discusses mechanics and points out its importance to physical educators.
Broer, Marion R. *Efficiency of Human Movement.* 2nd ed. Philadelphia: W. B. Saunders Company, 1966.
    Discusses basic laws governing movement and the application of basic mechanical principles to fundamental skills, sports, and dance.
Davis, Elwood Craig, and Logan, Gene A. *Biophysical Values of Muscular Activity.* Dubuque, Iowa: Wm. C. Brown Company, 1965.
    Categorizes biophysical values using scholarly reviews of the effects of muscular activity and philosophical perspectives in identifying the importance of physical activity.
Johnson, Warren R. (ed.). *Science and Medicine of Exercise and Sports.* New York: Harper & Brothers, 1960.
    Provides an excellent compendium of knowledge of the various aspects of exercise and sports and the variables affecting them.
Karpovich, Peter V., and Sinning, Wayne E. *Physiology of Muscular Activity.* 7th ed. Philadelphia: W. B. Saunders Company, 1971.
    Theoretical aspects of human physiological functioning are treated and applied to physical activity; ergogenic aids are analyzed in regard to their use in performance.
Kuntzleman, Charles T. (ed.), Eyanson, Paul F. (ass't ed.), and Olson, Arne L. (consulting ed.). *The Physical Fitness Encyclopedia.* Emmaus, Pennsylvania: Rodale Books, 1970.
    Emphasizes the role of exercise in relation to fitness, and includes explication of a great many concepts related to exercise and sport.
Larson, Leonard A. (ed.). *Encyclopedia of Sport Sciences and Medicine.* New York: The Macmillan Company, 1971.
    Prepared under the sponsorship of the American College of Sports Medicine, this is an ambitious work that contains articles on an extremely wide range of topics concerned with the human organism in relation to physical activity.
Mathews, Donald K., and Fox, Edward L. *The Physiological Basis of Physical Education and Athletics.* Philadelphia: W. B. Saunders Company, 1971.
    Deals with direct applications of physiological principles to movement problems.
Rasch, Philip J., and Burke, Roger K. *Kinesiology and Applied Anatomy: The Science of Human Movement.* Philadelphia: Lea & Febiger, 1971.

Presents anatomical and physiological structure of muscles in relation to the application of mechanical principles to human movement; analyzes muscle actions involved in various types of movement.

Smith, Hope M. (ed.). *Introduction to Human Movement.* Reading, Massachusetts: Addison-Wesley Publishing Company, 1968.

Analyzes human movement according to biophysical and cultural variables. Guidelines for learning movement sequences and experiments in movement and perception are included.

Wells, Katharine F. *Kinesiology: The Scientific Basis of Human Motion.* 5th ed. Philadelphia: W. B. Saunders Company, 1971.

Includes basic mechanics of human motion; action of joints and muscles; major categories of motor skill, and the applications of kinesiology to movement.

Describing Movement (Sociocultural Aspects)

Alpenfels, Ethel. "An Anthropologist Looks at Dance." *Journal of Health, Physical Education and Recreation.* November-December, 1966, 65-66.

Discusses dance as cultural expression and analyzes culture in its effects on our understanding of dance.

Bacon, Lucille S. "Sport Script: A New Language for the Kinesiologist." *Journal of Health, Physical Education and Recreation.* February, 1968, 83-85.

Suggests modifications of the Labanotation system for recording sport movement.

Birdwhistell, Ray L. *Kinesics and Context: Essays on Body Motion Communication.* Philadelphia: University of Pennsylvania Press, 1970.

Uses linguistic concepts and techniques as a basis for an analysis of body motion as communication; includes detailed analysis of research and recording techniques.

Boyle, Robert H. *Sport—Mirror of American Life.* Boston: Little, Brown and Company, 1963.

Considers the social influences that foster sport and analyzes some social variables.

Cassidy, Rosalind. "The Cultural Definition of Physical Education." *Quest IV.* April, 1965, 11-15.

Focuses on the importance of human movement in cultural context.

————. "Societal Determinants of Human Movement—The Next Thirty Years." *Quest XVI.* June, 1971, 48-54.

Describes the social influence on movement in both historical and contemporary perspective, and projects the future relationship of movement to society.

Clark, Sharon L. "The Changing Scene in Social Dance." *Journal of Health, Physical Education and Recreation.* March, 1967, 89-91.

Analyzes cultural change and its impact on dance forms.

Cozens, Frederick W., and Stumpf, Florence Scovil. *Sports in American Life.* Chicago: University of Chicago Press, 1953.

Discusses the role of sport and physical education in American culture, and treats the impact of various social institutions on sport and physical education.

Edwards, Harry. *The Revolt of The Black Athlete.* New York: The Free Press, A division of the Macmillan Company, 1970.

Focuses on attitudes toward the black athlete and the nature of the protest during the 1960's; includes appendices documenting protest activity in many contexts of sport and society.

Fast, Julius. *Body Language.* New York: M. Evans and Company, 1970.

Explores gesture and movement, and analyzes their meaning found in communication.

Hart, Marie. "Sport: Women Sit in the Back of the Bus." *Phychology Today.* October, 1971, 64-66.

Deals with the effects of social attitudes on the actual and perceived roles of women in sport.

Hutchinson, Ann. *Labanotation: The System for Recording Movement.* New York: New Directions, 1961.

The classic work that explicates the Laban system of notating movement.
Ibrahim, Hilmi. "Character of American Sports." *The Physical Educator*. March, 1968, 147-149.
   Examines national traits in relation to American sports.
Jokl, Ernst. "Sport As Leisure." *Quest IV*. April, 1965, 37-47.
   Justifies the role of sport in contemporary society.
————. *Medical Sociology and Cultural Anthropology of Sport and Physical Education*. Springfield, Illinois: Charles C Thomas, 1964.
   Consists of essays on the role of sport in culture, data compiled of worldwide athletes, and the impact of sport on human development.
Lippincott, Gertrude. "The Cultural Explosion and Its Implications for Dance." *Journal of Health, Physical Education and Recreation*. January, 1965, 83-85.
   Analyzes dance and increased interest in the arts in relation to culture.
Loy, John W., and Kenyon, Gerald S. (eds.). *Sport, Culture, and Society: A Reader on the Sociology of Sport*. New York: The Macmillan Company, 1969.
   Contains selections that reflect the sociology of sport in various theoretical frameworks; treats sport as a subsystem of a more inclusive social system.
McIntosh, P. C. *Sport in Society*. London: C. A. Watts and Company, 1963.
   Emphasizes the interrelation between sport and the life and philosophies of man.
Mordy, Margaret A. (ed.). *"The Cultural Context of Physical Education."* *Quest XVI*. June, 1971.
   Contains articles that treat sport in relation to culture, society, and aesthetics.
Obertueffer, Delbert. "On Learning Values through Sport." *Quest I*. December, 1963, 23-29.
   Discusses games as a means of transmitting social values. Views the role of organized athletics and its impact on these values with consideration given to the element of competition.
Sage, George H. (ed.). *Sport and American Society: Selected Readings*. Reading, Massachusetts: Addison-Wesley Publishing Company, 1970.
   Deals with sport and physical activity as a psychological and sociological phenomenon; explicates the relationship of social variables to sport, and includes research studies.
Singer, Robert. "Status of Sports in Contemporary American Society." *The Physical Educator*. December, 1966, 147-149.
   Analyzes sport in relation to the quality of American life.
Ulrich, Celeste. *The Social Matrix of Physical Education*. Englewood Cliffs, New Jersey: Prentice-Hall, 1968.
   Considers man and his motor activities in relation to sociological variables such as social groups and social stratification, and deals with implications for physical education.

Chapter III

STUDYING MOVEMENT FORMS

The idea of "forms" transcends the understanding of man's movement pursued in the previous chapter. While the study of movement is concerned with its substance, the study of forms focuses on the contour or shape of movement as it has been developed by man. Even if our knowledge of movement itself were complete; if we knew how it occurs, how it is used and understood, and its most minute effect on every capillary, we would still not understand such forms of movement as sport, dance, or exercise. The analysis of sound and its production would lead to only fragmentary understanding of music, and would not yield insight into the nature of symphonic form. So it is with movement and its forms. Because "form" refers to a holistic concept, it is a more encompassing notion than the sum of its parts suggests.

The identification of dance or sport or exercise as a recognizable phenomenon that exists suggests the idea of "forms." The actual study of forms centers around explanation and discrimination with reference to these phenomena. To seek to explain what dance is or to consider whether or not such things as fishing, billiards, or mountain climbing are sports, is to approach the study of forms. Such study deals with the essence of something rather than its matter; it seeks to explicate the modalities of its existence rather than singular occurrences. Forms, then, have shape or design or pattern, and these are recognizable and manifest in both the conception of the form and its existence. The study of forms is not concerned directly with performance in sport and dance, nor with choosing exercises to produce certain results. Rather, the focus of such study is the essence and modalities of forms of human movement. It is important to remember, however, that understanding of things proceeds both from experiencing them and from analyzing them. Whenever we discuss nonverbal forms, we are abstracting conceptions about experience; that is, we are using words to talk about something that is not dependent upon language. Our study of movement forms is directed toward defining, explaining, and characterizing them, and the dimension of experience is treated in a later chapter. The field of study of human movement is concerned with both academic and experiential modes of knowing, but the focus here is on forms as they are classified on the basis of ideas about their essences.

Physical education has been concerned with particular kinds of movement forms. As the field of study is refined, the boundaries of concern and focus may shift. At present, the movement forms of principal interest may be said to be sport, dance, and exercise. All of these are recognizable structures involving movement as a primary medium for exploration, experimentation, and experience whose function is symbolic in nature and emphasizes the definition of self in relation to the capacity to sense, feel, and perform movement. Further, the forms of sport, dance, and exercise have perceived cultural and personal significance, and that underscores their importance in relation to both knowledge and education.

Although sport, dance, and exercise are clearly definable as forms in which movement plays a dominant role, movement alone is insufficient as a basis to explain or differentiate among them. As forms of human activity, they have sources and relatedness to other large categories of human endeavor that do not necessarily emphasize movement to the same extent. It is, for example, easily granted that card games or word games have something in common with sports; that theater or music are similar to dance; that scales and catechisms bear relationship to exercise. This implies that sport, dance, and exercise, as well as being movement forms, are forms of something else.

It is important to clarify how each of the movement forms may differ or share commonalities with respect to their human sources and functions in order to determine relevant areas of study that should be pursued in order to understand them. Just as the study of movement is insufficient for the complete understanding of each form, so the complete study of one form is insufficient for understanding the others.

One of the first steps to clarifying the larger frameworks of movement forms depends on a distinction between work and play. Each mode has enjoyed both good and bad reputations at one time or another. Perhaps the frequent need to distinguish between the two stems from the polarity of values associated with them. It is also probable that the pursuit of human undertakings under one identified category or the other is influenced by their perceived relative worth. Our purpose here is not to evaluate or compare them in terms of their virtues but rather to distinguish between them.

Play is characterized by activity which arises from the self as a whole feeling, thinking, acting organism and operates on a closed-loop, self-regulating principle of pleasure. Its spirit is both experiential and experimental, meaning that it continues as play so long as it provides valued sensation and progress in the sense of discovery or diversity. It is always associated with a primary sensibility, ability, or capacity acting either on itself alone or in relation to external objects or contexts. Though play serves to define relationships which can be said to be very

3

important, the player's overall intentions are not perceived to be critical by him. He invests himself totally and voluntarily, submitting himself to a reality frame of his own choosing.

Play seems to be socially unnecessary, irresponsible, and self-indulgent, and so it is in its processes; but as a phenomenon, it is very necessary and responsible for creation and much of what is recognized as personal and cultural growth. Necessity may be the "mother of invention," but lack of it is the mother of *creation* working miracles through the pleasures of play. Play only works when it is not working.

Work, on the other hand, is characterized by responsibility, necessity, and mutual social obligation. It is activity directed by the ego in the long-range interests of the self, and it is associated with controls imposed from within or from without. It continues to operate on the basis of power whether it be from ideas, dogma, man, the society, or God. To the extent that these powers are accepted, and there is evidence of progress, work can be experienced as pleasurable, satisfying, and voluntary. Though the results of work can be viewed as unimportant, the overall intentions of the worker are to accomplish something of significance. Though the worker may submit himself totally to his undertaking, the framework itself and its significance and operation are greatly dependent on outside definitions and sources. Work as a phenomenon is every bit as important as play. It is necessary for growth, learning, and progress, not in the sense of creativity but in the sense of actualization and implementation.

It should be apparent that work and play are as much distinguished by modality or approach as by the distinct outlines of particular activities. Riding a bicycle, discussing the origin of the species, drawing a line, or smelling flowers cannot be identified on the continuum of work or play unless much more information is known about the person engaged in the activity and the context of his engagement. Yet, as we look at forms, knowing the nature of work and play allows us to relate the functions and demands inherent in their structure and enables us to determine when they are consistent.

Play, art, and ritual, which are the sources of sport, dance, and exercise, are best understood within the philosophical realm of axiology, which treats the nature of valuing. As such, their relationship to human experience is their primary characteristic, and this is treated in the following chapter. For our purpose in clarifying the study of movement forms, only a few distinctions need be made.

Art and play are concerned with sensory experience, but play forms exemplify an emphasis on the "acting out" phases, and art forms concentrate on perception. Art, then, implies a dimension of judgment having to do with beauty and sensibility, and when this refers to the experiencing of art it is termed "aesthetic." It is fairly clear that art works such as the surviving cave drawings of paleolithic man were not intended as beautiful creations for their own sake or as expressions of the artists' conceptions of beauty. Rather, we suppose that they functioned in some religious or mystical way at the time. The important distinction, however, is that art may be considered any modification of the world of nature in ways that affect the sense of beauty. Play, then, may certainly be indistinguishable from art, and the difference between them lies in the emphasis of art on perceptual elements and the emphasis of play on effectual or action dimensions. Even within art itself we distinguish between the artist as a creative individual and the artisan as one whose skills are primarily manual. And surely the dancer who actualizes the creation of the choreographer may be more like a player than an artist.

Sport clearly derives from play, and its essence depends on the same elements that characterize play. Sport also creates beauty, and certain sports, such as gymnastics, diving, surfing, and the like, depend upon aesthetic judgments in their overall evaluation. One may view sport as though it were art and seek satisfaction in the effects on perception; in fact, the study of sport with reference to sensibilities of "appreciation" is clearly rooted in aesthetic concerns. The use of sport as a subject of art also confuses the distinctions between these two phenomena. When a discus thrower is depicted in sculpture and judged aesthetically pleasing, confusion results as to whether it is the creation of the sculptor that is the art or the discus thrower himself. Even if we were to see a film clip of someone engaged in movement, it would not be readily apparent whether we were viewing dance or sport. But sport is not art in that the intent and symbolic content of the form derive from the effective domain. The form of sport is clearly a sophisticated actualization of play. When its appropriate modalities and approaches are being enacted, sport does not exist as art, though both the participant and the viewer may experience aesthetic meanings in relation to it.

Sport, dance, and exercise are symbolic forms in that they have a recognizable and continued existence in expressing human capacities for motion, perception, experimentation and manipulation, interaction, and actualization. Their similarity rests on the modality of movement as the source for developing, refining, and actualizing these capacities, and they all involve ability and sensibility in their processes. The understanding of sport, dance, and exercise is incomplete without treatment of them as experience, but their classification as forms refers to their sources and intent. It is possible to conceive of sport, dance, and exercise as related cultural forms arising from man's freedom from the necessities of work and his impulses to play and to create. Maheu (1970) certainly expressed this point of view when he suggested that sport and culture, used in the sense of artistic sensibility, both derived from leisure as the primary source. It is probably more accurate, however, to pursue the study of sport, dance, and exercise as forms that differ in that their emphasis implies sources of sport in play, dance in art, and exercise in ritual. The ritualized source for understanding exercise as a form suggests its focus on compelling replication of experience, though this may derive initially from creative or aesthetic sources geared toward effective actualization. All of these movement forms must be understood apart from "work" in that both art and play do imply the freedom to pursue nonproductive, in the workaday sense of the word, avenues of development and expression.

SPORT

Sport has recently become not only acceptable but even fashionable as a subject for scholarly study. Although both the study of play and the analysis of games have prevailed since the nineteenth century, social scientists, philosophers, and physical educators have pursued a similar focus on sport only in the last decade. That is not to suggest there was not some interesting speculation and some study prior to that, but it was not an identified domain for widespread application of theory and scholarship.

The "work-play" dichotomy expressed by the Puritan ethic and the traditional concerns of scholarship with classical and serious studies implied the allegation of "trivial" with reference to sport. Many of the activities of man have been rejected as topics for serious scholarship because of their widespread popularity. Even the study of science and technology was not found in institutions of higher education in the United States until the late nineteenth century, and their entry exemplified a change in the conception of academic studies. The study of sport, then, was simply not considered "dignified" or "academically respectable" until very recently.

Contemporary approaches to the study of sport are diverse. In general, and at different times, philosophers, psychiatrists, psychologists, sociologists, and physical educators alike are concerned with (1) investigating and explaining the nature of the sport experience, and (2) identifying and classifying the characteristics of sport that define and explain it. There is, of course, a great deal of confusion about which discipline is most appropriately responsible for the study of sport. Currently, such courses as "The Sociology of Sport" may be found in departments of either sociology or physical education, and the same is true of concerns with the history of sport, the philosophy of sport, the psychology of sport, and so on. In the preface to his book *Sport: A Philosophic Inquiry*, Weiss (1969) suggests that he has written a book "in philosophy, and not in sport," but his book is used primarily by people more interested in sport than in philosophy. It is unlikely that the study of sport will become the domain of any one discipline, and there is no reason why it should. On the other hand, the integrity of a field of study depends on the clarity of its focus and concerns. There may be interdisciplinary study, and various disciplines may also borrow techniques and modes of inquiry, but studying movement forms as a focus implies a central concern with the phenomenon of sport itself. As sport has become a focus for scholarly consideration, a host of new avenues for speculation and investigation have been proposed and explored. The growing possibilities for pursuit of academic majors in "sport science" and "sport theory" are evidence of a changed attitude toward sport itself as well as toward the field of study of physical education. There are those, of course, who would find it very attractive to major in the playing of a sport, but the treatment here rests on the analysis and understanding of sport as a movement form.

Sport, then, may be conceived as a phenomenon that contains some identifiable and persistent elements and essences and at the same time exists as a source of significant experiences for man. Because sport has been institutionalized; that is, given importance in the life of society, it may also be studied as a social institution. In fact, it is the recognition of the importance of sport in society that is responsible for some of the scholarly attention and research that have developed. Sport simply occupies a lot of the time and interest of large segments of society. Newspapers continually devote a high proportion of space to sport matters; billions of dollars are spent on sport and its related concerns and accouterments in the United States, and sport provides a basis for common understanding and communication. In addition, the importance of sport is also manifest in its use as a vehicle for political and racial protest and in the ways it has been institutionalized in communities, schools, recreational pursuits, and professional categories of all kinds. Social change, problems, and conditions are of great interest today, and more attention is accorded social phenomena than ever before. As this has occurred, the actual and symbolic importance of sport in the life of American society has become more and more obvious. The use of the contexts of sport for protest gestures by black athletes at the Olympic Games, young athletes on the college campus, women athletes on the tennis tournament circuit, and so on is all testimony to that importance. In addition, there is a growing body of sport literature written by athletes rather than scholars. Almost all of these books are about the individual's experience in sport, and the public at large seems to have an insatiable interest in such books as Jerry Kramer's *Instant Replay, Farewell to Football,* and the one he edited, *Lombardi: Winning is the Only Thing.* On the other hand, there is another category of books by athletes or others involved in sport that are highly critical, and Jim Bouton's *Ball Four,* Dave Meggyesy's *Out of Their League,* and books like them have also had a wide appeal. All of these books, which are largely personal and anecdotal, are important sources for studying sport, but, of course, they must be understood in relation to the intent of their authors, and not confused with those works that have been written for the purpose of broadening our understanding of the phenomenon in general.

The search for acceptable definitions of sport is still going on. Most conceptions of sport begin with ideas about play, because there is fairly general agreement that sport is a higher form of play. The classic treatment of play is, of course, *Homo Ludens: A Study of the Play Element in Culture* (Huizinga, 1950). There is no substitute for reading this book, but Huizinga suggests that "the very existence of play continually confirms the supra-logical nature of the human situation . . . We play and know that we play, so we must be more than rational beings, for play is irrational." (pp. 3-4) Huizinga also supplied oft-quoted characteristics of play that are used as a definition:

> We might call it a free activity standing quite consciously outside "ordinary" life as being "not serious," but at the same time absorbing the player intensely and utterly. It is an activity connected with no material interest and no profit can be gained by it. It proceeds within its own proper boundaries of time and space according to fixed rules and in an orderly manner. It promotes the formation of social groupings which tend to surround themselves with secrecy and to stress their difference from the common world by disguise or other means. (p. 13)

Schmitz (1968) suggested that although sport and play were different, sport "is primarily an extension of play," and he identified an important and pervasive aspect of sport as "suspension of the ordinary." Metheny (1969) offered a comprehensive definition of sport that transcended the aspect of play, included the notion of a specified "pattern of organization" known and agreed to, and differentiated among "individual performances," "side-by-side performances," "comparative parallel performances," and "face-to-face oppositional performances." It is apparent that sport must be differentiated from both play and games.

Part of the differentiation of sport from play has to do with the nature of the experience. Slusher (1967) suggested that "sport is more than play. It includes devotion, care, respect, concern and responsiveness toward the desired outcomes. It is serious." This is not to deny that play can also be serious, and perhaps this distinction would have to rest on the seriousness with which sport has been institutionalized. Insofar as "play," "games," and "sport" are used interchangeably, they refer to those elements they have in common. The characteristics of play as *free, separate, uncertain, unproductive,* and governed by both *make-believe* and *rules*" (Caillois, 1961) are common to sport and games as well. The "suspension of the ordinary" pervades play, sport, and games even when "players" are being paid, winning or losing large amounts of money, or breaking very ordinary arms and legs in the process of playing. These activities are bounded by their own distinctive orders and are not part of the "real" or pragmatic world of commerce, sociality, or attention. "Game" implies structure, and playing a game means to apply the characteristics of play within a defined and bounded procedure. A game has been defined in just that way, as "*an exercise of voluntary control systems in which there is an opposition between forces, confined by a procedure and rules in order to produce a disequilibrial outcome.*" (Sutton-Smith and Avedon, 1971) Some sports are games, but all games are not properly sport. Weiss suggested that this was because sport is a contest, "and despite the contesting there are no contests in a game." (Weiss, 1969) The analysis of sport rests on the assumptions discussed here, and is not intended to clarify these issues much more, but is intended to provide a model that can be used for study.

ESSENCE

One approach to classification models lies in identifying the essence or essential qualities of a phenomenon. In this way, definitions include those activities that express the identified essence *as a focus* and exclude those activities that do not. Certainly, the characteristics of play identified by Caillois and others are central to the essence of sport. Because they do not adequately distinguish or explain sport, however, they may be considered crucial characteristics of sport; that is, play itself is not the essence of sport but the elements of play are always present.

The essence of sport is found in *contesting* and *performing with excellence.* Sports are contests, and man struggles and competes against an opposing force whether this be other men, animals, nature, or measurements of time and space and force. Excellent and superior skill and performance express and define the contest no matter what other faculties or abilities contribute to such excellence.

In various sports the elements of contest and performance may hold differing degrees of importance. Some sports, like gymnastics and diving, preserve a focus on form or skill as part of their formulation even when structured in competitive situations. Other sports, like surfing and skiing, are most often pursued simply in the interests of increased skill. Sports that are also games, like football and basketball, focus clearly on the contest between performers. In a similar way, the mountain climber, fisherman, or runner is contesting nature whenever he is performing.

STRUCTURE

Sport has structure; it is not an amorphous activity, but is carried on within its own bounded order. Most simply, structure is the set of rules and procedures by which a sport is understood and carried on. The essence of sport is preserved and expressed by its structure. In that sense, rules define the contest and preserve the qualities of equality of opportunity to succeed and uncertainty of the outcome until it has been realized. Whenever rules become inadequate to that task, they are changed and refined so that the sport can endure. In recent years we have seen the "advantages" of height in basketball equalized by the introduction of rules regarding "dunking" and "goaltending." There have been radical changes in the structure of women's basketball so that the essence of the contest would be exciting and excellence of performance would become a standard that was not easily attained.

The essence of sport as contest and performance implies excitement and excellence and continual challenge. The structure of each sport must insure these qualities. For centuries, for instance, the sport of archery has persisted because of its demands for skill mastery and refinement, and its structure has not changed very much. Today, however, technology has improved the equipment available to such an extent that *perfect* performances in competition are occurring. It is the structure of archery that must change to provide for its essence as contest to be realized, and to account for the use of mechanical releases and other devices.

CONTEXT

Whenever sport is carried on, there is some context that affects it. Obviously, individuals can pursue sport on their own as a one-time occurrence, and they are not bounded by any considerations other than the structure of the particular sport. Even so, the restrictions and goals they set for themselves probably derive from some context in which that sport is carried on, or by regulations about the use of courts or fields or the number of fish that one may catch that do derive from an existing organization or regulatory body. In general, sport is regulated and controlled and affected by a variety of contexts that exist as sponsoring organizations or structures, regulatory or legal policies and rules, and institutionalized agreements. In other words, baseball is played as a sport on sandlots, in schools and colleges, in Little Leagues and Lassie Leagues, in park and city leagues, in minor leagues and major leagues. Each of these contexts has some effect on who shall play, how play is actually carried out, and what performance and contest mean. Within these various contexts there are different agreements; there are seasons and pre-season games, there are practice and contest; there are game winners and league champions, and there are team standings and individual records.

Although we refer to generalized notions of sport and of particular sports, the context is an important aspect of understanding sport. Beyond certain general agreements, the actual structure of a sport, its rules, may be modified according to the policies derived from the context. Pop Warner football, college football, and professional football differ with reference to certain rules, and that means that the essence of that sport is being expressed in somewhat different ways. The determination of eligibility—that is, specifying who may participate—is a crucial effect of the context.

STYLE

Essence, structure, and context serve to explicate the nature of sport; "style," because it refers most directly to human expression, focuses on the sport experience more clearly. The structure of sport provides for the expression of contesting and performing, and it is the individualized expression of these, whether as the skill or strategy of individuals or teams, that may be called "style." There are, of course, styles of play or performance that become fashionable and institutionalized. The use of the forward pass in football is a good example of an aspect of style that revolutionized the game itself. Eventually, the structure of football was modified to accommodate and enhance the use of the forward pass, and we must conclude that this happened because it contributed to the expression of the essence of the game. Other developments of style have not been permitted to persist; "dunking," for instance, was outlawed instead, though there are some current efforts to change the rules to permit it once more.

The style of a player or a team is related to contesting and performance. Style is developed, whether consciously or not, in order to contribute to excellence and effectiveness of performing and to success and winning. The "Fosberry Flop" as a stylistic approach to the high jump gained great currency because of its effectiveness in the Olympic Games. On the other hand, some aspects of style relate to actual performance only indirectly. "Style," as a term used about athletes, teams, or sportsmen, may refer to appearances, images, and attitudes. In this sense, style comes to be associated with people or sports even though it may seem to have no relevance to the actual conduct of the sport.

PROBLEMS IN THE STUDY OF SPORT

Because formalized study of sport is relatively new, there are a great many problems that are either discouraging scholarly effort or limiting it. The whole question of professional athletics, for instance, is sometimes arbitrarily ignored because it seems that it does not fulfill Huizinga's characteristic of play as "connected with no material interest." There are those who use the terms "sport" and "athletics" to represent differing categories. In that view "sport" is used whenever all of the connotations surrounding the activity are those most clearly associated with play, and "athletics" is used to represent those situations in which sports are highly organized and there is some element of "profit" or "spectacle" surrounding them. The thesis here is that the focus for attention in studying movement forms is the *phenomenon* of sport. Sport itself cannot be connected with material interest, and there is no profit in the sport experience except insofar as the *context* is organized in such a way as to produce income or pay players for their performance. This may be an arbitrary distinction that is difficult to accept because the motivations of the athlete have, in fact, been considered in defining sport contexts. That is to say, conceptions of the athlete as a "professional" or an "amateur" have been important considerations in the organization of sport, and such distinctions imply that sport is different according to who is involved in it. For purposes of study, however, it is better to focus on the broadest conception, and sport would exist whenever it was played, with the understanding that *contexts* do vary and do affect *essence, structure, and style*. If they affect the essence or structure of sport to a point where they are not recognizable or important, then the phenomenon may be spectacle or entertainment, but cannot be identified as sport.

The judgment as to when sport does or does not exist is a complex one. Social variables have affected sport greatly, and if social factors continually determine sport decisions, the essence of sport may be corrupted. This relationship of sport and society is, of course, an important concern in the study of sport. Technology and mass media affect sport in many subtle and obvious ways. Certainly, simplified systems of scoring and sudden death tie-breakers in tennis are probably an outgrowth of the demands of television programming. The taking of time-outs not related to the structure of soccer or football but necessary for television commercials is not a sport decision. The secrecy of strategy in sport suffers in a world where the camera and the microphone can intrude the bench and the huddle. Somehow, the study of sport must focus more clearly on the phenomenon itself so that we truly understand the relationship of sport to such things as social class, status, roles, race, sex, economics, and technology. Within the field of study, our understanding of sport is the important focus; if our study leads to more insight into society or socialization only, it is not sufficient.

The model presented here could be helpful in classifying data about many of the things that influence sport. As such a model was developed more completely, it would permit us to postulate constructs derived specifically from our understanding of sport and classify other variables and data. Presently, there is a mass of data relevant to sport, but there is a dearth of commanding structures that provide insight into either needed avenues of research and study or ways of organizing existing information.

If we perceive sport according to the model of *essence, structure, style and contexts*, it helps us explicate the sport phenomenon. There is, for instance, some confusion about those sports that depend upon human skill primarily and those like horse racing and auto driving where the actual power is that of an animal or machine. There is question, too, about the actualizations of the sport form; that is, if someone skis or swims in a random and unstructured manner, for his own pleasure, is it sport that he is engaged in? There is even question about the rules or laws established by fish and game commissions with reference to the structure of hunting and fishing as sports. Some have suggested that such things as football are clearly sport, but activities like golf "are only games."

It is, of course, the purpose of the study of sport to develop theoretical structures that lead to clear distinctions and answers to these questions.

Both sport and the sport experience must be studied from all the relevant perspectives: that of performer; spectator; coach; and scholar as well as that of the phenomenon itself. The first step to such study is an inquiring attitude that transcends the internal aspects of sport; that is, understanding sport implies asking "why?" and "what does that mean?" as well as "how is that done?" and "what is most effective?"

DANCE

Edrie Ferdun

In this section our attention will be focused on dance and how it can be studied. Each of us starts with some idea of what dance is, having had personal experiences with the word and the phenomena to which it refers. If we searched through our images, we might recall a darkened room where friends alternately arose and returned from a few minutes of rhythmic moving about in an area staked out for that purpose. We might have in mind a grand opera house with highly skilled people turning, leaping, and posing on a stage far away in a flood of light. We might be able to recall the feeling of stretching and bending, pointing and turning, exhilaration or despair, all under the watchful eye of the dancing teacher.

Images of this kind provide some personal data for you to use in understanding what dance as a field of study might include, but you need a great many of them, and you need to know how much of your image is truly attributable to dance and how much might be you. For those who have extensive experience with dance in all its facets, defining the subject is a search order in the sum total of their images. To make this process more easily accomplished some guidance is provided in the form of an overall perspective on dance. This should help you either in constructing your experiences with dance or in understanding them.

DANCE AS MOVEMENT, FORM, AND MEANING

Dance is something people do; we can see it and feel it. Some go to great lengths to participate in or watch it. It is identifiable and, therefore, has some distinguishing features of form in our perceptions. Since the form of things has direct relation to their function and nothing comes into existence or persists without meaning or the promise of fulfilling certain needs, we must recognize the necessity of considering both function and form in defining dance.

The most obvious characteristic of dance is movement perceived as having a special quality in direct relation to something felt. Terms like "rhythmic," "graceful," "expressive" point to our heightened awareness of these factors in the presence of most dance. Our attention is shifted from practical outcomes of particular movement patterns to what they are as unique organizations of space, time, and energy, as evidence of the capacities and sensibilities of the dancers, and as meaningful human constructions with the potential to reveal and illuminate something of the sense of living.

Movement, then, is an important phenomenon in the field of study of dance. The main interest in movement from the dance perspective has to do with its roles as a source of awareness, feeling, and understanding and as a medium for discovering, formulating, and sharing it. Concern for movement as experience dominates interest in movement as behavior, as man's primal technology, or as a means to physiological well-being.

Experiencing movement requires attention to interactive sensory information which is perceived from either of two alternative positions, as mover or viewer. "What is movement?" becomes primarily a question of what there is to experience about movement—associated bodily sensations; a sense of space, time, and energy; and all the connotations of meaning derivable from the active perceptual and cognitive processes.

This point of view is reflected in the typical language used by dancers and audiences in describing movement. It is seen as "fast" or "slow," "even" or "uneven," "big" or "small," "high" or "low," "hard" or "soft," "round" or "straight," "smooth" or "sharp." Analogies and feeling relationships like "bouncy," "bubbly," "deflated," "attacking" and endless others describe movement in the fluid vocabulary of dance experience. This does not mean that there are no shared words which refer to specific movements or relationships, but these too are based on meaningful perceptual groupings, not isolated elements prerequisite to precise scientific investigation.

Patterns of relationships (or form, which is the mode of perception) become at least equally as important as movement in the subject of dance. "Form" as applied to dance can refer to any number of aspects of organization. In developing or comprehending a particular dance form, one is capable of ordering his perceptions or actions on the basis of (1) dancers, their number and sequence of grouping, (2) time and its rhythmic flow and sequential organization, (3) space and the shape of its development, (4) energy and the dynamics of its evolution, and (5) meaning, the development of its symbols or themes. These alternatives rarely represent a pure or conscious choice, but operate in relation to the nature of the dance itself and the individual style of artist or audience member.

Form is a consideration in all fields in that it is the basis of identification and differentiation, but in the arts it is a central aspect of subject matter. The same kind of concern for form is shared by all the arts regardless of their media or the initial sensibility which may dominate them. When sound, shapes, images, words, or actions are dealt with as experience and manipulated for perception, new forms emerge, though they may bear close relationship to forms previously known from the natural or humanly constructed world. The study of dance forms and their function in experience which is specific and meaningful is in the realm of the subject matter of dance.

Meaning as it is expressed in or derived from movement pattern, form, and context is a third dimension of the interactive concerns of dance. Movement may be the most objective stuff we see and feel in dance, but it must be formed by the dancer or audience to be perceived, and this is done on the basis of meaning and value. Movement is an outgrowth of something felt or understood, and our grasp of it acknowledges this relationship and at the same time depends upon our own personal resources and systems of meaning. What we come to know of a dance is a complex interaction between what appears to be given as sensory symbolic material from a source outside ourselves and the unique materials of ourselves which we acknowledge as having come from our life experiences.

Our understanding and appreciation of a dance represent an integration of what we believe the dance to be and the personal relationship we find with it. The role of meaning, then, is significant in forming the dance, whether as artist or audience, in responding to it, and in appreciating it. Because this is so, dance forms and reactions to them provide a resource for understanding the processes, meanings, and values of those involved. Dance both reflects and formulates the sensibility and sense of a people in the context of their time and place.

Of particular interest to the field of dance are those meanings which are relevant to understanding dance itself. Evidence is sought regarding the concepts of the body and movement, form and meaning, the role of the various participants in the dance cycle, technique and craft, and the relationship of dance to other experience and situations. Both the processes by which feeling and ideas are expressed, communicated, or derived and the resultant conclusions appropriate to dance are within the subject framework of dance.

APPROACHES TO THE STUDY OF DANCE

"Dance" cannot be defined satisfactorily without reference to characteristics which have been termed here as "movement," "form," and "meaning." The process of qualifying these and the phenomena to which they refer is the task of those engaged in the field of study. There are two approaches to this study. One method is to engage directly in dance, actively manipulating and experiencing its various dimensions and relationships. The second method is to remove oneself sufficiently to observe the whole or parts, analyzing or deducing the structures and operations involved. The following discussion focuses first on study from within.

Dance as a field of study embraces movement, form, and meaning primarily as these relate to each other in the experience of the choreographer, the dancer, and the audience. These three roles, whether fulfilled by one or more persons, must function for dance to exist. Studying dance as a participant means exploring and developing oneself in relation to movement, form, and meaning as they operate in the making, the performing, or the grasping of a dance.

In the recent history of the performing arts, each of these roles has been quite distinct, being fulfilled by clearly designated individuals, but this need not be so, and there is a trend away from this kind of specialization. The functions considered separately, however, provide a basis for understanding the frameworks of responsibility and goals which influence perception and the kind of experience sought in dance study.

Studying dance from the point of view of the dancer necessarily emphasizes moving and movement. It is the dancer who shapes himself and his powers in relation to the formal and expressive demands of particular dances or types of dance. The usual specificity of these demands makes accomplishment or proficiency in dance performance a matter of extensive and specialized study, most often as immersion in the technique developed by artist-teachers.

Different types and styles of dance like ballet, modern dance, jazz, and folk dance emphasize different skills and sensitivities; they often use different movement vocabularies and proceed according to different aesthetic, cultural, and process values. Some dance forms, especially those of a religious or theatrical nature which have developed over centuries, are so articulated and refined as to require many years of study for participation. When dance forms are derived from cultural sources different from those of the dancer, even simple dances ordinarily considered recreational are inaccessible except through concentrated study.

Regardless of the complexity or uniqueness of particular dance forms, a dancer's study involves the discovery of interrelationships between form and meaning as they relate to his own capacities to actualize them in performance. This means that a dancer must study himself. His focus of attention must alternate among the variables of himself as a sensing, moving body, movement as physical-perceptual pattern, and dance as a framework of aesthetic and expressive goals, values and processes.

With choreography as a frame of reference, dance study focuses on aspects of forming in relationship to movement and felt or declared meaning. The choreographer forms what the dancer performs. He defines the goals and designs the events which are the dance. It is his responsibility to discover and evaluate what is meaningful and worth exploring in terms of movement, thematic ideas, and sensory relationships, and to invent, shape, and mold materials into an integrated form for experience.

Studying dance as a choreographer involves exploration of those processes of the self and perception which facilitate creation and effective presentation. Like the dancer, the choreographer must study himself, but the emphasis of his attention lies with his capacity to discover and envision meaningful relationships in conjunction with the craft to actualize them in concrete perceptual form. To do this, the student of choreography usually explores the work of many others, the personal methods of a few, and, most important of all, tries his hand at making dances.

To study dance for the purpose of enhancing one's capacity to function fully as a member of the audience is to concentrate on the challenge of deriving maximum meaning in relation to a perceived form. The audience member does not shape himself as does the dancer, nor does he determine movement and form as does the choreographer; rather, he operates on and forms his perceptions into a synthesis of meanings which in turn shape his experience and himself.

Aspects influencing perceptual inclusion and depth, such as openness and sensitivity, especially respecting movement, are important considerations in determining the audience's experience. Knowledge and understanding of dance, the arts, and the social and cultural conditions past or present relevant to a particular dance experience not only influence what is perceived in the dance but provide a context for potentially related and shared meanings and associations from which significance may be derived.

The process of study involves experiencing a great many dances in the role of an audience member. Guidance can come from more aware members who share their methods of apprehending, resultant feelings, and insights. The professional critic provides one source for this comparison. The cognitive study of movement, form, the arts, dance history, and the works and lives of particular dance artists if synthesized into a human and cultural consciousness, functions to extend awareness and appreciation of dance.

For dance to maintain itself and grow in significance as a personal and cultural source, there must be people actively engaged in it. The quality of its functioning is dependent upon informal or formal study on the part of those participating directly in it: choreographers, dancers, and audience. This kind of study depends upon immersion and the active pursuit of the ever-changing interrelationships of movement, form, and meaning as evidenced in particular dances. It represents a cultivation of self in relation to dance as it is experienced from the inside.

There is another point of view from which to study dance. One can look at dance from outside its experiential operation in the fashion of a scholar. This approach seeks to define relationships between and among dance and other phenomena. Dance provides certain kinds of data which can be examined for purposes of understanding man, society, and culture. Dance or aspects of it can be of interest to both the humanities and the sciences depending upon the general purposes and methods of the study. History, anthropology, psychology, philosophy, physiology, and education are among the fields sharing an interest in dance.

Questions arise as to the subject boundaries and proper placement of studies in their respective academic fields when interests and methods overlap. Is dance history a study of history or dance? Is rhythmic analysis a study of music or dance? Is consideration of body image and the dancer properly psychology or dance? The criterion which generally provides guidance in this consideration has to do with the primary orientation or purpose of the study. If something is studied for reasons of better understanding something else, it is properly placed in the framework of the subject of which it is a topic. It is quite obvious that a transposition integrating information from one field to another is not only possible but desirable as a means to achieving understanding.

To study dance as a scholar means to seek definition, clarification, and explanation of dance, its processes and forms, its innerworkings and relationships with other phenomena, as they have existed in the past, appear in the present, and may develop in the future. The goal of this study is understanding, in the form of satisfactory explanation acceptable to all in contact with the data. Generalizations, principles, concepts, and classifications are constantly tested in the face of all particular instances which can be observed. A body of knowledge about dance is developed which undergoes elaboration and reorganization on the basis of continuous study. An extensive vocabulary develops as differentiations become more precise.

Since the systematic study of dance in this manner is of relatively recent origin in comparison to other fields, its body of knowledge is not highly developed, integrated, and organized. Even the most cultivated areas, such as the study of dance history and motor performance, are in need of much further study. Aesthetics and dance criticism, dance ethnology, and kinesics are developing rapidly. As transposition of concepts and material takes place from other fields to dance and as the interests and tools for study such as Labanotation, Effort-shape analysis, choreometrics, and kinemorphics are extended, the body of knowledge of dance is expected to grow and become more functional in providing greater understanding and guidelines for more effective application in the improved life of man.

EXERCISE

All of the various definitions of the word "exercise" suggest connotations of duty, obligation, improvement or strengthening, and some kind of exertion. There are specific exercises, whether in movement or music, designed to improve some aspect of function or ability. In that sense, whenever one is engaged in movement for the purpose of improving some aspect of capacity or ability, he is exercising. Exercise as a form, however, transcends an emphasis on specific aims for improvement. When we refer to "forms" of exercise, we are using that word in a way that is related to some concept of ceremony or traditional rites. Forms of exercise are like such things as commencement exercises, with an implication of the importance of ritualized behavior as the essence of the form.

Most simply, exercise exists as a movement form whenever particular movement patterns have been described, even named, and are learned and performed by diverse groups or succeeding generations. "Jumping jacks," "squat thrusts," "windmills," and the like are easily recognizable names for specific movements known to many people. Whole exercise routines, such as the "daily dozen" or the "Air Force exercises," may be similarly recognizable and engaged in regularly or from time to time by various individuals. Other, more vague categorizations may be used to refer to various combinations of specific patterns; "calisthenics," "setting-up exercises," or "endurance activities" are examples of these. There may even be specific actions that are used as exercise forms, and these might include "jogging," "running in place," "walking," or the like.

In its emphasis on improvement and exertion, exercise is a rationalized form of movement. This implies that the effect of exercise and of specific exercises is known and beneficial and that exercise is pursued for the purpose of gaining those benefits. The essence of exercise as a form, then, is its effects on the body or its functioning or capacities. Exercises can strengthen various body parts, increase range of motion, improve cardiovascular endurance and function, and in general contribute to the enhancement of the organism. Exercise can be manifest as isometric or isotonic and can involve particular body segments or the body as whole.

Most exercise is predicated on replication as a requisite dimension to the attainment of its benefits. In its repetitive nature, or its requirements of effort over long periods of time, the connotations of exercise are more like those of work than of play. These are heightened by the fact that exercise has been used in many kinds of situations as a form of punishment. Because of the principle of overload, it is also generally believed that the benefits of exercise are available only when the individual is experiencing pain, fatigue, or some other kind of physical discomfort. In the face of all this, the wonder is that exercise persists as one of the most popular and widespread movement forms.

The individual who participates in exercise as a form usually incorporates it into his activities in some planned and repetitive manner. There is a dimension of virtue and compulsion attendant to regular exercise in that its essence is fulfilled only through frequent, repetitive, energetic immersion in it. Most exercise patterns also have at least pseudo-scientific overtones which lend a sense of greater importance to their routinization. Those forms of exercise that are based in medicine have the most scientific credence, of course, but almost all proponents of exercise systems claim a scientific basis for their programs. Because this is so, the compulsive aspect of exercise is increased; that is, full benefits are believed to accrue only when the system is followed faithfully and performed according to its explicit structure. At one time in the history of physical education, that field was characterized by exercise programs such as the "Swedish movement cure," "Danish gymnastics," and even "wand drills."

Conceived in its medical and scientific bases, exercise systems seem to foster a mind-body dichotomy. The exerciser may develop attitudes about his participation that seem to suggest that "he" must take care of his "body" and improve and exercise it. Exercise, then, can become a highly mechanized expression of its essence; the use and improvement of the body. Even the "use and disuse" principle that is a basic one underlying the importance of exercise has connotations of the body as distinct from the self, and as a kind of instrument that must be "tuned" or refined and kept in good order. All of these connotations reinforce exercise in relation to values that express an ethic in which hard work, self-improvement, and essential good are known and pursued.

"Physical fitness" has been an important concept during the past two decades in the United States and has reinforced the importance of keeping the body in good shape. With its attention to testing and assessing the status of the body, the physical fitness movement is geared toward making people aware of their limitations and, hopefully, being willing to work toward improvement. Not only are dualisms of mind and body reinforced within the notion of physical fitness, but the movement itself employs techniques designed to foster national shame and individual guilt as motivating factors.

The essence of exercise is found in its contributions to "improvement" and the satisfactions attendant to fulfilling obligatory responsibilities toward the body. "Improvement" may be understood differently in the various ways in which exercise is used. Physical therapy programs are rehabilitative, the purpose of exercise may be maintenance of function, or the goal may be increased abilities. At the same time, exercise for men suggests goals of strength and vigor, while it is usually conceived as having goals of weight control and increased attractiveness for women. This is less true as the values of vitality in general are recognized and considered important for all.

Interestingly enough, exercise, which depends primarily on the use and efforts of the body, is surrounded by an array of technological aids. Commercial gymnasiums and spas abound, usually under some title of "health club," and the exercise consumer can be assessed and programmed toward improvement. These establishments are characterized by their equipment, designed for every conceivable effect on the body, and by the presence of pools, saunas, sun rooms, and the like. In contemporary society, it would seem the Spartan connotations of exercise are fulfilled simply by using the body at all, even in lovely, fully carpeted, and comfortable environments. The exercise consumer responds to both the television personality and the health spa entrepreneur because they direct his efforts and affirm the alleged effects of them.

The concern of Americans with their bodies is obvious, and the health-attractiveness-aid industry is booming. Some years ago, millions of couches that moved and supposedly "exercised" the body in doing so were bought by a gullible public. Presently, "sauna pants" that are supposed to cause great weight losses, "jogging machines," "exercycles," and a host of other items of equipment are being used widely. The home sauna is in widespread use, and exercise and weight-control programs of all types are found everywhere.

In addition to the expression of its essence of exertion-toward-improvement, forms of exercise must have ritualistic dimensions. Like sport and dance, exercise as a form must provide a domain that can be entered and re-entered and in which the individual knows that he is immersed and involved in that form. Because the structure and contexts of exercise are so variable, its forms are not as easily recognizable as those of sport and dance. People employ the rituals of jogging around the park at dawn, or practicing isometrics as they drive cars, or performing an exercise series every morning and all of these may be participation in the form of exercise if, in fact, it is done for self-improvement and becomes ritualized.

There is another domain of exercise form that is not characterized by the pragmatic, rational, mechanistic framework just described. In Oriental philosophy, although the mind and body were seen as somewhat discrete aspects of man, both were considered crucial in the development of higher states of being. The martial arts of judo and karate, and the Oriental body disciplines of Yoga, Tai Chi, and Zen awareness training are all exercise forms that are gaining currency in the Western world. All of these, of course, are the most highly ritualized exercise forms we know, and in their purposes of achieving "perfect knowledge" or "Nirvana" have an advantage over solely bodily-based systems. In these disciplines, the connotations of punishment are replaced by a need for "control," and their practitioners sometimes accept new modes of behavior and lifestyles as a result of their immersion in Yoga or Zen.

Other exercise forms have developed recently as body therapies; that is, psychotherapeutic methods have traditionally seemed to suggest a mind-body dualism just as medical therapies have, and this is not completely acceptable in relation to present theory. Although not exercise forms, sensitivity and encounter experiences are good examples of the way in which movement and touch are being used in relation to personal and emotional expression. At Esalen Institute in Big Sur, California, the structural integration theories of Ida Rolf are being applied. Based on a theory of the importance of posture and its relation to character, this technique depends upon stretching, palpating, and manipulating the body. Dance experiences are being used as therapy in mental hospitals and in the culture at large, and movement improvisation or dance is pursued as one of the forms requisite to therapy or self-integration. Alexander Lowen, a psychoanalyst, directs the Institute for Bioenergetic Analysis in New York, and has developed therapy programs that rely heavily on postural awareness and the repositioning of body parts.

"Exercise" as a form, then, becomes more and more complex. Its essence lies in its contributions to improvement of the human organism, but this may be understood as prescribed effects on body functioning or ability, or as representative of a whole state of being. It does presuppose a need for improvement, but that, too, may derive from concepts of either remediation or extension. As part of the field of study underlying physical education, exercise has not been attended to as a form to any great extent; rather, it has been studied either specifically as discrete movements or vaguely as undifferentiated from sport.

DISCUSSION

Statements relative to knowledge in the field of study as descriptive of movement forms. The emphasis here is on the symbolic nature of "forms" and their connotations.

Studying Movement Forms

1. The notion of "form" implies a concept beyond that of the movement itself; that is, even the most complete utilization of biomechanical and sociocultural analyses of movement would yield incomplete understanding of the form within which they were undertaken.

2. Traditionally and conceptually, the concerns of physical education center around the movement forms of play, sport, dance, and exercise, although there are aspects of physical education which do not deal with these.

3. If a form is to be understood, its connotations and symbolic uses must be examined; the forms of play, sport, and dance are almost totally nonrational and nonproductive in their essence.

4. "Exercise," of course, is based in rational concerns, but when we consider *forms* of exercise, the symbolic content is extremely important.

5. Basically, the forms with which physical education is concerned derive from frameworks of either play or art, and certain activities deal with both of these concepts.

6. The characteristics of play provide a basis for sport, and the characteristics of art provide a basis for dance, but surely sport can be aesthetic and dance can be playful; movement is a crucial characteristic of both, but alone does not make something either dance or sport.

7. Forms are characterized by an "essence" which expresses the symbolic content; by a "structure" which explicates that essence, and by "style" as a mode of behaving within the form—they are carried on within "contexts" which provide for performance and may affect their connotations.

8. The structure and function of sport and dance may parallel structures and functions in "real" (as opposed to symbolic) life, but they must be understood as symbolic forms if the knowledge about them is to be valid.

9. Theorizing about movement forms is not the same as participating in them, but crucial understanding of them probably depends upon both since they are, by definition, nonverbal forms.

10. Knowledge about movement forms depends on insight into philosophical processes of symbolizing and experiencing as well as *knowing* and finding meaning; analysis derives from systems of classifying and synthesizing knowledge gleaned from the widest range of empirical data.

SELECTED BIBLIOGRAPHY

Studying Movement Forms

Brown, Evelyn. "An Ethological Theory of Play." *Journal of Health, Physical Education and Recreation.* September, 1968, 36-39.
  Builds a theory of play based on the premise of territory, pecking order, and weaponry, and applies these elements to the consideration of sport.
Caillois, Roger. *Man, Play and Games.* New York: Free Press of Glencoe, 1961.
  A classic work suggesting various classifications and approaches to understanding play and games.
DeGrazia, Sebastian. *Of Time, Work and Leisure.* New York: The Twentieth Century Fund, 1962.
  Defines leisure within constructs of time-usage and other classifications and deals with its role in society.
Ellfeldt, Lois Elizabeth. "Dance Is Many Things." *Anthology of Contemporary Readings: An Introduction to Physical Education.* 2nd ed. Edited by Howard S. Slusher and Aileene S. Lochkart. Dubuque, Iowa: Wm. C. Brown Company, 1970, 236-241.
  Explicates dance within the two primary categories of participation and performance.
Eyler, Marvin H. (ed.). *Toward a Theory of Sport. Quest X.* May, 1968
  A valuable collection of scholarly articles on sport that seek to define it, deal with its essence and characteristics, and suggest the importance of sport as a focus for study and physical education.
Fraleigh, Sandra Horton. Unity of Design: Modern Dance in Physical Education." *Journal of Health, Physical Education and Recreation.* November-December, 1971, 31-33.
  An analysis of modern dance as movement form, art, and education; deals with concepts of play and art, and suggests the need for a central role for dance in a unified academic discipline based on the art and science of movement.

Gates, Alice. *A New Look At Movement: A Dancer's View*. Minneapolis: Burgess Publishing Company, 1968.
Provides an understanding of movement from the dancer's perspective; offers suggestions for reviewing and analyzing movement forms.

Hart, M. Marie. *Sport in the Socio-Cultural Process*. Dubuque, Iowa: Wm. C. Brown Company, 1972.
A valuable collection of readings that treat sport in relation to social systems and variables and in the context of culture and experience.

Huizinga, Johan. *Homo Ludens: A Study of the Play Element in Culture*. Boston: The Beacon Press, 1950.
The classic exposition of Man the Player, and the integration of concepts of play and culture.

Keen, Sam. "Sing the Body Electric." *Psychology Today*. October, 1970, 56-58, 88.
Analyzes the new body therapies in relation to their theoretical sources in play, unified views of the mind and body, and existentialist views of man.

Kovich, Maureen. "Sport as an Art Form." *Journal of Health, Physical Education and Recreation*. October, 1971, 42.
Accepts a definition of physical education as the art and science of human movement and emphasizes aesthetic meanings derived by sports performers and spectators within a broad concept of art.

Lansley, Keith L., and Howell, Maxwell L. "Play Classification and Physical Education." *Journal of Health, Physical Education and Recreation*. September, 1970, 44-45, 59.
Summarizes the research which has attempted to define and categorize the phenomenon of play activities and the socioculture relationships of sports, games and physical activities.

Maheu, Rene. "Sport and Culture." *Anthology of Contemporary Readings: An Introduction to Physical Education*. 2nd ed. Edited by Howard S. Slusher and Aileene S. Lockhart. Dubuque, Iowa: Wm. C. Brown Company, 1970, 186-197.
Uses a concept of cultural expression as art as the basis for a discussion of sport and play, and concludes that sport is not presently manifest in culture for logical and aesthetic reasons.

Metheny, Eleanor. "The Excellence of Patroclus." *Anthology of Contemporary Readings: An Introduction to Physical Education*. 2nd ed. Edited by Howard S. Slusher and Aileene S. Lockhart. Dubuque, Iowa: Wm. C. Brown Company, 1970, 63-67.
Suggests a basic view of the essence of sport connotations.

————. "This 'Thing' Called Sport." *Journal of Health, Physical Education and Recreation*. March, 1969, 59-60.
Defines the characteristic structure and composition of activities known as sport.

Miller, Donna Mae, and Russell, Kathryn R. E. *Sport: A Contemporary View*. Philadelphia: Lea & Febiger, 1971.
Explores the manifestations of sport in various contexts through data which are primarily phenomenological and contemporary.

Ryan, Allan J. "Yoga and Fitness." *Journal of Health, Physical Education and Recreation*. February, 1971, 26-27.
Discusses the nature, purpose, and techniques of Yoga practice and evaluates the contribution of Yoga to physical fitness as minimal.

Schmitz, Kenneth. "Sport and Play: Suspension of the Ordinary." Paper presented at the Thirteenth Annual Meeting of the American Association for the Advancement of Science, Dallas, Texas, December, 1968. In *Sport and the Body: A Philosophical Symposium*. Edited by Ellen W. Gerber. Philadelphia: Lea & Febiger, 1972.
A philosophical treatment of play and its forms and characteristics and sport as a distinctive modality.

Slusher, Howard S. *Man, Sport and Existence: A Critical Analysis*. Philadelphia: Lea & Febiger, 1967.
A theoretical analysis of the sport experience from the perspective of existential philosophy.

Sorell, Walter (ed.). *The Dance Has Many Faces*. New York: Columbia University Press, 1966.
> A collection of essays treating a variety of forms and contexts of dance.

Sutton-Smith, Brian. "Games-Play-Daydreams." *Quest X*. May, 1968, 47-58.
> Considers problems of taxonomy, boundary states such as playfulness and gamesmanship, and relationships with nonexpressive phenomena.

————, and Avedon, Elliott M. *The Study of Games*. New York: John Wiley & Sons, 1971.
> An excellent contribution to the scholarly study of games; includes a wide range of readings and studies, and comprehensive bibliographies.

————, and Herron, R. R. *Child's Play*. New York: John Wiley & Sons, 1971.
> A companion volume to *The Study of Games*, this collection provides a basic introduction to the scholarly literature on children's play, and contains some readings that are highly relevant to physical education; i.e., Gregory Stone's "The Play of Little Children," which is also contained in *Quest IV* (April, 1965), appears as the introduction to the work.

Turner, Margery J. "The Shape of Contemporary Dance." *Journal of Health, Physical Education and Recreation*. January 1965, 23-24, 85.
> Discusses several characteristics of "space age" dance and provides a framework for dance.

Weiss, Paul. *Sport: A Philosophic Inquiry*. Carbondale: Southern Illinois University Press, 1969.
> Considers many aspects of sport and the athletic experience in relation to philosophical perspectives that provide insight into the nature of the phenomenon and its relation to man.

Chapter IV

EXPERIENCING THE FORMS OF MOVEMENT

In its focus on man in his pursuit and engagement in movement activities, the field of study underlying physical education is ultimately characterized by its humanistic concerns. Mechanistic approaches to understanding movement do contribute to both descriptive and prescriptive applications of knowledge and have been important in the field of study because of their long history of accumulated data. In fact, one of the ironies surrounding physical education lies in its concern with knowledge about man as a biomechanical system or object in light of its attention to man as an experiencing and behaving subject in its actual existence.

The nature of experience, of course, is an appropriate subject for philosophical speculation, and has not ever been defined very clearly. Human experience is always personal and singular, and, yet, studying it depends upon assumptions of universal characteristics and some commonality of meanings inherent in various phenomena. It is important, therefore, to recognize that any individual's experience is unique to him, but that our analysis of experience presumes some generalizable concepts and abstractions.

EXPERIENCE AND MEANING

Edrie Ferdun

From his beginnings, man has been endowed with physical systems that provide the means for his experiencing and behaving in such relation that he can learn, grow, adapt, or create. His sensory modalities are capable of providing him a range of data that, when acted upon in the phases of perception and cognition and experienced in the phase of action, can become functionally integrated and usable in his future. The interdependence of the systems in any human functioning and the cyclic nature of its operation is apparent. The human being acts or behaves, and in doing so certain information becomes potentially available to him because of his capacities to feel, perceive, or experience. Regardless of the route initially emphasized, whether sensory or motor, this is the process through which meanings are built and modified as potentially permanent points of reference within the individual.

Movement has primary relevance to the experiential process because it both provides unique sensory information and is a means to action. It is through his own motion that the human being can alter what is outside of himself and thereby change whatever is available to him to experience. The experience provided to the human being in the act of moving yields information about himself in relation to that upon which he acts.

Man's capacity to move and to experience movement is so important to his successful functioning as an organism that it is accompanied by pleasure in and of itself which insures its development and refinement. This is also true of other primary modalities of sensation, organization, and integration as well as methods of action. Man simply needs to use and develop his capacities, and he derives satisfaction within the processes of doing so.

The concept of man refining his abilities in relation to his experiencing of satisfaction is exemplified most obviously in play. When a child or an adult plays, he enters a self-regulating cycle of experiencing and experimenting that continues only so long as valued sensation and awareness of progress or diversity result. In play, it is obvious that sequences of engagement ensue as they are appropriate to the level of development of the player. Playing with fingers and toes, babbling so-called "nonsense syllables," and "peek-a-boo" are all examples of rudimentary definitions of sensory-motor relationships. External objects, people, and contexts become aspects of experimentation with an ever-increasing sophistication of methods to ultimately extend the arena of play to the most advanced levels of human genius. The dimensions of increased endurance for concentration and the ability to suspend satisfaction within the over-all span of play are part of this development.

Play, then, functions in such a way as to enhance and extend the various capacities and abilities of man in relation to his ever-increasing cultural interdependence. The modes of play are both experiential and experimental, and these are correlatives, or complementary and reciprocal aspects, to the basic human processes that have been described as perceptual and effectual. Play proceeds for its own purposes and satisfactions, and these are inherent within its operations. Because this is so, the products of play are likely to represent the most creative acts of which the human being is capable, in that they are rooted firmly in the central and primary sources of the human being and have evolved through each person's own accepted and constructed regulation.

In general terms, "creativity" refers to the capacity of an individual to make new and unique integrations and formulations. This is most likely to occur when the processes of perception, cognition, and action are freed from previous integrations or organizations which ordinarily serve to facilitate the efficiency of dealing with others and the environment. The process of "freeing" these processes is necessary when the existing organizations lose their intimacy with the primary and experiential data upon which they were built. The freeing process is characteristic of play which arises from the self as a whole freeing, thinking, and acting organism in pursuit of its own definition of relationships.

Creativity and play are closely associated with the activities and responses of children. Because children are in the initial stages of building their abilities and meanings and, for the most part, are not obligated to fulfill a large number of pre-programmed responsibilities, they play and create as a function of both necessity and opportunity. Adults, on the other hand, as they progress by building steadily upon their initial structures of beliefs and abilities and enter roles with predictable demands, usually reduce the extent to which they employ either play or creativity as a modality.

There are, however, institutionalized forms of play and creativity that provide for the continuous actualization of these phenomena and their resultant positive functions for both the individual and the culture. Both sport and art are such forms; they operate according to the prerequisite conditions of play. As forms, sport and art must be entered into freely and fully, with the primary sensibilities and abilities in close interaction. They are symbolic forms and as such are themselves not responsible for immediate practical values or efficient uses, while at the same time they hold inherent potential for intense meaningfulness.

Though they are related, sport and art differ in several important respects. As advanced cultural forms, they reflect specialized functions in relation to the dual characteristics of play, the distinctive emphasis on sensory modalities, and the means of human action. Art emphasizes the perceptual experience; that is, the hearing, the seeing, the feeling, and the making sense of it. The dominant concern of art in its play phases is the quality of the sensory experience as it comes back in perception or what is referred to as "aesthetic values." Experimentation and mastery of action or the effective systems proceed in the interest of creating sensory aesthetic experience. Art is marked by creativity in a continuing search for new forms of perception and contemplation. Each form of art, whether music, dance, painting, sculpture, poetry, drama, or literature, further emphasizes a particular sensory or symbolic modality or hierarchy of modalities for its primary or initial data for manipulation and comprehension. In the processes of perceiving and making sense of what is given, all of the modalities are welded together to provide for the experience and the meaning.

Sport emphasizes the action experience; doing and being able to do are its dominant concerns. As play, sport uses perception and experimentation in the interest of effective action. Because movement is the dominant effective system of man, sport is a more singular form than art and focuses clearly on contesting elements of skill, ability, and performance. The creativity evidenced in sport does not lie in the development of new forms for experiencing and mastering action principally, but rather is found in the striving to discover new and more effective methods of actualization. Sport, then, might be considered a kind of human technological art in the sense that man pursues the refinement of his skills and abilities.

It is important to distinguish between the overall orientation provided by the forms of art and sport and potential shifts and flow in the focus of the experiencing players or spectators. As totally functioning human beings in activities which progress through time, singular approaches to experiencing and deriving meaning and power are more than unlikely. The individual in any circumstance may shift between the aesthetic mode and the effective mode. The athlete can and does become aware of the quality of his feeling, the form of his action, and its symbolic significance. The artist can and does focus on his abilities to act and effect, attending almost exclusively on occasion to his powers to accomplish.

The spectator or audience may be even more free to respond to the sport or art presentation in alternative modes, and by doing so may change the primary character of the experience to that ordinarily associated with the other. The individual who experiences a football game primarily as a ballet of costumed men creating patterns in space and time, struggling with forces of good and evil, acting out a drama of violence and repose, and whose satisfactions from this experience are found mainly in the qualities of the perceptions provided, has approached football as aesthetic experience. By the same token, if a dance is seen primarily as a series of physical feats or skills with a focus on how many turns can be accomplished in the air, how high a dancer can jump, how effective the use of groups, or lights, or props is, and the satisfactions from the experience derive mostly from these qualities of effective functioning, one can assume the dance was approached for the most part as athletic experience.

Although the richest experience for any individual probably includes both modes, the achievement of the fullest potential from the form as a unique and specialized opportunity in its own domain demands a framework of orientation consistent with the form. This orientation can yield particular heights of experience not otherwise easily obtainable in things or events.

Movement can be considered an ability and a sensibility. Both are developed in the recurrent demands of living, play, and the sophisticated cultural forms of sport and dance. The focus of the experiencing of movement or feeling qualities, formal values, or actual effective results represents heightened potential for advancing sensibility and ability respectively. Dance and sport are forms which provide for experiencing and creative forming of movement in symbolic context. Each is distinguished by a characteristic emphasis on perceptual intake or physical output and demands a similar orientation from its participants for its fullest functioning as a form. The emphasis of dance is on the "what" and "why" in qualitative perceptual experience and that of sport is on the "how" in qualitative actual experience.

PSYCHOSOCIAL ASPECTS OF MEANING

Because the human being develops his capacities in social situations, the modes by which he seeks and experiences meaning are socialized, and his individual psychology is modified and shaped by social processes. Personality and motivation are the key concepts used most often to describe the individual, but the ways in which these are assessed and evaluated depend on common agreements about how they are manifest. Both personality and motivation are "constructs," which means that they are ideas that are assumed and not available to direct study or assessment. They are useful assumptions in the process of understanding and explaining behavior, but they must not be thought of as identifiable and actual entities. Some of the ways in which personality, particularly, is used and applied as a construct in explaining human behavior are especially open to question. Although it is most commonly thought of as a configuration of all the characteristics or qualities of a person, it is frequently studied as though it was simply a collection of "traits," any of which can be considered singly. Furthermore, while personality is usually assumed to be personal and individual, many studies attempt to define and deal with some notion of the collective personality of particular groups. We refer easily to the "athlete's personality" or the "coach's personality" as though this construct can be applied as an abstraction.

One of the most clear aspects of experiential meaningfulness has to do with the idea of personal relevance. Man finds those things meaningful that have some kind of direct relationship to himself. The finding of "personal meaning" in experience is basic to any extension of meaning. On the simplest level, one does not get involved in nor does he pursue those things that are not recognizable to him as somehow within his scope of concern or attention. People tend to "screen out" or ignore those aspects of the environment that are not intelligible to them. Studies have shown that even visually in the process of reading, individuals are not aware that they have read words that are not familiar to them.

Personal relevance is associated with attitudes toward the self. In this view, the self-concept or "self known to the self" is the basic aspect of both personality and perception. The concept of self includes both what one thinks he is and the values that he attaches to those things. Each individual, then, develops a frame of reference for his own behavior that implies the parameters of personal relevance and goals and standards for his own personality and behavior.

The aspect of the self-concept that is concerned with the body is important in relation to participation in movement activities. Like the concept of self, the "body-image" is a useful construct for dealing with the perceptions and attitudes held by an individual with reference to his body. Obviously, self-presentations depend on the body first, and each person develops a host of personal and socialized ideas and values about himself. People are able and willing to reveal their self-characterizations in such statements as "I am tall," or "I am too tall"; "I am fat," or "I am thin"; "I am athletic," or "I am clumsy." In this way, the body-image can be said to extend to include movement abilities as well as physical characteristics. Because the body is so obvious, and until recently in the United States there were fairly narrow cultural agreements as to standards of attractiveness and acceptability of the body, body-images can be said to be positive or negative. It is generally accepted that most people would change some aspect of their bodies if they could, and this suggests that the body-image has slightly negative connotations. Even in the case of individuals considered highly attractive, this may be so since it is the person's own evaluation that is the crucial one.

Because most individuals are motivated by pervasive goals of self-enhancement, they tend to avoid or withdraw from situations in which they are likely to be evaluated by others in less than positive ways. The frame of reference for these evaluations is any syndrome of socialized values about "what is good" or what desirable behavior is. Depending on his self-concept, an individual establishes acceptable standards for his own behavior in relation to these "norms" or standards. Although this process is not always conscious, if the importance of self-enhancement as a human motivation is accepted, it does explain why individuals choose to enter situations or avoid them when they have their choice. Since most human situations can or do yield evaluative data about the individual's performance or behavior, the notion of "enhancement" is an ever-present variable in experiences. Personality, defined as the characteristic qualities or ways of behaving of an individual, develops in relation to the perceptions of self and situations. It is a complex syndrome of development that is dependent on the interactions of self and situation as they occur and as they have occurred throughout the life history of a person.

Motivation, like personality, is used to express complicated ideas about the goals and values that seem to explain the characteristic responses and behavior of an individual. It is always personal and internalized, and when we refer to "external" or "extrinsic" values, we are really suggesting that an individual seems impelled to behave in ways likely to yield recognition or rewards that are overt. In the sense that values are socialized and shared by groups of people, approval and positive evaluations of personality or behavior do, indeed, exist outside the self. These may be internalized, and there are people who do not seem to seek or require the stated approval of others in relation to their motivation. In other cases, we have seen people who consistently reject the evaluations of others even when these are positive, and seem motivated by their personal standards and evaluations.

Any individual, then, may be said to behave within a framework of his own motivation and personality, with self-concept and body-image as the crucial constructs that provide consistent explanations of behavior and personal relevance. Perceptions underlie behavior, and behavior provides feedback and perceptual data. Although individual psychology and behavior are not entirely cultural, it is society that provides for a certain commonality of values and perceptions, and it is, therefore, the social experience that allows us to use personality and motivation as generalizable ideas.

Each phase that leads to action, that is the perception and cognition that underlie experience, is available to the effects of socialization. In fact, the affective or feeling-centered component of experience is a result of socialized values and attitudes in part. All of man's behavior does not derive from enculturation processes, but these do affect perceptual organizations in many ways and do provide frames of reference for cognition. Any feedback about behavior, because it is most often provided by other people, also expresses a social context. Most importantly, however, it is the socialized agreements about man and his behavior that provide generalized understanding. This means that our understanding of personality and motivation and meaning is based on the experiences that we share rather than on those that are unique to the individual. This is an important point because it suggests that while experience may be personal and noncommunicable, it is its commonality that receives attention. Whatever dimension of experience has been socialized, it is that which is understood by others; insofar as we respond in socialized ways or attach socialized meanings to experience, our experience is understood by others. Furthermore, in attempting to integrate his own experience, the individual is drawn to social sources simply because these are the most explicit and available to him. The concept of "alienation" expresses the feelings of the individual who cannot integrate his experience with reference to socialized sources and understandings. In complex and discontinuous societies, individuals often feel alienated from their surroundings and those around them simply because their personal experience is not reflected in rationalized ways in the apparent social experience. Some kind of "social contract" breaks down, and the existential philosophy of experience as isolated and personal becomes more understandable.

MOTIVATION THEORIES

There are theories of motivation that are based on assumptions about the human being as a "reactor"; that is, man is thought to act in such

4

ways as to maintain his organism and maximize his experiencing of pleasure in relation to the stresses of the environment. "Motives" can be viewed as either conscious or unconscious behavioral dispositions leading to protection or enhancement of the organism. "Learned motivations" in this view are seen to be rooted in biologically caused tensions but manifest in objects or goals that have come to signify tension reduction. These theories, which all depend on some notion of disequilibrium as a result of environmental stress, hypothesize resultant drives as explanations of motivation. Behavioral variability is then studied by creating disequilibrious conditions through some form of deprivation, and assessing behavior. Much of the experimental support for this position has resulted from studies with animals, and it is considered by many to be too narrow and mechanistic a view of human behavior. Whether they deal with motivation as a construct for the explanation of behavior or not, the most often identified theories of behavior that express this frame of reference are S-R theory, drive-reduction theory, hedonistic theory, homeostatic theory, and even the operant conditioning theory of B. F. Skinner. Some of the prevailing theories of "motor learning" seem to depend on these mechanistic assumptions of behavior, and have been criticized for hypothesizing motor behavior as a nonhumanized concept. Cybernetics, as a mathematical approach to understanding the nervous system, has been getting increasing attention, and considerations of differences between closed-loop and open-loop feedback mechanisms seem fruitful for study.

The importance of motivation as an explanation of human behavior has been stressed by such theorists as Carl Rogers, Gordon Allport, Donald Snygg and Arthur Combs, and Abraham Maslow. These theorists have hypothesized a broad view of the human organism striving to enhance and actualize a "phenomenal" self in his behavior and experience. Rogers' "fully-functioning person," Allport's "creative becoming," Snygg and Combs' "phenomenal self," and Maslow's "self-actualizing person" all share innate capacities that are ideally expressed in some notion of striving toward self-realization. In these views, the human being is not a "reactor" only to the environment, but his behavior is thought to function in relation to his individual perception of reality. There is some question as to the role of unconscious perceptual dispositions in these theories; however, because these theories are humanistic and not either mechanistic or deterministic, they are attractive bases for dealing with human behavior.

It remains for the field of study of psychology to pursue understanding of human behavior, and to yield both verifiable data and cohesive theories. The field of study underlying physical education, however, is vitally concerned with man's motivations in relation to his movement behavior and

his engagement in movement forms, and depends on the continual generation of hypotheses to explain and predict man's relationship to these
phenomena. In doing so, we are not concerned with accounting for all
human behavior, and have found it somewhat fruitful to deal with experiencing movement as a focus for consideration.

MEANING AND MOVEMENT FORMS

Although not always crystallized, questions about why man creates and pursues movement forms have always been germane to the field of study underlying physical education. Because sport and dance have been characterized as nonrational and nonproductive activities, there are not obvious logical explanations for man's continued absorption with them. Whether we believe that the human organism is impelled by drives to reduce pain and maximize pleasure or by needs to enhance his organism, neither sport, dance, nor exercise forms provide obvious opportunities for fulfillment. In fact, many of the experiences in these forms can be described only as "unpleasant" in that they produce actual pain or physical discomfort. Yet, man does pursue sport, dance, and exercise in the face of both discomfort and failure and the nonimportance of these activities in everyday reality. Kretchmar and Harper (1969) suggested that man would play even if such activity held no alleged benefits to health or well-being, although the individual in a rational world does not often admit that and seeks acceptable reasons for his own participation. Metheny (1965), especially, has focused on the idea of "meaning" as central to explanations of sport and dance as phenomena and as experience. In *Movement and Meaning* (1968), she differentiated between the meanings available to the participant and the observer by using the concepts of "performance" and "presentational form" in her descriptions of movement forms.

"Meaning" is a vague conception of the sum of cognitive and affective connotations having to do with personal relevance. As such, meaning may derive from either perception or action, and may be considered to emanate from personal or socialized sources. At the same time, though usually construed as a positive construct, especially when used with reference to motivation, meaning may operate as a negative construct that signals avoidance behavior on the part of the individual. When we refer to dance as a source of potential meanings or to the sport experience as potentially meaningful, we are generally alluding to those aspects of experience that are shared or commonly understood, and these are most often those that have been socialized.

Many of the socialized meanings of sport simply accrue to individuals as a result of the values that surround sport in the society. For the young male particularly, sport offers opportunities for the enhancement of personality and accomplishment in ways valued by society. That is to say that success in the interactive experiences of sport implies certain abilities and personality attributes that are considered desirable both at the time and in relation to how adult roles are perceived. The immediacy of the sport experience is important in view of the fact that many youthful activities are preparation for other "real" roles in later life. Contests in sport, on the other hand, are seen as important at the time, and the positive evaluations from adults and peers that surround success may, therefore, have greater relevance because they are unqualified. Success in sport, then, and especially in organized athletics is a powerful source of self-documentation, social approval, and social status in relation to various groups of both peers and adults. This is, of course, not as true for women. There is not unqualified approval offered to the successful athlete who is a girl or woman. On the other hand, there may be approval for specific sports or generally for such activities within the family or particular geographical location. Dance represents a different situation in that dance is applauded for the female and viewed suspiciously for the male. Participation in sport or dance may be affected by these kinds of socialized values, but they are not the substance of the explanations for these experiences. Exercise, insofar as it represents a more amorphous form, is usually also viewed differently for men and women; that is, men are presumed to be seeking one kind of benefit and women another although both of these are considered desirable.

The meaning experienced by an individual may stem from a variety of related values. "Success" alone is a crucial social value, and the obvious evaluations provided by sport and dance allow one to know that he "has done well" in the situation and in comparison to others. The approval of his activities is another kind of reward for the athlete or dancer, and he may find great meaning in his acceptance and recognition by others. Beyond approval is the resultant status in social groups and situations that frequently accrues to the performer, and sport or dance may serve as vehicles to meaningful social position and interaction. In a society that values achievement and excellence as seriously as we do in the United States, any individual is likely to find his own achievement meaningful. Sport, because its structure clearly defines achievement and because it is a valued area of human endeavor, becomes a fruitful source of actualizing achievement needs and motivations. Long after their days of athletic participation, adults still prize the medals and trophies and other symbols that attest to their participation and success in sport. Dancers, on the other hand, frequently find the same satisfaction in performance.

The realms of sport themselves are particular social situations. In some ways, sports as well as particular sports are subcultures and have the characteristics of small societies. The individual athlete pursuing his own achievement is, nevertheless, part of a social interaction as well. This is most obvious in organized team sports, of course, but when they are organized, even the so-called individual sports are competed in as teams. Some sports, like fishing, mountain climbing, maybe even surfing and skydiving, can be considered almost "solitary" sports, and, yet, these too are rarely pursued by the individual alone. It is apparent, therefore, that some of the meaning in sport may have to do with social interaction; with the fulfillment of affiliative as well as achievement needs. The somewhat related concept of "identity" may also be involved. Youth seeks to define self in social as well as personal ways, and roles and positions are one important way in which we do define who we are. To be an "athlete," a "football player," "a dancer," or "a jogger" may be the most meaningful source of identity for a young person, and as that also implies the existence of a particular and an abstract social group to which he belongs, that identity is affirmed and enhanced.

It would be simplistic, however, to view meaning in movement forms as entirely related to social values and socialization. The nature of sport implies some potential sources of meaning that may be viewed as more personal than social though the personal-social context is a mutually interactive dimension. Contesting is characteristic of sport, and that implies that the sport situation always contains elements of challenge and opportunities for mastery. It is true that we tend to think of competitive situations most often in terms of their outcome in winning and losing with the attendant connotations of success and failure. Within that concept of competition, however, any individual is experiencing the challenge to perform, to rise to the task, to overcome obstacles, and, thus, to actualize his abilities and gain mastery over the situation and its variables. The dancer does not compete directly, but performance is obviously a similar kind of context in that the demands and standards of the situation are clear. The expressive functions of dance simply add a dimension to the notion of mastery insofar as performing excellence depends not only on skill but on communication as well. Exercise as a form rests almost wholly on developing control and improving the abilities to master and perform. Even mastery of the body alone, especially during adolescence with its great bodily changes, may be an important aspect of meaning. If the human being is impelled toward actualization of himself in any way that might be understood, then surely movement forms provide opportunities for that, and these may be considered potential sources of meaning for the individual. The social implications that surround this mastery may provide another kind of gratification.

Mastery, of course, is inextricably related to skill and excellence of performance. Since this is the other dimension of the essence of the sport experience and is central to dance, it is difficult to suggest which aspect holds the greater potential meaning. Perhaps because different sports seem to lend themselves to various degrees of emphasis on contest or performance, discriminations could be made about the nature of potential meaning as a function of that. In either case the experiences of sport, dance, and exercise provide opportunities for the most crucial kinds of self-definition within challenges and demands, and it seems likely that meaning and personal relevance must emanate from the discovery of self and the actualization of skill and ability. Obviously, the nature of these forms suggests only potential meaningfulness for the individual. Sport can be organized and carried on in ways that negate this potential. Striving toward mastery and finding it highly meaningful, for instance, is difficult when the imposed competitive structures are not compatible with the abilities or motivations of those participating. This is most obvious when we recognize that in the spontaneous activity of youngsters, competition is abandoned when stress, whether psychological or in relation to performance demands, becomes too great. Yet, adults frequently organize competition for youngsters in imposed structures; that is, a baseball game may be established as having seven innings and the responses of those engaged in it become irrelevant. Some individuals find that they cannot cope with certain kinds of challenges, and instead of striving toward mastery, they withdraw. The stereotype of the rigid "ballet master" has provided a model for many who structure dance experiences, and when this obtains, dancers, too, may simply abandon the form.

There are, however, certain prescribed roles and values associated with the modes of participation and striving in movement forms. Perseverance, for instance, is a characteristic value of sport participation, and to "quit" or not to try, for whatever reason, results in negative evaluations by others. In view of this, "meaning" must be viewed as a complex concept; for within sport one may experience the most crucial kinds of feelings of inadequacy and negative self-definition. Challenge becomes "threat" when the individual feels totally inadequate or is afraid that to enter the situation is to insure failure. Interestingly enough, as social constructs, there is a relationship between the need to achieve in our society and the need not to fail. Depending on certain personality variables and, perhaps, the strength of the concept of self-worth, individuals may be impelled to seek achievement or to avoid failure. Those with the latter motivation tend to avoid testing situations in which one, by definition, either succeeds or fails. Sport, of course, has many, many more "losers" than winners, and this may explain why the athlete is usually characterized as having stable, positive motivations; those who do not, simply do not choose sport as an endeavor. Ogilvie and Tutko, in their article "Sport: If You Want to Build Character, Try Something Else" (1971), suggest that the athlete gets only a few chances to prove his worth. They ask, "What sort of personality structure supports the person who can face this blunt reinforcement of reality?" Although dance and exercise do not contain as rigid criteria for success and failure in their structures, these forms do usually adopt models of excellence and in organized contexts, at least, depend on comparisons that imply these criteria.

The structure of sport seems to suggest some other possibilities for meaningful experiences to accrue. The individual is freed from a host of concerns by the very structure of sport itself. Within the rules, and in relation to the ways they are supervised and manifest, the crucial areas of striving and performance are clear. Certainly, this is partly why mastery is a viable notion in sport; only those things directly relevant to defining it are allowed to be considered. In addition to the clarification of the nature of the task and challenge, however, there is also the idea that the individual may experience a sense of freedom in relation to the clear goals and demands of sport. In sports not so clearly defined and in dance, experiencing an actual sense of exhilaration and freedom is available and has been described by surfers, sky-divers, divers, and even trampolinists and gymnasts. It is an interesting idea that one can clarify and structure one's own efforts in order to experience "being out of control" in the sense that he has committed his performance to the laws of physics in defiance of gravity. These kinds of sensation-producing or "sensational" experiences may be more appropriately considered meaningful in relation to the experiencing of movement itself than freedom.

Surely, movement of the body produces pleasurable sensation. In the most concrete sense, performing, moving, acting are satisfying to the individual. Reaching the limits of skilled movement or of endurance capacities provides experiences of the self and the body in meaningful ways. Even the experience of sore and stiff muscles is not entirely unpleasant, and, for many, all of the effects of using the body are pleasing and hold personal relevance. Movement behavior is expressive and is, therefore, directly related to the meanings the individual holds. Whereas in infancy and childhood, even random, exploratory movement seems wholly satisfying, development seems to proceed toward seeking more complex and structured movement situations. Sport provides clear situations in which the demands of movement and performance are known and understood and, yet, which provide opportunities for the individual to pursue those tasks in somewhat free and expressive ways.

The understanding of meaning and movement forms is far from complete. Within the field of study underlying physical education, knowledge and insight about the phenomenon and experience of sport, dance, and exercise must be pursued. There is a growing body of data that deals with the concepts involved in understanding motivation and meaning in sport particularly, but the theoretical modes have been limited. We do, of course, seek to understand the athlete and the functional relationships and effects of participation in sport. It would be desirable, however, to seek understanding of the phenomenon of sport as a source of meaning as well. Toward this end, the uses and understanding of sport in our world must be investigated. Some attention must be given to the applications of normative values in sport and the potential benefits and dysfunctional effects that result.

Much of our understanding of the meaningfulness of the sport experience has depended on the phenomenological descriptions of athletes, and these are a valuable source of insight. Affective and cognitive processes cannot always be described in ways that communicate them directly, however, and modes of inquiry into the nature of experience must be refined. Case studies and even personal experiences also help us understand meaning, but these sources, too, are limited in their general applications.

The study of sport as experience must be extended beyond a focus on the contest alone. Essence, structure, style, and context are all aspects of the sport phenomenon and understanding sport depends upon consideration of all the variables that affect understanding and experience. Any individual experiences his particular relationship to sport within the values associated with sport in all the ways that it exists. That is to say, the Little Leaguer's experience is somehow related to the existence of major league baseball, and the various contextual connotations of sport are important sources for understanding it. In the pursuit of knowledge about sport, it is important, too, to be concerned with the dysfunctional uses of sport, with the ways in which it distorts and corrupts socialization and social values, and influences individual personality in negative and harmful ways. The complexity of the construct of "meaning" requires sophisticated and valid data and theory if it is to be understood.

DISCUSSION

Subject: Statements relative to the field of study; perspectives of knowledge as experiences in movement, dance, and sport. There is a dual emphasis here on a view of human behavior (which will be re-affirmed in the next area) and the nature of movement and sport as sources of meaning and experience (with psychosocial considerations).

Experiencing the Forms of Movement

1. Man is essentially rational, but behavior can be understood only within the personal perspective of the individual; that is, each person behaves within his perceptual framework, and his behavior "makes sense" only as his values, beliefs, attitudes, and needs are known and understood.

2. Our perceptual frameworks are personal and socialized; although each individual is unique and individual differences are important, human beings are more alike than different, and social experiences within the culture have much in common.

3. Behavior is an expression of the individual-in-his-frame-of-reference, and, as such, may be said to express personality, style, motivation, etc., but behavior itself may be misunderstood because the perceptions of the observer become involved as well.

4. In addition to the variables of perception, the most important determinant of behavior, especially in a long-range sense, is the notion of *personal meaning;* that is to say, people act, react, and are motivated to pursue and/or experience those things which have relevance to them. It might be said, we cannot even *perceive* unless there is some personal meaning involved.

5. Movement may be meaningful in a variety of ways; certainly, the use of movement as an *instrumentality* is obvious, but it has social connotations and uses beyond the personal ones.

6. The persistence of movement activities, especially sport and dance, throughout man's history is eloquent testimony to the essential meaningfulness of these activities. Somehow, man simply finds ways to pursue his involvement in these activities despite the diverse ways in which they are used and valued by cultures.

7. Meaningful involvement which provides for the actualization of human abilities and potentials seems to be a key concept in understanding human activity, and movement seems a rich source of experience in this light.

8. Sport and art differ in their emphasis on sensory modalities, and distinguishing between them is important in understanding the nature of experience whether as participant or spectator.

9. The sport experience can be dysfunctional, and the study of experiencing movement forms depends upon analyzing the forms as well as the individual.

10. Understanding man-in-movement as an experiential concept is, perhaps, the most crucial concern of the field of study of physical education; it depends on philosophical considerations of man, social and psychological insight into behavior and experience, and a humanistic view of movement and sport.

SELECTED BIBLIOGRAPHY

Experiencing Movement Forms

Beisser, Arnold R. *The Madness In Sports: Psychosocial Observations on Sport.* New York: Appleton-Century-Crofts, 1967.
Reports case histories of various types of athletes and psychological problems related to their participation in sport.

Brown, Roscoe C., and Cratty, Bryant C. (eds.). *New Perspectives of Man in Action.* Englewood Cliffs, New Jersey: Prentice-Hall, 1969.
Includes various approaches to physical education as an academic discipline focused on the nature of man in action and in relation to participation in sport.

Felshin, Jan. "Sport and Modes of Meaning." *Journal of Health, Physical Education and Recreation.* May, 1969, 43-44.
Deals with meaning in sport and the ways in which modalities for finding experience meaningful depend upon socialized sources.

Gerber, Ellen W. *Sport and the Body: A Philosophical Symposium.* Philadelphia: Lea & Febiger, 1972.
An excellent collection of papers on diverse considerations of sport and the body; includes treatment of philosophical and aesthetic aspects of particular value with reference to the sport experience.

Houts, Jo Ann. "Feeling and Perception in the Sport Experience." *Journal of Health, Physical Education and Recreation.* October, 1970, 71-72.
Deals with how the sport experience is perceived by the performer during a peak performance.

Hubbard, Alfred W. "Some Thoughts on Motivation in Sport." *Quest X.* May, 1968, 40-46.
Describes motivation and movement in relation to participation in activity.

Kretchmar, R. Scott, and Harper, William A. "Must We Have a Rational Answer to the Question Why Does Man Play?" *Journal of Health, Physical Education and Recreation.* March, 1969, 57-58.
Considers the rational bases for the pursuit of play and raises the question as as to whether or not man would pursue play even if it did not result in rational outcomes.

Lowe, Benjamin. "The Aesthetics of Sport: The Statement of a Problem." *Quest XVI.* June, 1971, 13-17.

Presents various classifications of definitions of both aesthetics and sport and attempts to establish a frame of reference for the development of a "sport-aesthetic."

Metheny, Eleanor. *Connotations of Movement in Sport and Dance.* Dubuque, Iowa: Wm. C. Brown Company, 1965.
A valuable collection of speeches, many of which treat the significance of movement and its meaning.

————. "How Does a Movement Mean?" *Quest VIII.* May, 1967, 1-6.
Treats movement symbolism in its forms.

————. *Movement and Meaning.* New York: McGraw-Hill Book Company, 1968.
Presents a cohesive statement of movement as symbolic form.

Mitchell, Brian (ed.). *Today's Athlete.* London: Pelham Books, 1970.
Includes selections relative to the social importance of athletics (track and field) in various countries, the role of the professional and the future of the Olympics; includes studies of interest.

Moore, Robert A. *Sport and Mental Health.* Springfield, Illinois: Charles C Thomas, 1966.
Views the history and theories of play, psychological development, and the function of sports in society.

Mordy, Margaret (ed.). *Psychology of Sport. Quest XIII.* January, 1970.
Contains several articles of interest and value in relation to the topic.

National Association for Physical Education of College Women. *Aesthetics and Human Movement: Report of the Ruby Anniversary Workshop* (June, 1964). Washington, D.C.: American Association for Health, Physical Education and Recreation, 1964.
Contains some valuable selections relevant to the topic including E. F. Kaelin, "The Well-Played Game: Notes Toward an Aesthetics of Sport," which also appears in *Quest X;* Seymour Kleinman, "The Significance of Human Movement: A Phenomenological Approach," and Howard S. Slusher, "The Existential Function of Physical Education."

Ogilvie, Bruce C. "The Unconscious Fear of Success," *Quest X.* May, 1968, 35-39.
Explores several major psychological reactions to high-level athletic competition.

————, and Tutko, Thomas A. "Sport: If You Want to Build Character, Try Something Else." *Psychology Today.* October, 1971, 60-63.
Discusses the personality traits of athletes and coaches and concludes that it is selective processes rather than the sport experience that accounts for similarities.

Slovenko, Ralph, and Knight, James A. (eds.). *Motivations in Play, Games and Sports.* Springfield, Illinois: Charles C Thomas, 1967.
Collection of articles analyzing psychological aspects relating to various types of sports and games; includes various theories of play and games.

Slusher, Howard S. "To Test the Waves is to Test Life." *Journal of Health, Physical Education and Recreation.* May, 1969, 32-33.
Describes surfing as a phenomenological experience consonant with the style and values of youth.

Willis, Joe D., and Bethe, Don R. "Achievement Motivation: Implications for Physical Activity." *Quest XIII.* January, 1970, 18-22.
Discusses a theory of achievement motivation, the personal attributes of a person with high achievement motive and gives examples of relevant physical activity.

Chapter V

APPLYING THE FIELD OF STUDY

Those who choose to study a field usually do so because of a pervasive concern with some use or application of knowledge. The field of study itself is rooted in an implied commitment to knowledge and understanding, but the people who pursue such study become practitioners within the field. There are scholars and researchers, of course, in all fields, but concerns with human movement and its forms are usually associated with a desire to work with people.

Knowledge in the field of study has obvious applications. Movement experiences can provide for a host of beneficial effects on individuals and groups and can be used to identify and remedy deficiencies. Through experiences in movement man's functioning can be enhanced and his sources of pleasure, joy, and selfhood expanded. The primacy of movement behavior in the experience of man means that its potential for improving and affecting the quality of living is vast. Because this is so, there are a variety of contexts within which movement experiences are utilized. Teachers, physical therapists, counselors and psychologists, dancers, athletes, coaches, doctors, and others all plan and prescribe movement at some time. The social director, choreographer, sportswriter, personnel director, and city architect are somehow concerned with the field of study of human movement.

Practitioners in diverse fields utilize the body of knowledge of physical education. The knowledge about human movement and its forms does not provide direct insight into how it should be applied. It is the human situations or professional contexts that determine what kinds of knowledge or understanding should be chosen, and what uses are indicated. As situations or contexts are analyzed, the nature of appropriate movement experiences becomes clear. It is the field of study, however, that serves as the pervasive source for selecting movement experiences. This means that when we deal with physical education, we are assuming a focus on knowledge about man as he pursues and engages in gross movement and its forms for either their own sake or his own enhancement. Movement can serve as an instrument or medium for the achievement of many kinds of desirable human goals, but if movement itself is not organically related to those purposes, they cannot be said to derive from this field of study, although that does not negate their importance. The field of study, then, as a basic concept of physical education, defines its proper concern. As this focus is explored and interpreted in appropriate contexts, purposes for the application of knowledge can be derived.

The city planner utilizes the field of study of physical education because he must understand patterns of play and the relationship of space to movement behavior. In his concern for the ultimate impact of his efforts on the people involved, as individuals and in groups, he shares the focus of all those who deal with movement experiences. The basic concerns and focus of city planning do not derive from the field of study of movement or its forms, and in that sense it is clearly not physical education. Physical education, then, is the application of knowledge from the field of study in planning or prescribing movement experiences. Analyzing the context within which knowledge is to be applied is a central aspect of the process. Although the identification of purposes for the application of knowledge derives from understanding the field of study, it is the human context involved that expresses what physical education is and how it should function.

FIELD OF STUDY

The pervasive assumption of dealing with a field of study is not its ultimate application or usefulness, but these are the usual concerns of those who seek or generate knowledge. Because this is so, and also because they are logical, the implications for applying knowledge emerge quite clearly from considerations of the field of study. Actual applications and rationalized purposes for programs depend on the contexts in which they will be used; that is, knowledge about the situations in which this field of study is to be used provides a framework for its use. In the larger sense, however, generalized commitments to human welfare and betterment simply permit us to recognize potential contributions of knowledge from the field of study underlying physical education. At the same time, if it is these contributions, identified directly from study of the body of knowledge of physical education, that are the crucial sources of purpose, we are aided in defining when we are dealing with physical education and when we are not. This is especially important in view of the fact that physical education has been defined in many ways: as activities and programs; as benefits and dangers; as purposes and outcomes; as prevention and rehabilitation; and as both education and non-academic services. Physical education has existed within all these definitions, and attempts to understand what this field really is are affected by its actual history and existence.

The whole notion of a field of study for physical education depends on the answers to two questions: (1) Is there an identifiable body of knowledge that is sufficiently unique in its concerns to warrant study? (2) Is this knowledge significant and worthy of study? All academic fields overlap with others in many areas, but as long as their scope of knowledge is based on a defined orientation that is not the core of another field and there is substantive content available in relation to it, they can be said to warrant study. Physical education does depend heavily on interdisciplinary study for much of its body of knowledge, but no other field has attended to a unitary focus on "man-in-motion," and the wealth of knowledge that needs to be ordered around that focus seems to support the assumption of an identifiable body of knowledge for physical education. Unfortunately, even when properly within the scope of other disciplines, the movement behavior of man has been largely ignored or treated in a superficial manner.

It is, in fact, the wealth and range of available knowledge and modes of inquiry related to the traditional domain of physical education that hamper efforts to structure an academic discipline. The study of human movement and movement forms implies a dual thrust that encompasses diverse insight into the ordering of key concepts. The failure of physical education to identify its field of study and pursue academic development was never due to a dearth of knowledge. Rather, its educational emphasis and historical assumptions about the "triviality" of its concerns based on an outmoded notion of "academic respectability" hindered the reflective development of the field. Dualisms of "mind" and "body" have been important bases for determining academic worthiness, and the things that were of concern in physical education have had connotations of "second-class" status. With contemporary insights into the nature of man, however, these obstacles to the academic development of physical education are becoming less and less important. In fact, there is some reason to believe that man's expressive activities may be viewed as most important. As more recognition is granted the humanistic concerns in the experience of man and his development, physical education, like the arts, may become a crucial aspect of academic and educational focus. It seems obvious that there has always been an available body of knowledge related to physical education, and that questions about its significance arose from academic fashion and, perhaps, the apologetic stance of its adherents.

In the final analysis, whether or not knowledge is considered significant and worthy of study depends on its usefulness in the life of man. The constructs of potential contribution to human well-being that emerge from considerations of the field of study underlying physical education are clear and substantive documentation of the importance of this field. All of the perspectives for considering knowledge in this field of study, those that describe movement in its biomechanical and sociocultural aspects, those that describe movement forms, and those that focus on experiencing movement forms, yield cogent guidelines for applying knowledge in the improvement of human welfare. As we seek to deal with prescribing and programming movement experiences, it is logical to precede an analysis of the contexts in which this is to be done with an identification of some of the emerging constructs of significance.

FITNESS

The application of knowledge about movement and its effects on the body in enhancing goals of improved functioning has long been recognized. "Fitness" is used to refer to a pervasive syndrome of concerns related to optimum functioning, health, and well-being. Effective and efficient movement as well as characteristic postures of the body, training for specific movement demands or capacities, developing endurance in relation to performance of everyday tasks, and even certain attitudes toward the body and its movement capacities and behavior may all be viewed as part of fitness. In the sense that movement is basic to all other human functions and necessary in the achievement of almost all human purposes or goals, it is unfortunate that physical education has, at times, identified its concern only with "physical fitness." Knowledge in the field of study clearly implies a central role of movement in human functioning and a conception of fitness in relation to the capacities of man as a unified organism and being.

There is no question about the relationship of the field of study underlying physical education to contributions to human goals and needs for fitness. All of our concerns with how movement takes place and its structural and environmental restrictions yield insight into standards for efficient and effective movement. Knowledge about the body and how it is affected and modified by movement and exercise can be applied directly in improving its condition and functioning. The connotations of movement in culture imply certain applications that have to do with the uses of movement in the lives of individuals and the attitudes that might best enhance those uses for greatest well-being. The construct of "fitness" is the most easily documented and demonstrated, and has been the most obvious contribution of this field of study to the improvement of human welfare. This concept is explained in more detail in the "Amplifying Readings."

SKILL AND MASTERY IN MOVEMENT

The dual concepts of movement skills and mastery over both the body and the environment are characteristic of knowledge in this field of study. It is simply apparent that man has innate capacities for developing skills and mastery in relation to movement, and that when these capacities are fulfilled, the quality of life is improved. Competence and confidence are related and valued concepts in our understanding of human behavior. At all stages of growth, the individual increases both his repertoire and degree of skills and in doing so is enabled to seek beyond his existing abilities and accept challenges to master other things. The healthy individual is not afraid of new tasks and approaches them with confidence in his ability to master them. Since movement is the primary mode by which both learning and accomplishment occur, skill and mastery in movement abilities must be crucial dimensions of development.

At the same time, if one has developed skill and mastery in forms of movement, he is able to use his abilities in their continued pursuit, thus making other values available to him. It is our skills that allow us to function in ways that contribute to our welfare. Being unable or unwilling is opposed to growth and the extension of abilities by which man develops. In some sense, the self is defined by its abilities, and feelings of self-worth are clearly associated with skill and mastery. These are also socially valued attributes and therefore enhance human interaction for the individual who possesses them.

Although the concept of skill and mastery might be defined differently, there is obviously an important application from the field of study implied by knowledge about gaining skill. Even when the skills themselves are not pursued throughout life, feelings of competence and mastery do generalize. The challenge of learning a headstand is not crucial in relation to the importance of actually doing headstands, but the recognition that skills can be learned and abilities developed is essential to the human being if he is to actualize himself. Skill and mastery in movement, as a concept differentiated from the application of these in movement forms, imply a dimension of personal response and appreciation that refers to the aesthetic mode. In this sense, "skill" refers to an appreciable model of excellence, and may provide emotionalized satisfaction to either performer or observer. There seems to be inherent pleasure in doing something well or seeing something done well; the efficiency and flow that characterize skilled movement are satisfying elements. Grace and ease in movement performance are recognizable and pleasing aspects of performance, and may be appreciated without reference to their ultimate effectiveness. An example of this occurs whenever a performer is applauded in a losing effort. As a form, dance relies heavily on the concept of skill and mastery. Many dancers pursue a lifelong commitment to the development of their movement abilities and mastery of the body and movement without reference to the structure of performance. Athletes and those who pursue exercise continually refine skills, and their obvious dedication to the processes of skill development testifies to the kinds of satisfactions that accrue from such pursuits. The concept of skill and mastery is a variable one. The young child may delight in gross performance and mastery of a particular and recognizable skill, while adolescents and adults may focus on known models of excellence and compare their performances to those and to the skill achieved by others. In movement behavior, mastery is manifest in more than learning isolated skills. Understanding movement structures, applying strategy, utilizing cooperative teamwork effectively, selecting from a repertoire of movement abilities, gauging demand and applying appropriate force and effort are all examples of the ways in which skill and mastery are related concepts and actualize effectiveness as well. All human striving depends on a view of skill and mastery as valuable, satisfying, and attainable goals.

CULTURAL PARTICIPATION IN MOVEMENT FORMS

The importance of the movement forms of sport, dance, and exercise in the culture of the United States is clear. Sports and games provide primary socialization models for children and youth, and are among the few youthful activities invested with immediate importance. Furthermore, movement activities are not only social institutions themselves but are elements of all social institutions. Cultural communication, especially as reflected in the communications media, depends in part on knowledge about sport, particularly. Social values are manifest in sport and affect sport, and sport affects culture as well in many ways, with language, dress, use of leisure time, and models for appropriate behavior as only obvious examples. The culture of art is using movement more and more, and there is a lessening distinction between dance and drama. Contemporary theater is sometimes really dance, and even popular entertainment of all kinds emphasizes dance more and more.

The point is that it seems obvious from the knowledge in this field of study that enculturation is partially dependent on knowledge and experience in movement forms. That is to say, ignorance of these forms may be considered cultural deprivation, and would inhibit full functioning within culture. Therefore, movement forms have potential contributions to make to the individual as part of society and affect his social functioning and his ability to participate in the culture. Beyond their psychological contributions, skill, mastery, and achievement in movement forms may enhance the individual with reference to social interaction, approval, status, and mobility, and provide him the means to relate socially and hence feel enculturated. This concept of cultural participation is also treated in the "Amplifying Readings."

MEANING AND SIGNIFICANCE OF MOVEMENT EXPERIENCES

The study of participation in movement forms suggests that it has personal relevance and becomes a source of meaning for the individual. Somehow, the symbolic forms of sport and dance provide opportunities for individuals to experience and actualize themselves and their abilities in important and satisfying ways. As both forms and experience, sport and dance are continually interesting to man and he consistently pursues engagement in them. Whether or not the athlete or dancer is able to refine his abilities and achieve excellence, he seems impelled to replicate the experience of the form. Meaningful involvement characterizes interest in these forms for many, many people and in the diverse roles of participant or spectator.

It is important to distinguish between the concept of personal relevance or meaning and that of the meaning and significance of movement experiences. Many things that are personally relevant to individuals simply may be said to have great meaning for them. In this sense, anytime an individual is involved or engrossed in something, he is pursuing his own sources of meaning, and this is a significant dimension of motivation and behavior. This occurs in movement forms when they are pursued for reasons or lead to satisfactions that are personally relevant, but it does not imply that these sources of meaning are directly related to the form of movement. For example, there may be great personal meaning attending participation when the motives are social acceptance, or glory, or being with particular people, but these motives might attend the pursuit of a variety of activities. The concept of the meaning and significance of movement implies that the sources of meaning derive specifically from the experiences provided by the movement form.

These two concepts are often confused or used interchangeably, partially because movement forms are potential sources for the actualization of a host of kinds of meaning. There is nothing wrong with this interchangeable use of these ideas, but as a key concept of the field of study, "meaning" and "significance" must refer to the focus of man in motion and not derive from considerations of the psychology of man alone.

No matter how experience is considered, meaning and significance are crucial for explaining human behavior. It is the concept that explains why man has created symbolic forms that are expressive and provide opportunities for his self-realization. Art, music, literature, dance, sport, and exercise forms are all examples of human expression that do not accede to rational explanation as forms, although individuals may pursue them for productive or pragmatic reasons. Individuals obviously find these forms meaningful in diverse ways and to varying degrees. The sport enthusiast may reject poetry as "silly," and the musician may view sport as a trivial amusement. We must recognize, however, that because of their endurance as human endeavors, the symbolic forms that man has created are apparent sources of meaning and significance. Applying our insights from the field of study of movement and its forms means understanding this concept and attempting to analyze it in ways that will help us understand why movement forms are sources of meaning and significance and what conditions are most likely to lead to the experiencing of meaning. This concept is developed further in the "Amplifying Readings."

ANALYZING CONTEXTS

The field of study of physical education contains implications for significant and broad contributions to human welfare. As has been indicated, knowledge from the field of study can be used in diverse ways for many purposes. When such knowledge is extrapolated from the field of study without reference to its central concerns, it is not necessarily physical education. This point cannot be emphasized strongly enough; for in mutual concern with many aspects of isolated knowledge, diverse fields have sought alliance with physical education. In their concern for the welfare and maintenance of the organism, physical education and health education share knowledge. Mutual concern with the protection and survival of the human being characterize both safety education and physical education. Effective movement and the rehabilitation and extension of movement capacity are the focus of both physical therapy and physical education. Driver education is concerned with skilled movement; nursing and medicine with bodily functioning; astronaut training with isolated muscle control, and so on. In confusing a concern with some aspect of knowledge with the central focus and commitments of either fields of study or programs, we become unable to discriminate among fields or to develop cohesive programs.

It is true that within any context or program there are times when the experiences of one field are more appropriately reflective of the knowledge and modes of another. It is an error, however, to think that when we are dealing with the attitudes of baseball players we are "psychologists," or when we are concerned about the relationships of offensive and defensive units of a football team we are being "sociologists." The key to understanding when a particular field is operating in programs or experiences is found in understanding the central focus and concepts of the particular application. In other words, when we use psychological or vocational tests in order to help someone gain insight into himself and make career choices, we are employing the modes and instruments of psychology, but the actual focus of the experience is singular and not devoted to a broad understanding of human behavior. In that sense, it may be "guidance" or "counseling" or even "education," but it is not really psychology because of the nature of the intent and the context within which the experience was provided. In the case just described, the field of study of psychology may be seen as providing a "service" in the interests of the individual. In fact, any time the needs of individuals are the starting point for planning experiences, knowledge is selected on the basis of those needs rather than understanding of the field of study. When this is done, knowledge as such is subservient to identified needs and is being used to serve them. Although the selected knowledge may derive from a particular field of study, the experiences or program cannot be said to express that field.

The notion of "service" is an important one simply because knowledge from the field of study of physical education is often used to serve the needs of children or youth or to serve the enhancement of related fields. When physical education is used in this way, the field can be said to be of "service" and may be serving functions that are very important and useful. Because such functions do not emanate directly from conceptions of the scope and concerns of the field of study of physical education, however, it is a logical error to confuse them with experiences designed specifically to express the nature of physical education.

Purposes for programs that are designed to reflect the nature and focus of particular fields are based on the key concepts of the field. In the broadest sense, then, physical education exists whenever movement experiences are pursued for the purposes of fitness, skill and mastery in movement, cultural participation in movement forms, or experiencing the meaning, significance, or aesthetic satisfaction of involvement in movement forms. Contributions to fitness, enculturation, or meaning that do not depend upon movement experiences, or the development of skill and mastery in areas other than movement, are not properly physical education. To be considered physical education, the use of movement cannot be an instrumentality, either; both the purpose for the experience and the substance of the experience must express the concerns of the field in order for programs to be considered physical education.

The suggestion was made in this book initially that "physical education" would be used to refer to school programs. This usage is indicated by the nature of that title and by the prior existence of physical education in schools.

This position should not preclude other theoretical considerations. If programs or experiences reflect the organic relationship to the field of study just described, it is possible to consider them physical education whether or not they take place in schools. It is an awkward concept, of course, because of the educational connotation of the title, and because fields of study are defined usually in relation to their academic pursuit. On the other hand, the concerns of this field of study are functional within the culture and may be both engaged in and studied in that context. Certainly, whenever we seek to understand the cultural functions of movement and its forms, we are dealing directly with the field of study; the question of whether or not the functions themselves can be called "physical education" remains.

All experience occurs within some context; that is, there is a situation in which particular events occur or behavior is manifest. Responding, behaving, or prescribing behavior for others depends upon the context within which it is to take place. We have all experienced the embarrassment of behaving inappropriately because we did not understand the situation well enough to make wise decisions. Actual environments are part of the concept of contexts, but there is also an implied understanding of an abstraction of all such occasions as well. In other words, we might be invited to a social occasion scheduled to take place in a garden, but the usual connotations for behavior of being outdoors are transcended if the event is a formal wedding. The understanding of "formal weddings" as an abstraction affects our behavior.

The point is that although a field of study is concerned with substantive content about a particular phenomenon, the application of the field is influenced by considerations of the context. The various contexts in which sport exists, for instance, determine such things as whether or not all the existing rules are utilized; whether infringements of rules are called by players or officials; how scrupulously records are kept; and even such things as who is eligible to play because of age, sex, ability, or even grade point average. Frequently knowledge of the context is simply assumed by the people involved or responsible, and as long as the context is well understood by all or allows for a broad range of choices with equal acceptability, this is adequate. The context, however, does serve to influence and modify the nature of the event, and when we are dealing with the applications of fields of study, it behooves us to plan such application with the most conscientious attention to it.

It might be more appropriate to talk about the school program in relation to a "contexture" rather than a context of education. The school program of physical education expresses the contexture or structure of the relationships among all of the variables that are relevant to designing that structure. The field of study, the individual as a learner, the society, and the role of the school are all relevant to deciding what physical education programs should be. Within the relatedness of these concerns insight into physical education as a school program is developed. Planning programs of physical education is treated in the following chapter, but because contemporary physical education developed in schools in an actual rather than a theoretical manner, it is necessary to understand its past.

AN HISTORICAL REVIEW OF THE CONCEPTUAL BASIS OF SCHOOL PHYSICAL EDUCATION

Ellen W. Gerber

The Association for the Advancement of Physical Education was organized in 1885. That occasion marked not only the establishment in America of the profession of physical education, but the culmination of a series of events and developing concepts which had pointed in this direction. The meeting was attended by about sixty people representing colleges, private schools and academies, organizations such as the YMCA and the New York Athletic Club, a hospital, and a gymnasium equipment company; famous writers on the subject of "physical culture" also were present. In their persons they typified the amalgamation of interests and concerns that provided the impetus for the formation of the profession of physical education.

THE IMPETUS TO BEGIN

In this country there were proponents of physical education as early as the latter half of the eighteenth century. Paralleling the writing of European intellectuals, Americans such as Benjamin Franklin, Noah Webster, Benjamin Rush, and Thomas Jefferson proposed the establishment of various forms and levels of educational programs and advocated the inclusion of exercise, military drill, and instruction in certain gentlemanly sports such as fencing. The earliest physical education programs per se were in a sense European imports; they took place in schools which were deliberately modeled on those of European educators. For example, Joseph Neef's school established near Philadelphia in 1809 promoted the principles of the great educator Johann Heinrich Pestalozzi and, like the master, Neef included calisthenic exercises, military drill, and natural (outdoor) play. The Round Hill School, which flourished in Northampton, Massachusetts, during the 1920s was modeled after the German gymnasium. Its founders not only provided opportunity for outdoor play, but included some form of Jahn (German) gymnastics within the prescribed curriculum. Throughout the nineteenth century a number of private academies emulated the English public school system and placed a strong emphasis on organized games for the young students. These endeavors, based as they were on European principles of education, took place in the beliefs that the school had some responsibility for the health and physical development of the students and that learning was enhanced if interspersed with relaxation or play.

However, the examples cited above, along with several others, particularly in the Northeast, were somewhat isolated occurrences. As an American system of education developed in the nineteenth century, it did not include any commitment to physical education. The public concern that was expressed for what was considered to be the deteriorating health of the American people focused on adults or college students. By mid-century, numbers of eminent figures had taken note of the poor health of the American people, using terms such as "weaklings," "pale," "cadaverous," "soft-muscled," "dissipated," "delicate," and "painfully nervous." Popular magazines began to carry articles urging better habits of hygiene and exercise. Health faddists advocated everything from vegetarianism to weight lifting as panaceas for overcoming the undesirable effects accruing to increasing industrialization and urbanization.

THE FIRST PROGRAMS

The largest educational bloc to adopt physical education programs during the nineteenth century was the American college system. Beginning in 1859 with the construction of the gymnasium at Amherst College in Massachusetts, gymnasiums and/or drill halls were constructed in colleges around the country. Hartwell lists forty-six such institutions in his report in 1885 (p. 140), but only about a third of these institutions actually required physical activity of their students. Amherst College also hired the first professor of hygiene and physical education, Edward Hitchcock (1828-1911), in 1861. However, it was eighteen years before another professional man, Dudley Allen Sargent (1849-1924) of Harvard, was appointed to a similar position on a college faculty. Many schools and colleges across the country demonstrated their concern for the health of students by requiring attendance at lectures on personal hygiene; frequently these lectures consisted of learned treatises on anatomy and physiology, based on the assumption that an understanding of how the body is constructed and functions leads to health care.

In the meantime, the public schools of the country had little or no physical education. In the last fifteen years of the nineteenth century the *Turners*, an organization devoted to the principles and practices of German gymnastics, introduced their system and started programs in the public school systems of approximately fifty cities, primarily in the Midwest. In other parts of the country, such physical education as existed consisted primarily of light gymnastic exercises. In the United States these were originally introduced as a system by Catharine Beecher (1800-1878), who called them calisthenics from the Greek words *kalos* (beautiful) and *sthenos* (strength). However, it was the colorful Dio Lewis (1823-1888) whose system of exercises was adopted by numerous schools and colleges. His book, *The New Gymnastics for Men, Women and Children*, was so popular that ten editions were published between 1862 and 1868. These light gymnastics* consisted of easy free exercises (e.g.,

---

* As opposed to the "heavy" German gymnastics, which utilized the large apparatus now commonly associated with gymnastics and which required of the performer a higher degree of strength and skill. Another form of "heavy" gymnastics was the weight-lifting program popularized by George Windship (1834-1876).

hopping in place or circular arm movements) and exercises with light hand apparatus (e.g., Indian clubs, two-pound wooden dumbbells, wands, and bean bags).

Since the "new gymnastics" of Lewis needed minimal equipment and space, it was easy to incorporate into a school program. Furthermore, since it did not demand a high degree of skill, neither did it demand highly trained leaders. With Lewis' book in hand and/or a little instruction, a teacher could break up the long day by standing the children in the aisle and directing five or ten minutes of exercises. It was probably because they recognized this possibility that in 1860 the prestigious American Institute of Instruction, composed of leading educators from all over the country, endorsed Lewis' work. It passed a resolution stating that his exercises were "eminently worthy of general introduction into all our schools, and into general use." (Leonard, n.d. pp. 47-48)

Just a few years later, in 1866, California passed the first law in the nation requiring the public schools of an entire state to include physical exercise. It was suggested that whole schools, grades one through six, do mass exercises; Lewis' handbook was suggested as a guide.

In 1890 similar conditions motivated the Boston School Committee to order that the Ling or Swedish system of gymnastics be introduced into all of the city's public schools. As in the earlier situations, the impetus was provided by forceful personalities, in this case Amy Morris Homans (1848-1933) and the Swedish Baron Nils Posse (1862-1895); they offered a concrete system which could be taught to large numbers of teachers in a relatively short time, and could be conducted for a few minutes daily within the confines of the regular classroom.

UNDERLYING ASSUMPTIONS

The aims of such systems* were necessarily limited, and the assumptions underlying the early programs were only vaguely defined by those engaged in the work. The keystone concept was the belief that the health of individuals was a proper concern of society, and therefore lay within the province of responsibility of society's agents; i.e., the schools. This principle, however, took hold slowly in America. Prior to 1900 only five states had passed some type of law requiring physical education; by World War I only sixteen states had such laws. However, in the three years following that war, the number more than doubled. Somehow, the war had brought home to the American people the utilitarian nature of

---

* The Lewis and Ling systems were not the only ones available or in use in the nineteenth century. Dalcroze eurythmics and Delsarte "gymnastics," for example, achieved some degree of popularity. And, in the century's last decade, the Sargent system of individually prescribed exercises, both free standing and on various pieces of developing apparatus, was quite popular, particularly in the colleges and athletic clubs which could afford gymnasiums. In 1889 Sargent claimed that his apparatus was used in more than three hundred and fifty institutions representing a total membership of over one hundred thousand. (*Physical Training*, 1890, p. 65)

fitness. It passed from an intellectual credo, espoused by far-seeing writers, educators, and doctors, to a concrete experience shared by large numbers of war veterans.

But it should be noted that a number of these laws provided that military drill be the basis of the physical education program. Thus it can be argued that coexistent with society's concern for the health of its children was an anxiety about the survival of the nation in a military sense. Throughout history one can find similar examples of societies establishing and maintaining physical education programs for the purpose of preparing for the future defense of their countries. For example, it has been amply demonstrated that the famous Swedish and German gymnastic systems of the nineteenth century were a direct outgrowth of military defeat followed by strong feelings of nationalism; sturdy youth were seen as the key to regaining and defending lost territories and a militarily strong homeland.

The concept that health and/or fitness and/or military training was a legitimate concern of school and colleges did not carry with it a belief in the educational value of physical education. In fact, even the physical educators of the late nineteenth century believed that their role in the schools was to prepare healthy bodies in order that young minds, and later adult citizens, could better carry out their responsibilities. In 1889, at the Conference in the Interest of Physical Training held in Boston, and presided over by the United States Commissioner of Education, this belief was clearly stated by Dudley Allen Sargent. Sargent, who was one of the most influential physical educators of his time, said: "The great aim of the gymnasium is to improve the physical condition of the mass of our students, and to give them as much health, strength and stamina as possible, to enable them to perform the duties that await them after leaving college." (*Physical Training*, 1890, p. 68) In other words, *mens sana in corpore sano*. This dualistic concept had been in evidence at least as early as the first century when it was stated by the Roman, Juvenal. In more modern times (the seventeenth century), it was given a new prominence by the philosopher Descartes, whose highly regarded theories were based on the belief that mind and body are substances which exist independently of one another. Following Descartes, John Locke (1632-1704), whose ideas carried great weight both in his native country of England and in America, advocated an educational system in which body condition had a prominent role in paving the way for optimum mental development.

A corollary concept was developed at this time in American physical education, probably due in part to the strong influence of Swedish gymnastics. It focused on a belief in the importance of the external structure of body and manifested itself in certain interesting ways. First, there was great concern with orthopedic deformities, particularly in relation to postural defects. Physical educators sought to correct these problems, and, in fact, even as great a visionary as Luther Halsey Gulick (1865-1918) remarked that "the first requirement of school gymnastics . . . [is] the correction of that faulty posture which is so frequently induced by the school desk." (Gulick, 1908, p. 381) And secondly, the early programs were marked by a tremendous interest in anthropometric measurement. The inspiration for anthropometry probably derived originally from the work of Sir Francis Galton, a well-known British anthropologist. The size of the chest, limbs, and so forth was believed to have some relation to the state of the health of the individual. Thousands of measurements were recorded and filed, and norms were established not only for the girth of numerous body parts, but for such things as height to the navel and length of the arm from the shoulder to the elbow.

The importance accorded to anthropometry by physical educators is evident not only by the extent of the practice, but by the fact that it was the first committee formed by the newly organized AAPE. From that first organizational meeting came a council to prepare a constitution and a committee on statistics and measurement. Perhaps this interest can in part be explained by the profession's need to establish itself as a science of the body. One way to achieve scientific respectability was to produce great numbers of figures. Some were, of course, useful. Measurements of strength and lung capacity served as a means to measure the progress of individual students. However, these more complicated measurements were not easily determined by teachers in the public schools who lacked the necessary equipment. Instead, they contented themselves with endless recording of heights and weights and several measures of girth.

THE FIRST PROGRAMS IN SUMMARY

It can be seen that the early school programs of physical education were characterized by a focus on health and the body in the context of a strongly dualistic philosophy. The rationale for this approach was rooted in the philosophy of seventeenth-century rationalism, especially as stated by Descartes, and applied by important thinkers such as Locke. The concern of the American society for the health of its citizens, along with the ever-present need to maintain military capability, led to the development of exercise programs in schools and colleges. These programs were selected, in part, because of their ease of administration, and were considered to be validated through the use of anthropometric measurements. The use of anthropometry further helped to create the sense of participation in a science of the body.

THE NEW PHYSICAL EDUCATION

In 1910 the Yearbook of the National Society for the Study of Education (NSSE) contained a chapter by Thomas Denison Wood (1865-1951) in which he enunciated the principles of what came to be known as "the new physical education." The expressed rationale marked a turning point in the profession—a change of focus from health and the science of the body to education and the science of child growth and development. The changed conceptual foundation suggested a new curriculum which added subject matter such as dance, play, games, and track and field athletics to the existing gymnastics or exercises.

Wood was a remarkably prescient man. As early as 1893 (when he was only 28 years old), he addressed his colleagues in the AAPE on the role of physical education within education, setting forth a distinct and new framework for the profession. He said:

> What is physical education? . . . Many people answer: "The training and development of the physical"; and they consider that the aim and end may be found in anthropometric apparatus, physical measurements, athletic contests and exhibitions, with graphic representations of measurements and of averages.
>
> Now these things are very well in their places, but if our science is to be worthy of the best efforts of men and women, and of the respect and recognition of the educational world, physical education must have an aim as broad as education itself, and as noble and inspiring as human life. The great thought in physical education is not the education of the physical nature, but the relation of physical training to complete education, and then the efforts to make the physical contribute its full share to the life of the individual, in environment, training, and culture. (Wood, 1893, p. 9)

The development of a professional philosophy stemming from this conception of physical education as an educational subject was, in part, an application of the speculative thinking advanced by a number of American and European philosophers, psychologists, and educators. Frequently cited and interpreted was the work of men such as Jean Jacques Rousseau, Friedrich Froebel, Charles Darwin, Edward L. Thorndike, William James, and John Dewey. Thus American physical education began to be related to the history of ideas, as well as to the findings of natural science which had motivated its inception.

The ideas of Jean Jacques Rousseau (1712-1778) were particularly influential, especially when coupled with the evolutionary theory of Charles Darwin. Rousseau's theories were based on the naturalistic belief that the child learned through experiences in nature, particularly in games which "exercised" the senses. The German philanthropic movement, which accepted the Rousseauistic precepts, therefore established schools which included programs in "natural physical education." For example, at the Schnepfenthal Educational Institute, Johann Christoph Friedrich Guts Muths (1759-1839) conducted activities in the out-of-doors, based primarily on skills which seemed "natural" to children, such as running jumping, and throwing.

Another significant idea developed by the European educational protagonists, and adopted by American physical educators, was that play is essentially a learning experience which touches upon the child's total being. Friedrich Froebel (1782-1852), a German who is best known for developing the idea of the kindergarten, stated this concept most beautifully when he said:

> It is by no means, however, only the physical power that is fed and strengthened in these games; intellectual and moral power, too, is definitely and steadily gained and brought under control. Indeed, a comparison of the relative gains of the mental and of the physical phases would scarcely yield the palm to the body. Justice, moderation, self-control, truthfulness, loyalty, brotherly love, and again strict impartiality—who when he approaches a group of boys engaged in such games could fail to catch the fragrance of these delicious blossomings of the heart and mind, and of a firm will; not to mention the beautiful, though perhaps less fragrant, blossoms of courage, perseverance, resolution, prudence, together with the severe elimination of indolent indulgence? (Hughes, 1901, pp. 122-123)

The American philosopher John Dewey (1859-1952) extended this concept to the social realm, making the point that physical activity is not only intelligent self-activity, but is socially intelligent—connected with the action of the other. Thus "the grounds for assigning to play . . . a definite place in the curriculum are intellectual and social." (Dewey, 1963, p. 195)

In order to accept the rationale for a new conception of physical education, it first became necessary to reject the exercise and gymnastics systems which were almost universally regarded as the primary curricular content. The exercise systems were inappropriate to the new ideas for two main reasons. First of all, they were "artificial"; that is, the requisite action or movements were not inherent in the behavioral instincts of the human being. Darwin's theory of evolution had been published in 1859, and educational theorists and psychologists such as G. Stanley Hall began to be interested in the play instincts of the child, and the inherited drives toward certain types of activities which reflected ancestral traits. The concept of "ontogeny recapitulates phylogeny" (the life history of the individual repeats the life history of the race) was interpreted to mean that the elemental activity drives necessary for hunting and survival in primitive society were still present in the nature of modern man. Physical educators such as Luther Gulick, Thomas Wood and Clark Hetherington argued, therefore, that the child's inherited "play instincts" should be the basis for the selection of program activities. This belief was typified by Wood's statement that

> the exercises should be natural in type, satisfying by their execution the play instinct and the fundamental powers and faculties as they develop, with due regard to the ancestral habits of activity and to the future practical needs of the individual. (Wood, 1910, p. 86)

Secondly, the concepts which it was hoped the child would learn through play could not easily be taught through exercises. Exploration of the environment, self-generation of movements designed to accomplish ends such as scoring points and, above all, social interaction with one's peers were all necessary to the vision of learning through play. Inherent in exercise programs, however, was limited freedom of movement in a confined area, action dictated by the teacher or the exercise prescription, and a minimum of social interaction. In fact, the discipline of moving in unison, according to teacher commands, without "peeking" at other students, was considered one of the desirable by-products of the gymnastics systems. Obviously the two approaches (gymnastic exercises and play) were incompatible. Nevertheless, the philosophical dualism lingered on, and programs in the early part of the twentieth century became a curious amalgamation of the twin concepts of body building and education through play.

EARLY TWENTIETH-CENTURY PROGRAMS

In the early part of the twentieth century, the primary curricular content of physical education in schools and colleges continued to be some form of exercises. A study done in 1905 at 225 public schools showed that 33 of the schools had compulsory gymnastics, 7 did military drill, and only one had compulsory instruction in athletics. (Lowman, 1907) Five years later another study of 2392 high schools showed 114 prescribing work in gymnastics and 28 in athletics. (Gulick, 1910).

However, a new dimension was added to the program in the form of physical education-sponsored extracurricular activities. In the colleges of the nation intramural and extramural sports competition had originally been organized and developed by the students. The first intercollegiate event was the Harvard-Yale boat race of 1852, and by the turn of the century the competitive sports program developed to include matches in football, soccer, fencing, track and field, swimming, golf, basketball, ice hockey, and other less widely played activities. When they became a large financial operation, they were taken over by athletic councils composed, usually, of students, administrators, and alumni of the institution. The hornet's nest of men's intercollegiate sports was severely criticized by professional physical educators who, by and large, had no authority to change it or even influence its direction. It was not until 1891 that Amos Alonzo Stagg at the University of Chicago, and later Clark W. Hetherington at the University of Missouri, first organized collegiate sports and physical education into a single administrative unit. This approach did not receive any great impetus, however, until 1931, when R. Tait McKenzie presented to President Gates of the University of Pennsylvania a plan for a comprehensive department of student health, physical instruction, and intercollegiate athletics. Known as the Gates Plan, it became the model for many colleges and universities which sought to make men's intercollegiate sports more educative.

Collegiate sports for women followed a slightly different pattern. Beginning with student-organized clubs for specific recreational activities such as walking or cycling, they progressed to physical education department-organized athletic associations. The first of these was organized at Bryn Mawr in Pennsylvania in 1891. The athletic associations sponsored intramural competitive sport in a variety of activities, among which were tennis, field hockey, ice skating, and basketball. The latter sport became the first large-scale, organized intercollegiate sport for women, the first game taking place in 1896. However, the opposition of professional physical educators succeeded in holding women's intercollegiate sport to a minimum, while promoting intramural activities as the most desirable supplement to the formal exercise programs in the curriculum.

In the early 1900s the public schools began to sponsor various forms of after-school sport. One of the earliest endeavors along these lines resulted in the formation of the Public School Athletic League (PSAL) in New York City in 1903. Under the leadership of Luther Gulick, the league was controlled and organized by volunteer teachers who recognized the need for providing some form of sports contests for the boys. The major events were competition in track and field, some competitive strength tests such as chinning, and also games such as baseball and football. By 1908, according to Gulick, the majority of boys in the grammar school grades (one to eight) were taking part in after-school athletic sports at least on an intramural basis.

The girls' curricular programs were also supplemented with after-school activities—in the case of New York City this was, at first, confined to folk dancing on the assumption that competitive athletics were not in keeping with the biological inheritance of females. The Girls Branch of the PSAL was organized in 1905. However, the desire of girls to participate in sports soon prevailed. Girls' athletic associations paralleled those of the college women and, like them, sponsored programs of intramural sports. Interscholastic competition was held to a minimum, largely due to the strenuous opposition of both male and female physical educators.

The rapid growth of extracurricular sports in the nation's schools was demonstrated in a survey of 225 public high schools in which it was reported that 28% of the 34,290 students in the schools surveyed were engaged in one or more sports including (in order of their popularity) football, track and field, rowing, baseball, basketball, ice hockey, tennis, and golf. (Lowman, 1907)

Another facet of the growth of extracurricular sport and games took place as a result of the burgeoning "play movement" in American cities. Although its roots were in the nineteenth century, the play movement received its greatest growth and public support in the early twentieth century. The need for playground facilities in urban areas was apparent, and municipal funds were expended to develop them. Since the school was the logical center of a child's life, playgrounds adjacent to schools were constructed. Unfortunately, these were often little more than concrete schoolyards providing a fenced-in area for play. Nevertheless, they provided facilities which made it feasible to carry out the extracurricular programs as well as providing a convenient place for games within the school curriculum when it was deemed desirable. Furthermore, by building playgrounds for schools, the play movement helped to legitimatize the connection between play and schools in the eyes of the lay public. Since the public at large was not particularly attuned to the theories of educators and psychologists, this was an important step in furthering the development of the sport curriculum in public schools.

THE NEW PHYSICAL EDUCATION IN SUMMARY

This second period in American physical education is marked by the development of a new rationale for school programs. In *addition* to accepting responsibility for the health and physical development of American youth, physical educators began to focus on the idea of the educational value of play, games, sports, and folk dancing. As the century progressed, there were increased pressures to regard these activities as being within the purview of physical education. The weight of educational theory suggested the idea; the desire of the profession to establish itself as an educational endeavor supported it; the students clamored for it; and the burgeoning play movement provided both rationale and facilities for it.

In practice, curricular programs of physical education continued to center on formal exercise or gymnastic systems, but a strong program of extracurricular activities was developed rapidly. Intramural sports in schools and colleges, interscholastic sports, and, in some cases, intercollegiate activities were given leadership by physical educators.

EDUCATION THROUGH PHYSICAL EDUCATION

For physical education, the next thirty years, from approximately 1930 to 1960, were a time of stability, unity, and growth. The conceptual basis of professional goals and programs, debated since the inception of school physical education, had culminated in the formulation of several well-accepted principles of physical education. Though these concepts were expanded, developed, and modified slightly over the years, nevertheless, they consisted of a central, stable core of ideas. From philosophy to curricular design and suggestions for teaching methodology, the literature of physical education evidences a remarkable unanimity of purpose and beliefs throughout this period. The main professional energies seem to have been applied to expanding the number and size of programs throughout the country.

The central conviction characteristic of this period was, in the words of Jesse Feiring Williams (1886-1966), that physical education is education *through* the physical rather than education *of* the physical. This concept was derived, first of all, from twentieth-century realizations that man is a unified or whole being and, consequently, the whole child is always a matter of concern in all phases of the education experience. Williams commented:

> When mind and body were thought of as two separate entities, physical education was obviously an education *of* the physical; in similar fashion mental education made its own exclusive demands. But with new understanding of the nature of the human organism in which wholeness of the individual is the outstanding fact, physical education becomes education *through* the physical. With this view operative, physical education has concern for and with emotional responses, personal relationships, group behaviors, mental learning, and other intellectual, social, emotional, and esthetic outcomes. (Williams, 1964, p. 8)

This concept carried with it some corollary ideas or implications. Thanks to John Dewey and others, the American educational system had learned to conceive of itself as a place to "socialize" the child. Specifically, this meant that in addition to mastering the knowledge associated with the various subjects in the curriculum, the child was, *at the same time,* expected to learn the fundamental values and behavior associated with life in a democratic society. Physical educators not only adopted this as a goal—they took it to be their *primary* purpose. The phrase "education through the physical" was interpreted to mean that through the medium of physical activities, primarily sports and games, the educational socialization goals such as loyalty, cooperation, sportsmanship, concern for others, equality of opportunity, and good winning and losing would be fulfilled. Williams remarked:

> The time is past when a physical education period is adjudged good or bad depending upon the amount of physical activity obtained during the period. A period is good or bad to the extent of desirable, useful, and pertinent intellectual knowledges, skills, and control obtained. (Williams, Dambach, and Schwendener, 1932, p. 81)

The logical conclusion of this idea was, of course, to recommend the complete negation of earlier professional focus on the physical. Williams did just this when he stressed that "cultivation of the body for the body's sake can never be justified." (Williams, 1932, p. 286) Or, as he put it later:

> What then, is to be said of the efforts of certain persons to develop large and bulging muscles or to pursue certain odd skills that have no useful function in life? The satisfactions derived from such exercises serve only whimsical values such as exhibitionism; at times they are outlets for maladjusted personalities. For example, the yoga devotees may finally acquire unilateral control over the *rectus abdominus,* but the evidence is lacking that this has in any way deepened spirituality. (Williams, 1964, pp. 186-187)

5

The belief of Williams and others that character traits and social values could be taught through a curriculum of sport activities was well accepted by the profession. The ideas agreed with those of contemporary educational theorists and behavioral scientists, and thus established for physical education a fixed place within the realm of public education. Physical education no longer had an important but different role—its objectives were now identical with those of education.

There were others in the profession, however, who were not willing to agree that "education *of* the physical" should be virtually eliminated. The foremost spokesman of the objective of body building and conditioning, and the learning of motor skills, was Charles Harold McCloy (1886-1959). He argued that the fundamental purpose of physical education was to assist the individual to develop organic power, particularly muscular strength and flexibility. McCloy's approach to body development extended beyond the earlier goals of health and the correction of orthopedic defects.* He conceived the development of skilled performance to be closely related to physical development and therefore placed great emphasis on mastery of skills as a primary objective of physical education. Furthermore, he argued that this type of learning also had cultural value:

> I believe that any worth-while activity executed skillfully enough to give the doer exquisite sensory pleasure is cultural. . . . Perhaps not more than a small percentage of our people will ever achieve culture in the humanities, at least as culture is defined by the humanists; but a very large percentage can achieve such culture in the motor field, for these skills reach far down into phylogenetic depths and touch a cord to which our beings easily respond. (McCloy, 1940, pp. 91-92, italics deleted)

An important adjunct to McCloy's beliefs about body and skill development was the use of research to determine exactly what an individual child should and could be able to do. He worked to develop standardized, objective tests of proven validity to measure performance and advocated that skill and physical capacity tests be administered by all teachers. In conjunction with norms established by McCloy and others, test scores could be used for purposes of classification, grading, and motivation. By this means it was hoped to avoid ungraded, heterogeneous programs with inexact standards of achievement.

The third major idea of this period was the conceptual and literal extension of physical education beyond the school program. As early as 1913, Clark Wilson Hetherington (1870-1942) had established a demon-

---

* In fact, professional health goals were so distinguishable from physical education goals that it became necessary to designate two distinct units in the one profession. In 1927 Thomas Wood became the first professor of Health Education so named, and in 1937 the American Physical Education Association became the American Association for Health and Physical Education. It also became customary to create departments and schools of health and physical education.

stration play school that was sponsored by the University of California, Berkeley, until 1934. It was "suggested as the extra-home institutional center of child-life in which the school and the playground are educationally fused." (Hetherington, 1915, p. 380) In other words, it blended what were then fundamentally two separate institutions—the school and the playground—into one, and furthermore, it enrolled pre-school age children as young as four years. This idea was later extended by one of Hetherington's protégés, Jay Bryan Nash (1886-1965), who conceived the school facility as a center from which both school and community recreation programs would emanate. Nash asked: "How can a line be drawn between class time and the time spent in activity at noon, after school, or even during the long summer vacation? These are all times for physical education." (Nash, 1928, p. 223)

This conception led naturally to the viewpoint that physical education is concerned not only with the whole child, but with the whole life of the individual—from early childhood through the years of adulthood. Thus physical education should take responsibility for developing skill in activities that would be enjoyed during leisure time. This led, of course, to the conception that programs should emphasize carry-over or lifetime sports—particularly those that had recreational and coeducational values. Appropriately, in 1938, the term "recreation" was added to professional titles, and the national organization became the American Association for Health, Physical Education and Recreation.

PROGRAMS FOR EDUCATIONAL PHYSICAL EDUCATION

One of the most striking characteristics of physical education during this period was its growth—both in size and scope. By 1949, legislation requiring some form and amount of physical education had been passed in 41 states. At that time a survey by the National Education Association indicated that 92% of all public school students had an average of 132 minutes per week of physical education. (Van Dalen and Bennett, 1971, p. 484) A survey taken just after the war found that approximately 60% of American colleges and universities required one or two years of physical education. (Hackensmith, 1966, p. 480) Another interesting indicator of the growth of physical education was the increase in membership in the AAHPER from 5733 in 1930 to 25,042 in 1960 (a figure which more than doubled in the next decade).

The curriculum was equally expanded to include a wide variety of sports, games, dance, aquatics, fundamental skills, classroom subjects, and even camping and outdoor activities. The growth of team sports in the schools was especially marked at this time because they seemed well suited to professional aims—particularly the social objectives. Unresolved was the problem of how to build a program around team sports and still prepare youth for the lifetime pursuits of sports. The limitations of facilities and large classes mitigated against the goal of including individual sports in significant amounts.

Modern dance was one of the new activities which developed in the 1930s, and in 1932 a Dance Section was organized in the APEA. Fifteen years later a survey showed that 42% of 526 colleges offered courses in modern dance; folk, tap, social, and square dancing, in that order of frequency, were also taught in the colleges. (Van Dalen and Bennett, 1971, p. 504)

The advent of World War II inevitably carried with it increased attention to physical fitness. Although there was some suggestion that physical education classes should return to programs of military drill, Secretary of War Henry L. Stimson prevailed upon physical educators to focus instead on physical conditioning. ("Letter," 1943, p. 368) *Physical Fitness through Physical Education for the High School Victory Corps* was an important guide booklet prepared by a committee of professional physical educators and representatives from the armed forces. It recommended calisthenics and other types of fitness activities, and provided tests and norms for male students. Women's programs also emphasized fitness, though they maintained more sport and dance activities. In this period McCloy's "back to the body" aim with its attendant testing program was much in evidence. Because of the patriotic spirit engendered by the war, this aim became closely related to the social goals of the profession. Williams had defined health as "that quality of life which enables the individual to live most and serve best" (Williams and Brownell, 1951, p. 6), and in wartime this meant attaining a level of conditioning suitable for entrance into the service.

Another phenomenon of this period was the broadening of the physical education curriculum to various related subjects, particularly of a theoretical or nonactivity nature. In the earliest programs, lectures on hygiene and the body had often been included in physical education. Now, in addition to this type of material, courses in health (total health including emotional aspects), safety education, first aid, civil defense, and driver education were scheduled as part of the allotted time for physical education programs. In keeping with a suggestion by Seward Staley, courses in "sports appreciation" were introduced in some places. During the 1950s, lectures in principles of movement achieved popularity, particularly in programs for college women.

An interesting aspect of programs during this period was the adoption of teaching methodology and class organization suitable to "education through physical education." The fulfillment of citizenship goals suggested an organization in which student leadership qualities could be fostered. Thus squads were organized, and student leaders or class captains were elected and given responsibilities. Discussion time was increased to place more emphasis on understanding the social implications of sport behavior. Even calisthenic and skill drills were organized in such a manner that students could be given opportunities to lead them occasionally.

Debate took place about the desirability of imposing activities on students if they were expected to develop lifelong interests in sport. Some believed the solution lay in forcing student exposure to the widest possible variety of activities with the expectation that successful performance and interest would be developed. Others advocated election of activities on the basis of "felt needs." In practice, the heterogeneous scheduling of physical education classes made it difficult to organize progressive, varied programs. The colleges were in a better position to offer classes in specified activities, and during this period they solved the problem by evolving a system of election within requirements. Students were expected to take a course in each area offered, such as conditioning, aquatics, team sports, and individual sports; the women's programs also added dance and fundamental movement to the list. In general, the trend toward recognition of general student interests reflected the prevailing educational shift toward student-centered programs, though it was group rather than individual needs that were considered important.

EDUCATION THROUGH PHYSICAL EDUCATION IN SUMMARY

Physical education between 1930 and 1960 was in a period of philosophical stability and concrete growth. The profession seemed united in its acceptance of a triad of goals that included learning of social values and attitudes suitable for citizenship in a democratic society; achievement of total fitness and mastery of concomitant physical skills; and development of skills, knowledge, and habits of, interest in, and positive attitudes toward activities suitable for leisure-time pursuit.

These goals resulted in the advocacy of programs of physical education that were diverse in nature, and conceived of in a progressive, developmental manner. However, in practice, the situational demands and the influence of national factors, such as the Depression and World War II, caused the activities to be somewhat more limited than was considered desirable. The largest blocks of class time were devoted to team sports and conditioning activities. As in earlier periods, extracurricular sports provided a means to extend the program. The introduction of a number of related theoretical courses also was evident in this time.

Increased use of testing for both fitness and skill levels and use of student leadership were characteristics of the manner in which programs were conducted. A trend toward student election of specific activities was apparent, particularly at the college level.

PHYSICAL EDUCATION IN THE LAST DECADE

The seventy-fifth anniversary of the organization of physical education in this country was celebrated by the profession in 1960. In its growth from a science of health and the body to "education through physical education," physical education reflected the changing emphasis in the social and behavioral sciences, in American education, and in social conditions and values.

Since that time further shifts have occurred. American culture has sought to change from its "melting pot" image to a society characterized by coexistent diversity. Within this framework, the individual has emerged as an entity free to pursue his "own thing," rather than goals decided by some amorphous social grouping. The objectives of education are now being stated in terms of the development of the individual qua individual rather than as part of a social unit.

The rationale and programs of physical education have begun to grow within this new focus. Sports, dance, exercise—heretofore seen for their instrumental values to be used in the service of society's goals—have become recognized as worthy activities in their own right. Rather than justifying sport for its social value or potential for character development, it is accepted for its contribution to the integrated, maturing individual in the manner that an understanding of poetry or a foreign language is now accepted.

Such a shift in rationale is beginning to cause a change in program content. Interest is turning from traditional games to sports such as the Oriental self-defense activities, to dance for men and women, to natural sport, to movement forms that are not inherently competitive.

The profession itself has refocused its attention on the nature and significance of its own activities. This development is a logical extension of the realization that values are centered within the participant-activity syndrome rather than in some external, instrumental objectives. Thus defining the art and science of human movement, or theorizing about sport and dance, have become important new professional considerations.

The meaning of the sport experience, or the movement experience, is found in an intensely personal response to the institutionalized experience of physical education. Thus it is evident that the future of physical education will be concerned with developing different means to enable students to find through its programs an experience of the self that they will find relevant to the life styles of the future.

REFERENCES

"A Letter from Mr. Stimson." *Journal of Health and Physical Education.* 14 (September, 1943), 368.

Dewey, John. *Democracy and Education.* New York: Macmillan, 1963 (First published in 1916.)

Gerber, Ellen W. *Innovators and Institutions in Physical Education.* Philadelphia: Lea & Febiger, 1971.

Gulick, Luther Halsey. "The Place and Limitations of Folk Dancing as an Agency in Physical Training." *American Physical Education Review.* XIII (October, 1908), 377, 382.

————. "Report of the Committee on the Status of Physical Education in Public Normal Schools and Public High Schools in the United States." *American Physical Education Review*. XV (June, 1910), 453, 454.

Hackensmith, Charles W. *History of Physical Education*. New York: Harper & Row, 1966.

Hartwell, Edward Mussey. *Physical Training in American Colleges and Universities*. Circular of Information of the Bureau of Education. No. 5, 1885. Washington, D.C.: U.S. Government Printing Office, 1886.

Hetherington, Clark W. "The Demonstration Play School of 1913." *American Physical Education Review*. XX (May; June; October, 1915), 282-294; 373-380; 429-445.

Hughes, James L. *Froebel's Educational Laws for All Teachers*. New York: D. Appleton and Company, 1901.

Leonard, Fred Eugene. *Pioneers of Modern Physical Training*. Reprinted from *Physical Training*. Published by the Physical Directors' Society of the Young Men's Christian Association of North America. n.d.

Lowman, G. S. "The Regulation and Control of Competitive Sport in Secondary Schools of the United States." *American Physical Education Review*. XII (September, 1907), 241-255.

McCloy, Charles Harold. *Philosophical Bases for Physical Education*. New York: F. S. Crofts & Company, 1940.

Nash, Jay B. *The Organization and Administration of Playgrounds and Recreation*. New York: A. S. Barnes and Company, 1928.

Physical Training, A Full Report of the Papers and Discussion of the Conference Held in Boston in November, 1889. Reported and edited by Isabel C. Barrows. Boston: Geo. H. Ellis, 1890.

Van Dalen, Deobold B., and Bennett, Bruce L. *A World History of Physical Education*. 2nd ed. Englewood Cliffs, New Jersey: Prentice-Hall, 1971.

Williams, Jesse Feiring. *The Principles of Physical Education*. 2nd ed. Philadelphia: W. B. Saunders Company, 1932.

————. *The Principles of Physical Education*. 8th ed. Philadelphia: W. B. Saunders Company, 1964.

————, Dambach, John I., and Schwendener, Norma. *Methods in Physical Education*. Philadelphia: W. B. Saunders Company, 1932.

————, and Brownell, Clifford Lee. *The Administration of Health Education and Physical Education*. Fourth Edition. Philadelphia: W. B. Saunders Company, 1951.

Wood, Thomas Denison. "Some Unsolved Problems in Physical Education." *Proceedings of the Eighth Annual Meeting*. Chicago: American Association for the Advancement of Physical Education, 1893.

————. *Health and Education. The Ninth Yearbook of the National Society for the Study of Education*. Part I. Chicago: University of Chicago Press, 1910.

DISCUSSION

Statements relative to the *application* of knowledge from the field of study in programming movement experiences. The emphasis here is on a view of the relationship of practice to theory, and on the relationship of the field of study to its contextual use, leading especially to a consideration of schools as one context.

Applying the Field of Study

1. Although the development of understanding within a field of study is not tied to applications of that knowledge, ultimately those who work in particular fields are concerned with how to *use* and *apply* knowledge.

2. The applications of knowledge about human movement are appropriate in many contexts; that is, movement experiences *can* contribute to many kinds

of beneficial effects on man and on groups and can be used to remedy existing deficiencies and problems as well.

3. Knowledge about human movement and sport alone does not provide insight into *how* such knowledge should be applied; rather, contexts other than the field of study indicate application, but key concepts of potential contribution to the welfare of humanity do emerge.

4. Although the body of knowledge may provide the insight and understanding that lead to appropriate applications, the *choice* of knowledge depends upon what the situation is, and an understanding of all the variables affecting it; from this kind of analysis, one derives purposes for his use of movement experiences.

5. If one wishes to utilize knowledge from within the field of study of physical education, the first task is to analyze the situation (context) within which he wishes to use knowledge or experiences; programs grow out of a contexture of understanding.

6. Within physical education, however, purposes which imply the use of movement experiences must also relate directly to the appropriate concerns of the field of study. Movement can be an *instrumentality* for the achievement of many kinds of desirable human purposes, but if movement *itself* is not somehow a crucial element in the process, these purposes cannot be said to derive or be intrinsically related to this field of study.

7. Programming movement as programs or experiences is a function of several professional groups; i.e., teachers, physical therapists, trainers, dancers and choreographers, dance therapists, coaches, and so on. Each of these is concerned with the body of knowledge of physical education in some way, but the professional context determines the purposes for which movement is programmed.

8. The practitioner within any of the fields utilizing the body of knowledge of physical education must understand the field of study, but he must also understand the other aspects of his concern. All of these fields deal directly with people, either as individuals or in groups, and all of them have some reference (obviously) to society and depend on understanding how people learn and behave, especially within the social context.

9. The "school" as a social institution implies certain other considerations as part of the context within which physical education is carried on, and assumptions about education provide a framework for the application of the body of knowledge and the identification of purposes for such application.

10. The history of physical education in the school program is an important aspect of the contexture within which the field is analyzed and understood.

SELECTED BIBLIOGRAPHY

History of Physical Education, Sport, Dance, and Exercise

Beck, Robert H. "The Greek Tradition and Today's Physical Education." *Journal of Health, Physical Education and Recreation.* June, 1963, 19-20, 50.
  Historical overview of the role of physical training in ancient Greece, the birth of physical education in the school program, and the current threat to its existence.
Brailsford, Dennis. *Sport and Society: Elizabeth to Anne.* Toronto: University of Toronto Press, 1969.
  Explores the impact of philosophical, medical, psychological, and social changes which affected attitudes towards sport, games, exercise, and physical education from the Elizabethan to Stuart period of English history.

Brasch, R. *How Did Sports Begin? A Look At the Origins of Man at Play.* New York: David McKay Company, 1970.
Discusses the origin of various sports and the Olympic Games.

Dulles, Foster Rhea. *A History of Recreation: America Learns To Play.* 2nd ed. New York: Appleton-Century-Crofts, 1965.
Traces the growth of recreation in the United States and considers social variables and mass leisure.

Eyler, Marvin H. (ed.) *Our Heritage. Quest XI.* December, 1968.
Includes selections by several authors on historical topics in relation to sport, exercise, and physical education.

Gerber, Ellen W. *Innovators and Institutions in Physical Education.* Philadelphia: Lea & Febiger, 1971.
Presents an historical perspective of the growth of physical education through the study of people who were primarily responsible for initiating its ideas; includes innovators and institutions that played significant roles in establishing physical education programs.

————. "Learning and Play: Insights of Educational Protagonists." *Quest XI.* December, 1968, 44-49.
Considers views related to the recognition of values resulting from the inclusion of physical education in the school program.

Hackensmith, Charles William. *History of Physical Education.* New York: Harper & Row, 1966.
Offers an historical perspective of physical education related to political, social, and educational background in various parts of the world, and treats leaders who influenced physical education.

Henderson, Robert W. *Ball, Bat and Bishop: The Origin of Ball Games.* New York: Rockport Press, Inc., 1947.
Traces the evolution of ball games, from their religious connotations, through the Christian religion which borrowed these rites, and to the present era whereby sport does not reflect the honoring of dead Gods. The myth surrounding the origin of baseball in the U. S. is exposed.

Kraus, Richard. *History of the Dance In Art and Education.* Englewood Cliffs, New Jersey: Prentice-Hall, 1969.
Analyzes the history of dance; examines contemporary theater dance, and reviews dance education as it developed in the United States.

Lawler, Lillian B. *The Dance In Ancient Greece.* Middletown, Connecticut: Wesleyan University Press, 1964.
Treats the role of dance in Greek society.

Leonard, Fred Eugene. *A Guide to the History of Physical Education.* 3rd ed. Philadelphia: Lea & Febiger, 1947.
Discusses the growth of physical education during the medieval period through the evolution of physical education in the United States.

Lewis, Guy M. "Adoption of the Sports Program, 1906-39: The Role of Accommodation in the Transformation of Physical Education." *Quest XII.* May, 1969, 34-46.
Views the relationship of sport to the physical education program and considers developments within education and changes in professional preparation which influenced their relationship.

Lucas, John A. "A Prelude to the Rise of Sport: Ante-bellum America, 1850-1860." *Quest XI.* December, 1968, 50-57.
Considers life in America during the Colonial period, the influence of English educational and sport views, the revival of the "whole man" concept, the desire for human perfection and the need for exercise.

Maynard, Olga. *American Modern Dance: The Pioneers.* Boston: Little, Brown and Company, 1965.
Includes biographies and histories of modern dance pioneers in relation to the growth of dance.

McIntosh, Peter C. *Games and Sports: How Things Developed.* London: Educational Supply Association, 1962.
Explains the origin of several competitive games and sports which have become popular in Britain.

Rice, Emmett A., Hutchinson, John L., and Lee, Mabel. *A Brief History of Physical Education.* 5th ed. New York: Ronald Press Company, 1969.
An historical overview of the position of physical education.

Schwendener, Norma. *A History of Physical Education in the United States.* New York: A. S. Barnes & Company, 1942.
Presents the history of physical education in the United States reflecting social, religious, economic, and political influences in each period of American life.

Sorell, Walter. *The Dance Through the Ages.* New York: Grosset & Dunlap, 1967.
Traces the development of dance from its origin to the present.

Terry, Walter. *The Dance In America.* New York: Harper and Row, 1956.
History of dance and people who contributed to its growth. Includes the role of dance in contemporary America.

Van Dalen, Deobold B., and Bennett, Bruce L. *A World History of Physical Education.* 2nd ed. Englewood Cliffs, New Jersey: Prentice-Hall, 1971.
Analyzes the historical phases through which physical education has passed; compares these periods within the history of particular countries.

Weston, Arthur: *The Making of American Physical Education.* New York: Appleton-Century-Crofts, 1962.
Discusses the historical development of physical education from its European heritage through the Kennedy administration; contains documents, speeches, and papers of outstanding leaders in the field who helped shape American physical education.

Ziegler, Earle F. *Problems in the History and Philosophy of Physical Education and Sport.* Englewood Cliffs, New Jersey: Prentice-Hall, 1968.
Treats physical education from an historical and philosophical perspective in relation to various characteristic problems.

Chapter VI

PLANNING PROGRAMS OF PHYSICAL EDUCATION

The school program is the result of a process of selection, which may be more or less rationalized depending upon the particular people involved in various programs. The role of the school is conceived within a culture, and the particularized conceptions that are expressed in programs derive from views of the elements involved. The formalization of the processes of education in the institutionalized existence of schools presumes a relationship to society, to individuals, to the functions of learning, and to knowledge and experience as the source of learning. Rationalized programs are developed within all these elements as a contexture for the educational process. Programs, themselves, however, are not stable and enduring; they are modified by their existence and interpreted differently as understanding of the sources is altered by new knowledge or insights.

Our general understanding of "schooling" is that it is a process of formalized enculturation. In any society, the young somehow have to absorb the knowledge and customs of the group in order to function within it as youth and as adults. When a society is homogeneous and integrative, that is, shares values and behavior widely and provides access for the individual to participate, enculturation may not even have to be formalized. In such societies, the young have the means for learning that which they must know as they participate in the life of the community within their capacities. Education is necessary to the continuity of all cultures, but it can be entrusted to informal processes, and the less complex the culture, the less time it takes to become educated.

Societies characterized by heterogeneity and complex culture have a great many problems that revolve around the concerns of education. The implications for what should be learned are not clear nor are they obvious to those doing the learning. Youth in the United States, for instance, cannot see the relatedness between what is being taught in schools and the means to a fulfilling and productive existence. As a result, education is sometimes seen as meaningless, and the young respond to it with apathy, indifference, and even hostility toward its restrictive dimensions. At the same time, because our society is discontinuous, that is, requires different behavior at various ages, *relevance* is not a clear concept. To structure education as relevant to the child's needs and interests may not satisfy the demands of enculturation, and when education is relevant to social needs, it may not be satisfying to the child. Nonintegrated societies simply cannot establish direct links between education and culture because of a host of factors.

The teacher in a complex society is often not the doer; that is, he is an "expert," of whatever degree, not in the field itself, but in the teaching of that field only, and this is another separation between the school and the society. With increasing frequency in our society, teachers are not even related to their students by virtue of community life, and, hence, have no real responsibility to either the previous or subsequent actual life of the student. Furthermore, when knowledge is abundant and complex, the school must introduce the young to knowledge and whole segments of culture which not only have they never experienced even indirectly, but which they may never experience at all. Education takes longer and is under constant pressure to hasten its processes, to include more and more, and to aid students in the development of understandings and abilities for which they have no actual frame of reference whatsoever.

There are various alternatives for education within the view that it is responsible primarily to enculturation. In societies undergoing rapid change, education may seek to provide a stable and enduring set of values, or to influence the direction and rate of change. Education may even influence change in unintentional ways; for we all know that there is frequently a serious divergence between what the school intends to teach and what is actually learned. Because cultural change does not occur in an even, symmetrical fashion, the role of the school is further confused by the fact that conflicting values are manifest at any time in a given culture; different values are held by different individuals or social groups, and each individual develops values within the unique configuration of his perceptions. George Kneller (1965) suggested that the three major issues for education in this context had to do with: "ideal versus manifest culture"; "traditional versus emergent values"; "dominant versus minority values." Regardless of how choices are made or, in fact, whether or not they are made, the role of the school does express some position with reference to these value dichotomies. The ways that school programs function in an emphasis on science or social studies, language or mathematics, literature or home economics, or include physical education and athletic programs, derives, in part, from how the school is conceived in relation to culture. In shaping individuals through the content or modes of the school, culture is shaped and values are expressed.

Besides the conceptions of culture and the relationships of individuals to society, the school program emerges from considerations of the individual and how he learns. Control, restriction, and repression were early characteristics of schools in the United States as an outgrowth of a Puritan ethic that presumed a lifelong battle against evil and the "devil," especially as these encouraged self-indulgence and bodily pleasure. Strict control and discipline were seen as adjuncts to the school that were necessary in the development of youth. They were also acceptable modes in relation to how learning was thought to take place, and the concept of education as "training" exemplified a cohesive point of view of the elements that formed the contexture of the school. Beliefs about the "higher" functions of the mind and the demands of literacy were also consonant with this point of view. Learning as a process always involves observing, listening, and doing; beliefs about how learning occurs and what is most worth learning determine the relative emphasis in the school.

The school program, then, is an outgrowth of a selective process based on beliefs and understanding of the individual and how he learns in relation to what he should become within a given society. Different philosophical views of man suggest various conceptions of what education is and its implied goals. Divergent views of the relationship of the individual to society suggest various goals for education, and these are especially conflicting with reference to implied positions about societal problems and the role of the school. Theories of learning and psychological development imply diverse educational modes. For subject-matter fields, the diversity of belief and opinion surrounding conceptions of the role of the school is simply compounded by any controversy that may also exist about the relative worth of knowledge in that particular field of study.

It is obvious that although the pervasive goal of education as "enculturation" is fairly acceptable, there is little agreement about what it means to be a functional and effective adult in the United States and which of the many diverse realities and values about the individual, society, and knowledge should be affirmed. Certain critics of education have suggested that schools are no longer a viable institution; Ivan Illich, for one, called for the "de-schooling of society," Paul Goodman, John Holt, Jonathan Kozol, Edgar Friedenberg, and other articulate educational critics who agree with this point of view suggest that de-schooling society is necessary. In their view, the school dehumanizes students and teachers, kills the natural desire of children to learn, and fosters the most undesirable attitudes toward humanity, society, and learning itself. Although these writers and others have been proposing "alternatives" to education as we know it for the last few years, none has proved viable. It would seem likely that the school will endure, but the processes of education may undergo radical transformations.

The point, finally, is that those responsible for educational programs must have cohesive views of what they are trying to do and why those aims are worthy ones. The selective processes that lead to programs in schools depend upon all the aspects of an educational perspective suggested. Despite the existence of national commissions, curriculum study groups within the profession at large, directives from state departments of instruction, and the like, school programs reflect the beliefs of those involved in them. This means that unless some kind of "performance contracting" is allotted to an outside agency, and this is a current reality in some school districts, teachers themselves must understand, define, and develop the programs they purvey.

For physical education, this task is complicated by the lack of clarity about its field of study. Somehow, the task of planning programs depends upon a clear contexture of beliefs about physical education in the school as an outgrowth of commitments to the pervasive goals of adulthood and the process of enculturation.

EDUCATIONAL COMMITMENTS

Of all social institutions, the school is most profoundly affected by stress and upheaval in society. A pervasive goal of "enculturation" demands, at least, some agreement about the kind of people we think are desirable if not about the kind of world in which we think they will live. Furthermore, the goals of education emerge from beliefs about the scope of responsibility of the school itself, and these are in question. The conception of free, universal, and compulsory education in the United States was a bold commitment to youth. Educational involvement in the United States today costs some $80 billion a year and represents more than 30% of the population in its endeavors. In a society that some have characterized as "breaking down" and "in despair," it is little wonder that the schools are controversial symbols of both our hopes and fears. As indicated, there are those who have called for abandoning the schools and seeking more viable educational alternatives. Others, like Charles E. Silberman (1970), call for a transformation of the schools on the basis of a reordering of commitments that transcend the mindless, dull, and limiting education based on specific tasks and job demand.

Erik Erikson suggested that:

> In youth, ego strength emerges from the mutual confirmation of individual and community, in the sense that society recognizes the young individual as a bearer of fresh energy and that the individual so confirmed recognizes society as a living process which inspires loyalty as it receives it, maintains allegiance as it attracts it, honors confidence as it demands it. (1968, p. 241)

This situation hardly characterizes the relationship of youth to society in the United States today, and if it is an important aspect of developing ego strength and "identity," it is no wonder that our society is sometimes said to be "schizophrenic" and "psychotic." In *Culture and Commitment: A Study of the Generation Gap*, Margaret Mead said that, "The idea of choice in commitment entered human history when competing styles of life were endowed with new kinds of sanctions of religious or political ideology" (Mead, 1970, xi). She has also identified contemporary Western culture as "prefigurative" in the sense that adults learn from their children. (Mead, 1970)

A major thrust of the school toward goals of socialization and an improved society was obtained as an outgrowth of the progressive education movement of the 1920s and 1930s and gained impetus as a result of World War II. Both society and the individual as a "whole" child were given cognizance, and education focused on the notions of "optimum development of the child" and the goals of education in a democracy.

Although this emphasis had lost some enthusiasm, partly because of the unacceptable "life adjustment education" that seemed to belie America's commitment to excellence and partly because of charges that "Johnny can't read," it was still viable until the 1950s. The successful launching of the Russian Sputnik I in 1957 ushered in a shift of educational focus from socialized goals to subject matter as the important mission of the schools, especially those areas most clearly related to technology. Those who espoused a philosophy of educational "fundamentalism" held sway during the early 1960s, and broad curriculum revision was carried on toward the end of defining the role of the school in clear relationship to knowledge areas.

The interesting point is that the 1960s were characterized by the greatest stress in both school and society of any decade in the twentieth century. Student rebellions became a commonplace; an "equality revolution" affected racial, ethnic, social, and sexual classifications; value dichotomies in relation to the "generation gap" seemed irrevocable, and, in general, American society faced problems of disaffection, disadvantage, and alienation more seriously than it had before. By the end of the sixties, the demands for "relevance" and "meaning" in both life and education seemed more like pleas, but education was left with compelling challenges to its commitments to the individual and society.

Many of the problems that revolve around youth and education derive from disparate value systems that have been polarized to represent "culture" as the establishment forms of adults and their expression of the past and the "counter-culture" representing the ideas and beliefs of youth as well as newly identified values of particular minority groups. This framework was presented most clearly in *The Making of a Counter-Culture* (1969) by Theodore Roszak and delineated in a romanticized and widely read treatise, *The Greening of America* (1970), by Charles Reich, a Yale professor. The literature of the seventies documents a noticeable change in life view that was apparent in its effects on all segments of society and its institutions.

"Consciousness" implies attitudes, opinions, and sensibilities, and to speak of a "new" consciousness or a "youth" consciousness is to suggest emergent views that contrast with older ones. Reich postulated three categories of consciousness as a "whole perception of reality" on which society depends. "Consciousness I" referred to the outlook of the free-enterprise system in relation to the individual, primarily as farmer or businessman. "Consciousness II" represented the organizational, technocratic society that presently symbolizes the "establishment." "Consciousness III," in Reich's version, was the values of youth in opposition to the repression and lack of meaning of the corporate state.

However it is viewed, it is obvious that the present state of society is such that individuals are not provided the means for their own growth and the development of satisfying identities easily. Social criticism has to do with the inordinate emphasis on economic growth and procedures as a primary value, and with the materialism, conformity, and externalization of values that ensue. As the United States became a mass society with competition as the primary modality for success, evaluations of individuals and their worth were based on external sources. The middle-class child, at least, was expected to absorb dispositions toward achievement and conformity and to value the rewards of his efforts. The approval and acceptance of others are important values in the society of the United States, but as they have come to mean being motivated to present an "image" and having a dichotomy between public and private behavior, it becomes the basis of the charge of "hypocrisy."

The newer consciousness also suggests that the easy acceptance of authority and so-called rationality is hypocritical. As the horrors of the Vietnam involvement, the economy, the obvious injustice to minority groups, and the failures of government became apparent, an older consciousness repressed cognitive dissonance with arguments that were seemingly no longer rational nor relevant. As a nation, our pride in our technological excellence turned to embarrassment as we realized the ecological damage that had been done. The intergenerational dispute was manifest in real hostility as youth came to view the expressions of affluence for which their parents had worked a lifetime as obscene symbols of the meaninglessness of existence and the lack of regard for humanity.

The rebellion against the establishments and authority was manifest in the actual uprisings in schools and colleges. Repressive and unjustified uses of authority were simply challenged by the young; for the first time, many of these challenges reached the courts. In cities like New York, the American Civil Liberties Union circulates booklets outlining student rights in both schools and colleges, and fairly well dispels the role of the school as a surrogate parent. At the same time, youngsters challenged their parents as well, and established their rights to express themselves in dress and behavior, and in doing so, altered the fashions of the whole society.

Selective criteria and processes were also attacked as supportive of an elitist and nonhumanized context for institutions. Many colleges and universities adopted policies of "open admissions" at the same time that degrees were losing their status and highly educated segments of society were among the unemployed. Certain groups also carried their fight for equality to the curriculum. Black studies programs were adopted widely and women's studies have also found their way into many educational institutions. The American trend toward homogenization of its people was reversed, and many minority groups, whether ethnic, racial, or sexual, affirmed their "pride" and demanded recognition in society and its schools. At the same time, the mindless repression of human behavior was attacked severely, and youth, especially, called for a social climate in which difference was truly valued and people were free to express and find themselves. All of these disaffections were given a sense of urgency by contemporary recognition of the problems of population and ecology as well as lack of order and controls that characterized the mass society.

THE HUMAN FOCUS

Certainly, in some ways it was unfortunate that the school system of the United States, which had always enjoyed a mystique that suggested it was the hope of our democratic society, was so successfully challenged as an irrelevant and even destructive institution. The effects of our changing attitudes toward the school are documented in the increasing numbers of schools being forced to close because their constituency will not support them with economic decisions. If the society of the United States can retain faith in its own future, however, perhaps there is an opportunity to reconstruct the institution of education in ways that will make it a viable social force. If that is to be, it seems clear that its first commitment must be to the notion that children and youth are human beings, deserving of respectful and dignified treatment, and the goal of education lies in their development. The democratic values that have always been "listed" as educational commitments must be actualized in all schools in ways that permit individuals to develop their talents, including those that are nonverbal, and to learn to participate responsibly in their own learning and the life of the group. The school must be sensitive and responsive to social needs and problems, but not to the demands of labor unions, corporations, and elitist professions as these groups have affected what goes on in education according to their own values.

The recent move to "informal" or "open" classrooms in many schools is an attempt to provide for the humanity and individuality of students. Somehow, the school must *not* discriminate between goals of socialization and humanism; rather, we must try to approach our tasks with a commitment that what is best for humanity is best for society, and the individual as a person is the concern. The human focus implies a hierarchy of values that cluster about the worth of those qualities that are characteristic of humanity in the finest actualization of capacities and interactions. To be "humane" is to act in ways that enhance the development of human potentialities and sensibilities. Recognition of the affective domain, or the importance of human feelings in behavior and interaction, is an important aspect of a humane environment. Although humane qualities are always developed in concert with other people, they rest on the importance of the individual and his capacities for self-awareness, growth, and expression. Within the human focus, rationality is prized as a human attribute and modality, but it is clearly understood to refer to the expression of the self as well. The individual, then, uses rational processes in ways that contribute to his own growth and his effectiveness in relating to both ideas and other people.

As an educational commitment, the human focus is consonant with such concepts as self-realization, self-actualization, the fully functioning person, and even individual development. It diverges from these concepts by its implied inclusion of a focus on humanity rather than on the individual alone. Although that focus is related to ideas about socialization, to speak of the "human" or "humane" is to transcend the effects of prevailing social customs or values. It is a broad commitment.

MEANING AND RELEVANCE

The controversy over whether education was "preparation for life" or "life itself" was stilled by the psychological and philosophical views of the child as an active organism behaving as an expression of all his capacities and abilities. At the same time, however, all human beings are in a state of "becoming" at all times, and this means that life itself exists and is actualized and also prepares. The human perceives, and feels, and thinks, and his behavior provides additional dimensions for these processes in a continuous cycle. The efficacy of the processes of human behavior and growth depends upon the energy and perseverance of the person. Although curiosity and inquiry as well as movement and action are thought to characterize the human, individuals accomplish growth and ability in highly variable degrees. People are said to have "different motivations" or different values as well as different capacities, and what each becomes depends upon his experiences and the unique configuration of perceptual, conceptual, and effectual elements.

It is generally recognized that human growth and the development of ability are enhanced under conditions of involvement. Whenever an individual is engrossed in something that challenges his capacities, he easily develops the ability he requires to satisfy the conditions of his involvement. When certain skills are requisite to the achievement of an important goal, they are pursued energetically and usually mastered. Engrossing activities transcend reality, and when we are involved we are prone to say that "the time just flew." To want to know something or to want to be able to do a thing are crucial elements in the pursuit of knowledge or skill. Under these conditions, learning contains a sense of excitement or anticipation, and both the process and the attainment are satisfying. Sometimes, we *need* to find out or develop a skill because other things that we want depend on it, and this too can be an engrossing process. Even the process itself may be the satisfying goal; that is, the human being can find excitement in the exercise of his abilities to discover, relate, and understand. The human can formulate, create, and express, and these abilities may be both his source of meanings and his actualization of them.

Education, in the sense that it is humanizing and enculturating, must enable individuals to discover and expand their own meanings. Its processes must take cognizance of self-definition and discovery as the basic aspects of meaning and relevance. It is, after all, only as culture or values or ideas become internalized that they can be said to relate to human experience. The experiential mode depends upon the individual relating things to himself, absorbing dispositions, and fomulating behavior as an expression of that process. The expansion of meanings implies that somehow the educational process must recognize existing meanings and then provide ways to help individuals seek new sources or modes of experiencing. The conditions of growth and learning are not always wholly pleasant and satisfying, but they can never be totally irrelevant to the individual or they will be "screened out" in the initial perceptual processes upon which they depend.

There are, of course, "gimmicks" for capturing attention and suggesting relevance, and education utilizes them because attending is the important first step to learning. There are also values or goals that an individual may have that are relevant to him but not necessarily to the learning situation, and these too may be used as bases for initial immersion or attention. Ultimately, however, the commitment of education to meaning and relevance suggests facilitating and enabling modes for human development. The selective processes upon which education depends must take cognizance of human meaning and relevance, and must result in programs that express this commitment. The relevance of contemporary social problems to education is obvious, but it is a narrow conception of the sources of human meaning. Within a human focus, the capacities and abilities that humanize and express are sources of meaning. The development of self and its actualization are the most relevant human activities. In fact, a meaningful, productive existence probably depends upon the integrative expression of the self. Education must be committed to enhancing these integrations.

CAPACITY AND ABILITY

Education, insofar as it is concerned with growth and becoming, focuses on potentiality and actualization; that is to say, the goals of education express notions of what people should be or be like in relation to what it seems they could be. Educational processes, of course, are formulated in relation to beliefs about how changes in human beings or their behavior take place. As one of the institutions of a society, education accepts primary responsibility for certain aspects of human growth, but its humane focus presupposes some concern with all development.

Although educational goals derive from concepts of enculturation and humanity, the school is a specialized and mediating environment. Its programs are representations of human experience within the limitations of their existence and are always outgrowths of selective processes. It is true that all experience educates, but the view here suggests that the school is responsible for planned, purposeful, and selective programs and is not comparable to the effects of mass media, social experiences, or community and culture in general. In fact, the purposes of education as an institution may diverge from the educating effects of cultural life in particular times and places. This is especially so when social life is disintegrative and its effects on the individual are dehumanizing.

In its commitment to fostering growth, the school must protect and enhance the individual. The educated person chooses behavior that leads to his own enhancement and development and avoids destructive experiences. It is important to note, however, that the *process* of learning may involve the testing of extremes; for it is in rebellious and even deviant behavior that one learns what his capacities are.

As recently as the early 1960s, rational and intellectual capacities were identified as the primary, if not only, proper focus for education. Charles E. Silberman, writing of his own arguments in 1961 for *"masses of intellectuals"* (emphasis in the original), suggested, "I was wrong. What tomorrow needs is not masses of intellectuals, but masses of educated men— men educated to feel and to act as well as to think." (1970, p. 7) It is the human focus, then, that provides insights into the capacities and abilities with which education is concerned. This implies a broad range of appropriate educational purposes and programs, but at the same time suggests that abilities are to be valued, and that they rest on the actualization of capacity or potential.

Education itself is a rationalized process, which means that it depends on awareness of the scope of available knowledge and ideas, and that its commitment to humanity is that it will seek truth and meaning in the realm of the whole heritage of man. This is an important point that denies the equal worth of all human behavior and capacity. If the ability to think is not the only concern of education, neither is the capacity to feel or act an acceptable source for human goals alone. There are social forces that are antieducational in their denial of knowledge, or taste, or the authority of truth or ideas. The whole concept of education as a formalized process rests on the assumption that there are human capacities that need to be nurtured and encouraged, and that their refinement and actualization in ability are important for the "good life" or a meaningful existence for either the individual or society. The development of these capacities depends upon experiencing demands upon them, and it becomes the role of education to provide cohesive experiences that lead to their development.

The self is defined by what it can experience and has experienced.

Each of us is known to ourselves as we are able to think, and feel, and act; and the discovery of capacity is crucial to the development of ability. The substance and processes of education are committed to the awareness and refinement of abilities and skills. The dimension of meaning and relevance must obtain for this to occur, and the human focus provides an inalienable framework for selecting and understanding how capacity and ability are related and when and why they are important.

RATIONALE AND PURPOSES FOR PHYSICAL EDUCATION*

Purposes are statements of intent that serve to represent the beliefs and values from which they derive and, at the same time, indicate direction for developing programs. Statements themselves, however, can be cryptic with reference to the theoretical responsibility they bear, and that is why diverse programs often seem to claim similar purposes. Curriculum contracting and learning packaging notwithstanding, it is important that those who purvey programs identify, clarify, and order the purposes upon which they depend. When this is done, individuals with program responsibility, whether as formulators or teachers, understand the rationale for the kind of experiences they provide or supervise. It is the understanding of what one is trying to do that is central to success in both teaching and learning. And when one's goals are not only clear but valued, there is little problem in deciding how to attain them.

Teachers, like machines and like students, can probably be programmed to behave in certain ways. The presumption of programming is that understanding is not a necessary concomitant to application. But if commitment and enthusiasm are crucial dimensions of the human and learning transaction, that assumption is abhorrent. It is, of course, the humanists who have always insisted that curriculum development should be an ongoing process and that all of those with program responsibility should be involved in it. That insistence has stemmed from democratic beliefs in the rights of individuals to participate in making decisions that affect them and from allegiance to principles of learning that suggest the relationships among involvement, understanding, and commitment.

There is, however, another reason for widespread and continuous efforts to identify purposes for physical education programs in schools. All of the beliefs and values that provide the sources for purposes are both changing continually, as knowledge is developed and as value priorities are redefined, and are always available for interpretative refinement. Physical educators have not agreed upon the theoretical concerns of the field; that means that purposes for programs, which are the most commonly used expressions of attitudes toward theory, have been confused. This confusion has had several unfortunate but familiar manifestations:

(1) Lack of ability to discriminate among purposes has resulted in purposes becoming additive; that is, new insights or formulations of intent have simply been added to existing ones with the resulting long lists of unordered purposes;

* The material in this section was prepared as a working paper for a workshop session of the Regional Conference for Curriculum Improvement in Secondary School Physical Education sponsored by the Physical Education Division, AAHPER, and held November 4 to 6, 1971, at Mt. Airy Lodge, Mt. Pocono, Pennsylvania.

(2) Confusion between intent and effect has led to alleged benefits of physical education being identified as purposes without reference to theoretical appropriateness;

(3) Beginning with the Seven Cardinal Principles of Education in 1918, physical education has accepted all educational obligations and commitments as its purposes, and the integrity of the field is frequently obscure in its statements of intent;

(4) The conventional wisdom of familiar purposes means that they are often ignored altogether, and curriculum process is likely to be approached by assuming that purposes are obvious and need no attention.

It is a tribute to the importance of physical education and to the efforts of its practitioners that it has survived in education and is represented by excellent programs in many places, in spite of the prevailing confusion about its worth and direction. As educational times change, however, diffuse and inarticulate justification for enormous and disproportional requirements of time, space, and money are not sufficient. If as we suspect in education, the "going is getting tough," then, it is clearly time for the "tough to get going." For us, this means developing effective programs based on rationales appropriate and important to our field and to education, and clarified in expressed purposes whose fulfillment in programs can be established.

As statements of intent, the validity of purposes does not lie in the worthiness of their concerns alone; that is, contributions to the welfare of humanity may all be valid as human goals, but all are not equally valid in their relevance to the role of the school. Any educational purpose must be evaluated in relation to knowledge and values about society, and about the individual and his learning, but is finally acceptable or not on the basis of its appropriateness to the role of schools. The rationale for purposes of physical education begins not only with the ways in which this field can contribute to the lives of children and youth but with answers to the question of why it should be in schools at all. And the potential of its contribution, no matter how great, alone is not an adequately logical answer to that question. "What *is* physical education?" —we have asked throughout this century, and we have answered with lists of activities, or purposes, or benefits, and occasionally even with the statement that it is, in fact, education itself—*of* and/or *through* the physical.

In the last decade, the profession of physical education has established clearly that in addition to its existence as programs in schools, it is also an identifiable field of knowledge and study. The framework for understanding physical education in schools and selecting purposes for programs depends first on cognizance of its field of study. That is to say that curriculum theory is based on ideas about what is to be included in the schools as content in relation to what the world is like, its relationship to the individual and his development, and what it is desirable for people to become. Pervasive goals for all education can be identified, but purposes for any specific area of the school program must be related to its unique and defined concerns.

The rationale for school programs of physical education expresses a framework of knowledge and belief about the nature of the field itself and about what aspects of the field represent it as appropriate and important educational concerns. As these are identified and selected, they are considered in relation to educational goals and commitments and modified to express purposes for programs.

Purposes, of course, can be stated in several ways. There are program purposes that suggest implications for the kinds of activities and experiences to be provided; teacher purposes that imply guidelines for organization and instruction, and student purposes that imply goals to be reached by individuals. All of these are important, and since each expresses its own guidelines for both action and evaluation, they may all be necessary aspects of curriculum definition. In general, though, we are coming to see that stating purposes as student goals, or objectives of behavior, contains the most promise of clear implication for program experiences and evaluating achievement.

The process of developing purposes can begin anywhere: with a purpose itself, with a guideline for school experiences, or with statements of belief or value about physical education, society, education, or about the individual and his learning. Ultimately, purposes are stated, but the foundational beliefs and implied program experiences must also be understood in relation to them. Purposes must be related to the nature of physical education and must be consistent with educational goals; after that, evaluating their validity depends upon theoretical views and available knowledge.

In order really to understand purposes as summations of theory and guides to action, it is necessary to analyze them with reference to the processes by which they were developed. This means that whether directly implied by the statement of purpose itself or not, some effort must be expended toward understanding the foundational assumptions about the school and physical education from which the purpose was derived. At the same time, the implications for program must be clarified to yield full insight into the intent of the purpose. Each statement of purpose must be questioned by those who developed it and by those who would understand it. "Why is that purpose important?"; "What assumptions about the role of education does it suggest?"; "Are its assumptions subject to validation either as an outgrowth of logic or evidence?"; "What are the bases in knowledge that support the purpose as appropriate and capable of being fulfilled?"; "What implications for student behavior are suggested by this purpose?"; and "How would this purpose be actualized in experience and evaluated?" are all questions that should be asked about every single statement of purpose.

Beyond the analysis of specific purposes for school programs or student behavior, the relationships among purposes must also be analyzed; for it is in identifying purposes that the framework and rationale for the whole program are expressed. Purposes, therefore, can provide an ordered expression of theoretical positions, and because of their viable and interactive relationship with program and experiences, they become crucial elements of the process of continual evaluation and refinement that are cornerstones of curriculum development.

Guidelines for the Development and Evaluation of Purposes

CONTENT

1. Purposes must be directly related to knowledge appropriate to the concerns of physical education.
   a. They may reflect the importance of knowledge about man as he pursues movement activities; the ways in which movement is related to human functioning; ideas about effective or efficient movement; the nature of sport, dance, or exercise as movement forms; or the experiencing of movement forms.
   b. They may reflect the importance of experience and/or development and functioning in relation to movement itself or sport, dance, and exercise.
2. Purposes must be defined and understood as contributions to broad goals and commitments of education.
   a. Foundational assumptions about the role of education, social realities and/or commitments, and beliefs and knowledge about individuals and how they develop and learn must be identified and related to purposes.
   b. The implications of purposes must be clarified so that the presumed effects of the experiences they suggest are explicit.

PROCESS

1. One approach is to use a model to show relationships:
   e.g., Foundational Assumptions ⟷ Purposes ⟷ Implications
   a. Internal validity would have to do with the relatedness of the knowledge and ideas involved, as well as meaning and accuracy.
   b. External validity would depend on the worth of the knowledge involved and judgments as to the importance of the ideas.
2. Purposes should be stated as student goals with the implied understanding that the goals of the program would be stated in terms of

providing opportunities for the achievement of these goals, and teacher goals would have to do with organizational and instructional dimensions of enhancing the possibilities of goals being achieved.

a. Goals can be stated so as to imply perceptual, cognitive, or effectual abilities.
b. Behavioral goals or objectives can be stated so as to be reflected in actual and observable behavior.

GOALS FOR PHYSICAL EDUCATION

Physical education is the study of man as he engages in movement and its forms either for their own sake or for his own enhancement. It exists as a field of study when the focus of knowledge implied by that definition is being pursued by students, scholars, researchers, teachers, or anyone else concerned with such understanding. Physical education exists as a school program whenever activities are planned and guided in educational institutions for the purpose of fulfilling the goals that the definition suggests.

There are a few additional discriminations that need to be made. Within the curriculum, the "instructional program" refers to carefully planned and organized sequences of learning experiences. As such, this program is expected to reflect the focus and goals of fields of study most clearly. At the same time, the school is a community and has an ongoing life of its own, comparable to cultural life, and the goals for these activities emerge from educational commitments but are modified in relation to varying contexts. In addition, the goals of all fields of study depend upon learning modalities and abilities for their fulfillment. In this sense, the content of one subject area becomes the means for learning or the medium for another. Physical education, then, must be understood as a distinct field of study with rational, carefully ordered goals for instructional programs; an important aspect of the life of youth during his years of school; and a basic medium of education in all of its concerns.

All education is committed to a humane focus, and the developing, thinking, feeling, acting person is its first concern. All of the activities and interactions purveyed by the school should reflect understanding of the imperatives of a commitment to the finest development of the individual and humanity. The concepts of meaning and relevance and capacity and ability are important in relation to the pervasive focus, and all educational effort should express rational and unfailing commitment to this focus. The school can never be forgiven for contributing to human waste or negating talent and ability. It fails whenever it does not contribute positively to the enhancement of the individual in relation to his human existence and capacities.

The framework for physical education in the school program is an integrated view of the key concepts of the field of study in their potential contributions to the quality of living, and the commitments of education. These concepts and commitments may be referred to in "catch phrases" for convenience, but their usefulness as a framework depends upon broad knowledge and full understanding of what they mean. The concepts of the field of study emerge from perspectives of knowledge and understanding about movement and its forms as scientific and aesthetic conceptualizations of those phenomena as significant human endeavors. Educational commitments derive from rational concerns with the individual and society, learning, and the role of the school.

FIELD OF STUDY	PHYSICAL EDUCATION	SCHOOL PROGRAM
Fitness	(man engaged in movement and its forms for	Human focus
Skill and mastery of movement	their own sake or his own enhancement)	Meaning and relevance
		Capacity and ability
Cultural participation in movement experiences	Instructional program	
	Culture of school	
Meaning and significance of movement experiences	Medium for learning	

It should be evident that this framework does not provide for a singular purpose for physical education; rather, key concepts may be ordered, educational commitments given emphasis, and program aspects attended to. When movement is a "medium for learning," it is not properly physical education because the intention underlying the use of movement does not accommodate the definition. When movement is used, for instance, to improve perceptual-motor abilities as an aid to reading effectiveness, it is *reading* rather than physical education. Even when movement activities are provided as a "release from tension" in relation to academic pursuits, these occasions are not properly physical education. The use of movement in relation to broad concerns with "health" is another example of movement itself as a medium. In an age where interdisciplinary study is important as an integrative approach to disparate knowledge, fields of study do relate to each other in many ways. For clarity of focus, distinctions must be made so that the increasing importance of movement in relation to learning does not obscure understanding of the goals of physical education. Whenever movement and its forms are the focus of knowledge and experience, physical education may be said to exist; when the focus is some unrelated understanding or ability, it serves as a medium.

The distinctions between movement forms as part of the cultural life of youth and school and as directly related to instruction in physical education are not so clear. To identify the concept of "cultural participation" in movement forms as a crucial concern of physical education is to suggest the importance of society in providing a framework for their significance. The whole notion of "lifetime sports" rests on this concept; that is, "lifetime" sports are those that exist in the society and, therefore, can be pursued easily throughout life. Those who promote the importance of "lifetime sports" as physical education programs may do so in relation to beliefs about fitness and significance as well, but cultural participation is the concept given highest priority in this view. At the same time, the symbolic importance of sport in the culture of the school most often is expressed in such team sports as football and basketball.

For many reasons, sport, dance, and exercise are important forms in the life of youth and in his relationship to the institutions of education. The acceptance of their importance was evident when the school system of Philadelphia attempted to abolish varsity sports and after-school programs on the basis of budgetary problems for the 1971-72 school year. The public and civic outcry was intense, and the programs were restored as everyone anticipated. All schools provide some means for noninstructional participation in activities, and programs related to the concerns of physical education are among those found most frequently. Because the framework for the existence of varsity and intramural sport, dance concerts, school dances, judo or jogging clubs *is* their cultural importance and recognition, the purposes for these activities derive from that fact. This is not to negate the personal significance of experiences in noninstructional aspects of physical education programs, but the ordering of program concepts begins with their cultural importance, and it is that fact that is crucial to the experience. It is very important that this be recognized, because if this distinction is not made, the indictment of athletic programs for their failure to contribute to all the purposes of physical education is tenable.

As cultural forms, sport and dance should be viewed more carefully in relation to the essence of their forms. Sometimes, the integrity of the essence of sport or of dance as a performing art demands practices of exclusion and emphasis on excellence that have been labeled "undemocratic" and not "educational." It is only as we understand both sport and dance as culturally symbolic forms and view their existence as noninstructional programs in this light that we understand the rationale for their provision and conduct. This is not to suggest that violations of the individual and his sensibilities are ever permissible in the educational context, but it does support the existence of dance and athletic programs, with their attendant emphasis on participation and excellence, within a framework of their own as part of the cultural life of the school. Decisions about the relative importance of programs in this domain are not resolved by this view, but neither is the instructional program the only responsibility of the school. The most desirable situation would provide for participation at all levels of ability.

It is the instructional program of physical education that is directly responsible to an integrated view of the concepts of the field of study and the commitments of education. Purposes for the school program depend upon rational conception and full consideration of all the impinging variables. Concepts are ordered, given priority, and understood as an outgrowth of knowledge and in relation to theoretical and philosophical views.

Insight into physical education, for instance, may begin with a view that suggests the primary importance of capacity. The human being, then, might be seen as an organism whose development rested on the refinement of condition and functioning, without reference to the accomplishment of specific tasks or the achievement of particular abilities. The human body would provide the exclusive framework for study and purposes, and the body would be seen as both a predeterminant and a symptom of motor activities. The focus of concern would be such things as the capacity to perform work as a result of energy output affecting the body or external objects in shape, space, and time. This view is, of course, a common one, and is expressed clearly in most statements of the purposes of physical education in relation to fitness.

Other views of physical education might begin with movement itself as the primary framework for study and purposes. This view might include goals of achievement in relation to motor tasks or patterns, and could assume the importance of either resultant satisfaction in competence and control or the processes of experience involved. Purposes would be derived from skill and mastery as the pervasive construct.

If the sociocultural forms of movement in their relationship to the individual are seen as crucial, the context of physical education derives from the symbolic structures of interaction, communication, and expression that are the significant elements of the forms. The use of the forms in society would be the framework for study and purposes, and the essence and structure of the interactions within the forms would provide purposes.

Individual experiencing of meaning and significance in movement provides another framework for purposes. In this view, the psychology of the individual in relation to the experiencing of movement, most often of its forms, is the focus for deriving purposes. Movement demands and sociocultural importance are elements of the framework, but purposes are derived on the basis of individual experience and significance.

The commitments of education in relation to the concepts of the field of study provide the framework for the purposes of the school program. These, of course, are derived as generalized goals. Specific purposes and objectives depend upon much more particular considerations of the actual settings and learners involved. Although purpose priorities are an outgrowth of individualized understanding and theoretical commitment, it seems apparent that the goals of physical education as an instructional program in schools should reflect consideration of all of the key concepts that it represents. At the same time, these goals are formulated as expressions of understanding of the commitments and processes of education. In this sense, it is especially important that they be based on cognizance of the bases of the selective processes of education, and that alternatives be recognized. There *are* differing conceptual views within which educational priorities may be ordered, and any framework for physical education in schools reflects a value orientation toward the key concepts of the field of study and educational commitments.

PHYSICAL EDUCATION PROGRAMS

As summations of both theoretical understanding and intentions, purposes provide the key to formulating programs of physical education. In addition to ordering priorities in relation to purposes, we must also be aware that our purposes relate to the feeling, thinking, and acting capacities of the individual. We are concerned, therefore, that students develop knowledge and insight; that they understand and perceive relationships; that they be able to apply knowledge in learning and understanding; that they be able to do certain things and possess requisite skills and abilities; and that they feel in particular ways, that is, appreciate, value, like, enjoy, and pursue our activities.

Planning a physical education program depends upon how well the purposes are clarified and understood. Our understanding of the key concepts is prerequisite, and depends upon sufficient knowledge about what they imply and how they are actualized. Because commitment to them is also prerequisite, those responsible for programs must develop purposes in concert. Although the whole range of possible purposes or objectives for physical education might be listed, this is fairly meaningless without reference to actual programs. If the key concepts are used as a basis for program, they can be modified to provide purposes for various educational levels and kinds of programs. Our knowledge of learning and human growth and development suggests the nature of appropriate experiences for individuals of various ages and experience, and our insight into the field of study allows us to identify the conditions relevant to the achievement of purposes at different stages.

Because the relationship between purposes and program is crucial, specific objectives are usually derived from broad statements of purpose and stated in terms of the actual behavior that would indicate their fulfillment. This process demands substantive and detailed knowledge both about the phenomenon and about learning as it relates to perceptual, affective and cognitive, and effectual process. Countless decisions are required to translate intention into guidelines for action. If objectives are stated well, they provide insight into how they can be fulfilled in experiences. The program itself can be viewed as those planned and guided experiences that are formulated in relation to purposes.

There are a host of related variables that must be accounted for in planning curriculum. Sequence, time, level, and design, for instance, contribute to the nature and shape of learning experiences. The facilities and equipment available affect the provision and design of experiences, and the abilities and personalities of the personnel are also crucial elements in programs. In general, these are modifying influences; that is

6

to say, that limitations in the availability of equipment must not be the point at which one begins to plan a program. The finest and most valid purposes and objectives provide guidelines for the kind of program that should be provided; limitations may affect the actual experiences but only in the sense that they modify possibilities as a practical consideration.

Even educational innovations must be viewed as modifying aspects of program planning. Modular or flexible scheduling, learning laboratories, video equipment, teaching machines, or any other technique must be recognized as precisely that. Program is a conceptualized design of learning experiences and clearly depends upon the nature of the goals to be achieved and the students involved; all else is the means to the most effective fulfillment of goals. Various methods, techniques, innovations, and so forth are *selected* for use when they are believed to contain the potential of contributing to the realization of goals, and for no other reason. On the other hand, everyone concerned with planning programs has a serious responsibility to awareness and knowledge of the widest range of possibilities for the enhancement of learning. New and innovative ideas are a significant source for our continual refinement of understanding of what we are doing and our ability to do it well. The important point is that whether we talk about "performance contracting" or "lifetime sports" we must understand that these are program modalities and not program sources. The sources for school program are found in the contexture of the school, society, the individual as a learner, and the key concepts of the field of study underlying physical education. The program itself is expressive of an integrated view of the potential contributions of physical education to education and youth.

DISCUSSION

Statements relative to the *relationships* among purposes of education and physical education and the variables which are *sources* for the derivation of such purposes, clarifying the *context* for purposes of physical education in schools, and the *process* of deriving purposes.

Planning Programs of Physical Education in Schools

1. Schools are created by societies when institutionalizing the processes of education is desirable; the alternative is to depend on informal educational processes conducted by the family, usually, or by other social groups.

2. In general, all schools are created for some purpose of "enculturation"; that is, it is considered necessary to institutionalize the ways in which the young of a society are prepared for their adult roles within that society.

3. Society in the United States is highly complex and heterogeneous, and "schooling" is the one common experience of all people.

4. The educational system in the United States is unique in combining its primary characteristics of being free, universal, and compulsory. "All of the children of all the people" *must* attend school without reference to socio-

economic differences or any other differences, and this implies some commitment to a common notion of "enculturation."

5. It is all well and good to identify "enculturation" as the pervasive goal of education, but there are vast philosophical differences in viewpoint as to what constitutes being a functional and effective adult in the United States and which of the many diverse realities and values of our society should be affirmed.

6. Any notion of educational commitment or purpose depends on how certain variables are considered; that is, what education itself *is*, what children or human beings are like and how they learn, and what kinds of experiences are best suited to these concerns.

7. Physical education has been conceived within education, and points of view about what physical education is and why it should be in the school are closely related to conceptions of education.

8. The shifts in educational thinking document the various ways of considering educational purposes and physical education, but the important point lies in identifying *why* certain views were held; that is, how they related to views of society, and the individual, and of education.

9. The teacher of any subject must develop commitments about the nature of education and his own field, and develop a cohesive point of view which will allow him to identify purposes and proceed with educational planning.

10. Educational practices can be evaluated and/or understood only within a theoretical view of their development—*why* something is being done is a crucial aspect of evaluating its use.

Sources for Purposes of Physical Education

1. There are certain "moral imperatives" for education in the United States that serve as assumptions of all aspects of the school program and find expression in such considerations as "personality goals"; democratic human behavior; intergroup goals and concerns, and other personal and social aspects.

2. Each subject field must clarify its worth and focus in ways that derive directly from its concern with knowledge and experience; purposes for a particular field, then, have reference to the concerns *of that field.*

3. Education as a social institution implies certain criteria for the evaluation of the worth of particular fields, and ultimately it is these criteria that determine whether or not a field is represented in the school program at all as well as the extent of its representation.

4. The commitment of schools to a primary concern with humanistic refinement has been established, and this implies a criterion of "educational" or cognitive complexity; that is, if something requires only "rehearsal" time or "practice" time rather than instructional time, it is probably appropriate as an adjunct to the school rather than an intrinsic part of the school program.

5. In its broad commitment to "enculturation," education does have the purpose of "exposing" youth to those aspects of culture which man has found significant and which are likely to endure, and at the same time, the notion of "optimum development of the individual" implies concern with those aspects of human experience that are likely to contribute to self-realization.

6. As physical education is conceived as a body of knowledge and a phenomenological experience of significance, its purposes can be identified in relation to its central concerns; these may be "agreed upon" by a whole profession, and school programs may represent varying assumptions of what is most important.

7. From perceptions of what is most crucial about the field of study, and

conceptions of what is most important for individuals and how they learn and develop, each of us perceives purposes for the use of physical education in schools.

8. Purposes for school programs may not be the same at all levels of education, and programs are surely different since they are developed in light of the purposes but modified according to the learners who are concerned.

9. The process of identifying purposes for the school program is the most important step in the process of developing programs; those responsible must *be responsible,* which means that actual experiences are *chosen* on the basis of rational consideration and the most valid understanding of the whole context.

10. Purposes serve as statements that represent both theoretical summations and guidelines for programs.

Deriving Purposes for School Programs in Physical Education

1. Purposes for school programs are identified (chosen) by those responsible on the basis of (a) the field of study, and (b) conceptions of the goals and commitments of education; they are modified in relation to the learners being considered.

2. Critical insight into the significance and potential contributions of knowledge and experience from the field of study of physical education depends upon some sophisticated awareness of the scope and nature of the field.

3. The perspectives of knowledge of physical education (biomechanical and sociocultural descriptions, movement forms, experiencing forms of movement) suggest the significance of this field for human well-being and actualization.

4. Depending on one's philosophical orientation, estimates of the value of the various perspectives may differ, but physical education itself must be defined in terms of its concerns; that is, the broad purposes of physical education are implied by its focus on man as he pursues movement and sport experiences to enhance himself (either the organism itself or the self), or to actualize himself.

5. Within the school, the field of study of physical education may be expressed in instructional programs, in the cultural and social life of youth, and in its usefulness to other curricular areas.

6. All purposes are subject to critical examination with reference to the criteria implied by the educational context; i.e., educational complexity, value in serving needs or development, and the extent of personal and universal contribution to generative considerations. The appropriateness of physical education in the school program is determined ultimately by the evaluation of its purposes.

7. Purposes for physical education may express the range of concerns of the field of study or may represent priority ordering of knowledge; this may or may not depend upon the educational level involved, but the planning of actual learning experiences does depend on considerations of the learner.

8. Analysis of purposes should provide identifiable guidelines for the program implications suggested, but the validity of these depends upon adequate understanding of the processes by which learning takes place and personal meaning occurs.

9. Assuming that one understands and values the field of study of physical education and continually studies the educational context, a method of intelligence is used in deriving purposes for the school program, and these are evaluated and re-examined in light of changing knowledge and changing views of man as well as changes in educational and social problems and priorities.

10. Developing programs to fulfill purposes is a difficult task, but it is this relationship that is crucial to educational appropriateness and excellence.

SELECTED BIBLIOGRAPHY

Planning Programs of Physical Education

Associations.
 Some of the most valuable references that relate to curriculum and programs are published by associations whose major focus is the preparation and dissemination of such material. It is, therefore, most desirable to obtain a current publications list since there are numerous relevant materials including yearbooks, position statements, research compilations, standards for program, conduct, and evaluation, and so on. The two most important associations for material relevant to this focus, both related to the National Education Association, are:
 American Association for Health, Physical Education and Recreation, and Association for Supervision and Curriculum Development. 1201 Sixteenth St., NW, Washington, D.C. 20036.
Barrett, Kate R. "The Structure of Movement Tasks—A Means for Gaining Insight Into the Nature of Problem-Solving Techniques." *Quest XV.* January, 1971, 22-31.
 Identifies components of a physical education lesson and discusses their interrelationship, and types of movement tasks.
Bennett, Joan. "Modules and Movement." *Journal of Health, Physical Education and Recreation.* April, 1970, 48-49.
 Discusses physical education classes in relation to modular scheduling.
Brown, Camille, and Cassidy, Rosalind. *Theory in Physical Education: A Guide To Program Change.* Philadelphia: Lea & Febiger, 1963.
 Presents a theoretical framework based on the art and science of human movement and the implications for program development; considers program experiences and design.
Erikson, Erik H. *Identity: Youth and Crisis.* New York: W. W. Norton & Company, 1968.
 An important work that treats the development of identity and the problems that surround it; includes some attention to contemporary issues.
Fraleigh, Warren P. "An Instructional Experiment In Actualizing The Meaning of Man As A Moving Being." *Journal of Health, Physical Education and Recreation.* January, 1969, 53-58.
 Describes the structure and assumptions of a basic instruction program in physical education.
Godfrey, Barbara B., and Kephart, Newell C. *Movement Patterns and Motor Education.* New York: Appleton-Century-Crofts, 1969.
 Discusses the role of motor activity in the schools and in the physical education program; analyzes various movement patterns, and suggests appropriate programs and techniques for movement education.
Jewett, Ann E., Jones, L. Sue, Luneke, Sheryl M., and Robinson, Sarah M. "Educational Change through a Taxonomy for Writing Physical Education Objectives." *Quest XV.* January, 1971, 32-38.
 Presents a structural taxonomy for the motor domain, and discusses the importance of taxonomies in developing curriculum and eliminating confusion regarding the evaluation of educational objectives.
Kleinman, Seymour. "What Future for Dance in Physical Education?" *Journal of Health, Physical Education and Recreation.* November-December, 1969, 101-102.
 Defends the role of dance in the school program and suggests that prospective physical education teachers acquire more experience in dance.
Kneller, George F. *Educational Anthropology: An Introduction.* New York: John Wiley & Sons, 1965.
 A basic and informative view of man, culture, and education.

Mackenzie, Marlin M. *Toward A New Curriculum in Physical Education.* New York: McGraw-Hill Book Company, 1969.
A cohesive exposition of a view of the field of study as a source for developing curriculum in physical education.

Mead, Margaret. *Culture and Commitment: A Study of the Generation Gap.* Garden City, New York: Natural History Press/Doubleday & Company, 1970.
An interesting treatment of cultural and generational differences.

Mordy, Margaret (ed.). *Teaching Physical Education. Quest XV.* January, 1971.
An excellent collection of articles with implications for studying, teaching, and planning programs in physical education.

Phenix, Philip H. *Realms of Meaning: A Philosophy of the Curriculum for General Education.* New York: McGraw-Hill Book Company, 1964.
Suggests that a philosophy of man and ways of knowing is necessary to consider when building curriculum; categorizes meaning into six realms which might be the basis of the curriculum, and offers suggestions for selecting and organizing content.

Reich, Charles A. *The Greening of America.* New York: Random House, 1970.
A controversial work that explicates three levels of consciousness in American society, and postulates that the changes initiated by youth are desirable and hopeful.

Roszak, Theodore. *The Making of a Counter-Culture: Reflections on the Technocratic Society and its Youthful Opposition.* Garden City, New York: Doubleday & Company, 1969.
A definitive statement of the values of youth as counter to established and existing culture.

Silberman, Charles E. *Crisis in the Classroom: The Remaking of American Education.* New York: Random House, 1970.
The result of a three-and-a-half year study financed by the Carnegie Corporation of New York, this is a comprehensive treatment of the schools and their problems and prospects.

"The New Physical Education." *Journal of Health, Physical Education and Recreation.* September, 1971, 24-39.
A series of articles on many aspects of educational innovations as they apply to physical education programs. The selections include "Independent Study Option" by Carolyn L. Stanhope; "Student Choice of Independent Study Units" by Gregory M. Sadowski; "Self-Directed Learning" by Patricia L. Geadelmann; "Goal-Centered Individualized Learning" by Sandra Dirscoll and Doris A. Mathieson; "An Elective Curriculum" by Lois J. McDonald; "The Quinmester Extended School Year Plan" by Hy Rothstein and Robert F. Adams; "Student-Designed Elective Course" by George Pastor; "Contingency Contracting" by Barbara L. Fast; "Individualized Approach to Learning" by Robert D. Shrader; "Performance Objectives" by Walter D. Sherman; and "Revitalizing a County-Wide Program" by Barbara A. Landers and James W. Ragans.

Chapter VII

TEACHING AND COACHING
PHYSICAL EDUCATION

Teaching was once considered a "calling"; that is, those who chose to teach were thought to do so on the basis of a strong inner impulse toward dedication that could not be denied. Perhaps because this was so, teachers, like clergymen, were viewed as somehow "above" material concerns, and their low salaries were consistent with this image. For many years, teachers were most often women, and that also confirmed the low-paying, low-status position of the occupation in social terms. All professions, of course, embody some notion of "social dedication," but medicine and the law were able to couple ideals of service with material rewards for their practitioners. These professions were able to organize and assume the responsibility for upholding their standards in ways that the teaching profession was not, and in doing so, constructed a strong image of importance and status for doctors and lawyers. College professors did somehow establish an image separate from that of teachers in the public schools, but the profession as a whole has occupied a humble social position.

A profession is, first of all, an occupation, and it implies an attendant technical body of knowledge, usually related to the academic arts and sciences. The complexity of the procedures for becoming certified as a teacher by state departments of instruction or the like according to qualifications based on academic degrees and credits is testimony to the academic relationship. Usually, there are several levels of certification leading to permanent attainment, and these are based on increasing educational demands. There may also be separate categories of teaching certification according to either specific school levels or particular subject areas. Again, college teaching has not been subject to these standards.

Because professions are always social and humanistic, their supervision tends to be in the hands of the state and community unless it is clearly handled by the profession itself. Professional service is perceived most often in relation to the local setting in which members of a profession operate. It is true, however, that the practice of a profession also permits great geographical mobility, and in the United States fewer and fewer people become professionally prepared to serve the communities in which they grew up. The higher the professional level, the more this is so.

All professions are characterized by ethical considerations impinging on their potential contributions to humanity. Even in today's world, where teachers and doctors on strike are a commonplace, and university professors and fifth-grade teachers belong to the same labor union, teaching is conceived as a moral enterprise. It could hardly be otherwise; for the relationship to youth, especially when responsibility is sought and accepted, is always a moral one. The teacher accepts a position of responsibility in relation to young people and, in doing so, implies that he is worthy of that role and the sanctions of trust and authority given him by both school and society. The potential influence on the personality and attitudes of the young throughout a professional career establishes teaching as a moral enterprise. In some ways, this influence includes subject areas as well; for it is the teacher's responsibility to use his knowledge in a rational and considered way as a contribution to human well-being.

The roles of the teacher are defined by the ethical, social, and rational contexts of education. The physical education teacher is obligated to both the body of knowledge and the profession of physical education. As a physical educator, he plans and provides learning experiences as an outgrowth of his specialized subject knowledge, and contributes to the profession itself. At the same time, all teachers are ethically bound to the development of youth, and fulfill roles in both directing learning and counseling that are based on the most valid understanding of human behavior and personality goals. Because the school provides an important environment for youth, teachers must also be cognizant of their roles as representatives of both culture and community. Insofar as the culture of education is to be a viable element in the life of the young, teachers must find ways to relate it to the culture at large. Finally, the physical education teacher, like all teachers, must recognize the common goals and tasks of those involved in the school, and define and fulfill roles that lead to cohesive and coordinated effort.

THE TEACHER

Although "teaching" can be defined as a functional activity, and teacher behavior and roles can be analyzed and studied, this has not proved to be a productive approach to understanding the teacher. To be sure, analyzing teacher behavior is necessary, but it is not sufficient as a commanding structure for the ideas and concepts that are involved in understanding teaching. The teacher behaves in relation to the learner, and many theoretical approaches to teaching begin with studying learning. This, too, is a requisite dimension for understanding because how one teaches is based firmly in beliefs about what should be learned and how learning takes place. Almost all the methodological considerations of teaching can be analyzed in relation to identified theories of learning, and they diverge from each other at the points where analysis fails or the assumptions about the learner are contradictory. In the history of school programs, learning has been assumed to be synonymous with mental discipline, conditioning, preparation for life, operant conditioning, and the development of insight and understanding at various times. Some theories have attempted to focus on both the teacher and learning and use such concepts as "teaching-learning behavior" and the "teacher-learner transaction."

Beginning in 1960, with Jerome Bruner's *The Process of Education* as the most expressive statement, educational reform was focused around the structure of the disciplines, and the methodologies of academic scholarship were stressed. A variety of "programs" found their way into the schools, and teachers, as the purveyors of "packaged" curricula, adopted models of teaching that were most closely allied to programming techniques. The claim made for some of these programs was that they were, in fact, "teacher-proof," meaning that the disciplinary structure represented was applied in a methodology that assured consistent teaching. In *Toward a Theory of Instruction* (1966), Bruner made it clear that programmed methodologies were not sufficient, and stressed discovery processes, but he retained his commitment to "experts" as the formulators of curriculum and to teaching as an outgrowth of the psychology of the subject matter.

It is clear that teacher roles, learning theories, or structures of academic disciplines can provide the basis for models for the teacher. Each of these bases, however, is challenged not only by the others, but more seriously by its failure to take cognizance of social and affective dimensions. The revolutionary critics demand recognition of education as a social and perhaps political force. In their view, there is no *neutral* education, and, therefore, experiences in the school enhance either conformity to existing systems or liberation in terms of individual freedom. Humanistic critics suggest simply that educational processes must derive from humane concerns and that the emotional development of the young is a more serious consideration than the structure of subject matter. In this view, intellectual matters and mastery are evaluated positively only when they are used to contribute to emotional as well as cognitive growth.

Humanistic education emphasizes that both teachers and students are persons. Somehow, the teacher, whether as facilitator or authority, must transcend the limitations of his functions and roles as a guiding theory for his behavior, and in doing so must recognize pupils of any age as persons as well as learners. This seems an obvious matter, but as more and more models for teacher behavior are developed and the literature and data relevant to teaching accumulate, it is clear that it is not so simple. Notions of "individual differences" and goals of "the optimum development of the individual" have pervaded educational thought throughout the twentieth century. Their interpretation and application in the school, however, have been largely discrete and mechanistic. Children have been treated as an outgrowth of attempts to identify their varying ability systems or progress stages, and developmental characteristics have been postulated for different age and growth levels. The teacher has accepted a responsibility to plan mass learning techniques that accommodate individual variation. Both teachers and learners have accepted status assessments as the basis for behavioral goals and the standard for achievement and growth.

The human focus for education is related to the human potential movement and to new insights in developmental psychology. Education is conceived not as a series of associative and inconsequential learnings, but as related to the self; that is, to the realization, actualization, and fulfillment of the self. The focus is on the nature of experience, and the person doing the experiencing. The "teacher-learner transaction" is seen as a human and inter*personal* interaction, and it is the humanity of pupils and teachers that provides the source for understanding behavior. Within a human focus, the concepts of meaning and relevance and capacity and ability are central and are understood to refer to the development of self and the relationship of self to subject. "Thinking" and "understanding" express slightly more humane concerns, perhaps, than "learning" which has been traditionally associated with rote and recall levels of knowing. "Cognition" and "affect" imply a relevant, holistic relationship with knowledge and the situations in which both pupils and teachers can explore and actualize themselves and their abilities. The human focus emphasizes the importance of being in ways that Abraham Maslow, Erik Erikson, Paulo Freire, Richard Jones, and the more revolutionary critics of education such as Ivan Illich have explicated so well. It rejects value-free and neutral scientific models for education and teaching, and suggests that our study and research need to focus on teaching and learning in alternative ways that postulate the relevance of humane factors in their initial conceptions.

The professional and program commitments of the teacher of physical education derive from the human focus of education. The teacher is a person who has come to know himself in ways that permit him to use his abilities and personality in the educational domain so that positive interactions occur. He is known, first, by what he is, and later by the ways he expresses this in his educational relationships and efforts as these are perceived in humane contexts.

AS SOMEONE KNOWLEDGEABLE ABOUT THE SCOPE AND CONCERNS OF THE FIELD OF STUDY

Education cannot be separated from its rational concern with knowledge. One of the failures of the progressive education movement can be attributed to the fact that many of its adherents focused exclusively on the "growth" of pupils and ignored subject matter. "Process" alone can become an irrelevant focus, and without some commitment to the importance of knowledge and ability, the educational milieu provides disparate "experiences" that do not lead to self-realization because they are neither cohesive nor relevant to any concept of the importance of knowledge. The physical education teacher must ultimately translate his knowledge of the field of study into purposes for the school program, but he is able to do this only as he recognizes its scope and values its concerns. Brief acquaintanceship with either ideas or information will not enhance the application of knowledge in school programs in meaningful and rational ways. Furthermore, knowledgeability implies that the teacher has related to his subject matter in significant and personal ways. Within the scope of physical education, this means that he is not only cognitively aware of knowledge, but also that he has experienced a valid relationship to it and understands his own field as experience. There is some real danger that scientific models for knowledge about movement and its forms will become too important. The physical educator who understands "sport science" as a scholarly domain, but does not understand "sport" as a profound experience will be a limited teacher.

AS AN "EXPERT" IN ASPECTS OF THE FIELD OF STUDY, COMMITTED TO THEIR IMPORTANCE AND ABLE TO INTERPRET THEM

"Specialization" has been charged with leading to depersonalization, but this would not seem to be necessary. Insofar as physical education is concerned with experiencing movement and its forms, the notion of being an "expert" has connotations of high levels of experience in a significant form. The experiences in physical education are centered around means of actualizing abilities and, thus, hold potential for "peaks" of significance and meaning in the realization of self and identity. Only as competence and ability are developed are inquiry and discovery facilitated. If the teacher of physical education is to be creative in relation to his own field as well as to teaching, some expertise with its attendant connotations of depth of experience seems requisite. Commitment does not always accompany excellence, but it frequently does. The teacher who pursues involvement in his field beyond mundane levels is usually the enthusiastic and committed teacher. If relevant and meaningful relationships to the subject matter experiences are to occur, the involvement of the teacher is an obvious first step.

It is generally agreed that people tend to teach as they have been taught, and the only means to transcending that modality is a creative relationship to the experiences of the field. Insight precludes imitation in that it personalizes the relatedness of the person to his own experiences. The teacher who is an "expert" then, and is committed to the importance of his concerns, is also likely to be able to interpret them in meaningful ways of his own. In doing so, he is also likely to contribute to knowledge and understanding whether only locally or to the profession at large.

AS SOMEONE COMMITTED TO YOUTH AND EDUCATION IN OUR SOCIETY AND AWARE OF WHAT THAT INVOLVES AS IT EXISTS AND CHANGES

If we accept that education is not neutral, then it is, in fact, value laden. The teacher, as part of a social institution, formulates his processes in relation to ideas about what it means to live in contemporary society, what kinds of values and abilities are appropriate, and how change does and should take place. Because physical education holds great potential relevance in the experiencing of youth and in the life of the school, it is particularly important that the teacher who symbolizes these activities is not "mindless" about their cultural significance, nor parochial about their potential impact on social life.

Teachers are frequently important representatives of adulthood and culture and community. As such, their attitudes and values may influence youth, and the responsible teacher accepts the importance of social goals and concerns. If schools are neither "preparation for life" nor "separate from real life" then it is the teacher's obligation to contribute to the life of the school in ways that reflect desirable social and human values. The concept of "confluent education," for instance, is based on the idea of a desirable synthesis between the affective and cognitive domain. In that sense, reality functions in the educational process in ways that enable the individual to accept existential responsibility.

The teacher's commitments to youth and education in a changing society must also transcend the culture's conventional wisdom. All social change is not desirable, and the school is more than merely a reflective social institution. Even conventional attitudes toward physical education must be evaluated and challenged when necessary. As attitudes toward the body and sport, dance, and exercise change, the physical educator, as an "expert," must not only respond to popular whims, even when these seem to support his field. Rather, his commitment is to the finest expression of his concerns in culture and community, and this implies preservation of the integrity of these forms in the social life of man.

At the same time, however, commitments to youth and education also imply that physical education activities will be used to contribute to the general welfare. The teacher must not allow his field to be used in ways that negate the social good or reflect practices of discrimination or exclusion that are socially untenable. There is an integrated view of the significance of physical education in the life of man that the teacher holds and exemplifies, and it is this view that becomes the expressive one in education.

AS A PERSON WHO CAN BE TRUSTED TO CONTRIBUTE TO THE LIVES OF OTHERS, THE GOOD OF SOCIETY, AND HIS OWN GROWTH

Despite educational bureaucracies, the teacher is essentially an independent agent with reference to the formulation of his roles and the interactions within the program. Obviously, existential responsibility is an important concept for the teacher. Somehow, teachers accept moral responsibilities and fulfill them only as they discover that all behavior reflects choices and decisions. The teacher behaves constantly within the human frameworks of interaction, conflict, and confrontation. There is not time to rationalize all behavior, so that it is some construct of the self that provides the modality for the countless decisions and actions that characterize teaching.

In its emphasis on the effective or action domain, physical education has expressed an external focus. This must be countermanded if the physical education teacher is to be in touch with himself and able to express an integrated allegiance to affective and cognitive elements. Teachers must be trustworthy human beings so that they can contribute to the self-realization of others; the alternative is disintegrative and possibly destructive.

Individual and social development depend upon hopeful, life-giving assumptions about self. The teacher affirms these assumptions in his commitments to democratic and personal sources for educational processes. Youth develops a vision of its goals and potentials as it is treated with dignity and hope and positive expectations. More than any other individual, the teacher is responsible to human views that stress growth and experience, and permit individuals to explore and experiment.

The teacher is not a therapist, and his human commitments are not abstractions. Rather, within his commitments to his field and his insight into himself, he is able to utilize creative enthusiasm that is the source of cognitive and affective integration. Many of the techniques of the body therapies and sensitivity encounter experiences are being understood in their appropriateness to education. Obviously, these are applied in schools in ways that do not directly mirror the experience of the encounter or sensitivity group. On the other hand, they are useful to the teacher who seeks to actualize his belief in the human being as a totality; a person who thinks and acts and feels and is able to learn and behave in integrated ways that contribute to his own actualization.

The physical education teacher represents activities that are personal and relevant to youth in that they are centered clearly around the self. The personal relevance of the activities frequently generalizes to the teacher as a symbol of them. If the cruciality of growth and identity is to be fostered, the physical education teacher must be aware of this aspect of experience, committed to its importance, and able to actualize himself in ways that contribute to the lives of others. Chessmen may be pawns, but football players are human beings, and the physical educator is responsible to the humanity of pupils and the contribution of his field to the quality of living.

Teachers are responsible for their own growth. Although schools may provide in-service activities or require numbers of credits as part of professional advancement, ultimately the individual teacher grows and changes, fulfills capacities, or does not. As tenure practices are being challenged, we understand that there is not permanent certifiability for being a teacher. The teacher must be committed to his own continual "becoming" and self-realization, or he cannot actualize the contributions of his field in the lives of others.

THE COACH

Stephen E. Stone

As Charles A. Reich pointed out in his book *The Greening of America* (1970), the rate of technological change in the United States has outstripped society's ability to understand and control its consequences. Reich argues that values dictated by the machine have taken over our lives. According to him, the solution to this complicated problem may be found if we can evolve a new consciousness to deal with run-away technology.

It seems that in physical education and coaching we also may need to develop a new consciousness. In these fields, we are faced with the same challenges as in the larger society, and have our own particular value lag, especially with reference to athletics.

The movie *Stalag 17* won an Academy Award during the '50s. The plot involved the attempt by prisoners of war to discover a traitor who was passing information to their German captors. The role of collaborator was played by Peter Graves. He portrayed a model prisoner with a very clean-cut image. The most shocking aspect of Graves' behavior and his subsequent exposure was the fact that we so believed in his image. He looked like the boy next door and *so* athletic. The casting was perfect, and the drama successful because of our utter faith in wholesome, athletic-looking people. It is disturbing to those of us involved in coaching to realize that many young people today would not be shocked by an athletic type portrayed as a traitor and a collaborator. The change has been a subtle one and seems to have overtaken us in less than a decade.

In a series of articles in 1969, John Underwood referred to the new problems and challenges facing the coach. Underwood supported the claim that the image of the athlete was under assault by certain segments of youth. The change can be explained in part by the fact that the heroes of the younger generation that developed in the '60s were taken from new sources of experience.

One symbolic function that athletics serve in society is to reflect and display certain cherished values. The marks of manhood as conceived traditionally were most clearly embodied in the arena. The athlete, possessing the traits highly valued in our culture, became a rather fixed symbol of dominance, sacrifice, striving, skill, and winning. Athletics have always been justified educationally because it was claimed that taking part in them developed character. Athletics have been perceived by many educators as a method of building certain personality characteristics that were valued highly.

As the counter culture developed during the middle 1960s, alternative values were posited. The ideals of love and community, sharing and co-operation, honesty and love were embodied in new cultural forms. The rock festival, happenings, and communes, for example, reflected these counter values in opposition to established values. The peace marches, "the movement" that organized against the Viet Nam War, the freedom marches, and civil rights demonstrations—all seemed to call forth an attitude of rebellion and confrontation among students. When large segments of young people began their vocal and sometimes violent rejection of much of the dominant value system, educational institutions were among the hardest hit by rebellion.

Athletics are valued highly by adults, but they are played primarily by youth. If the athlete had been a beloved symbol of adult values, and athletics a distilled establishment in miniature, then as the traditional image and value system these represented were questioned, the symbolic function of athletics was likely to lose some appeal with young people.

It is not the primary purpose here to explore the relative merits of this complex and changing social picture. It does seem important for the prospective coach to realize that athletics are being challenged in a new way. The coach could usually count on some limited opposition from certain quarters of the academic community; charges of "overemphasis" and "anti-intellectualism" have been part of the history of athletics in this country. These kinds of criticism were external. Now new voices are being heard from within; the athletes themselves are expressing dissension in relation to problems of dress and appearance and changing codes, racism, and brutality. These are internal problems that reflect the larger society.

This state of affairs is both disturbing and potentially promising. Confrontation carries the risk of permanent hostility. Battlelines may be drawn in such a way as to tear athletics apart. This danger seems real. The coach can become defined by the young in a way that will "turn them off" to all institutionalized athletics.

The central question facing coaches is how to reestablish an authority position with the new athlete. The first important step in dealing with this question is in realizing that coaches simply do not have any authority, except as it is based on sound theory and logic. The coach is appointed by the school and in that sense he has been granted official sanction. It is this kind of justification, however, that needs to be transcended as the basis of the coach's authority. We need to develop alternative models to coaching that incorporate the ability to change and grow as our culture changes.

Before we consider coaching models, we need to clarify certain demands the coach must meet. The particular coach in an area of specialization will develop his own style and system of teaching. Much of this process is rather rigidly determined by the nature of the sport involved and the age and skill level of the performers. The demands of the task do dictate that a coach solve certain similar problems regardless of the wide diversity of sport.

On another level the coach is concerned with the demands exerted by particular social contexts. As indicated earlier in this discussion, and as Governali has discussed in an article in *Quest* (December, 1966), we do live in a competitive social order that equates winning games with coaching competence. The boy or girl who plays on a winning team, according to this formula, is learning to win and developing the proper character to win in the "game of life." The coach must develop a style of coaching that can achieve a certain degree of success as measured by the number of games won or lost in competition with other schools. In dealing with the pressures that the coach feels from alumni, fans, and from his own high achievement needs, a great deal of tension and seriousness is added to the coaching situation. Some coaches are trapped eternally at this level of professional involvement. The problems that are perceived to be the important ones by those who see coaching from this single perspective focus on the rather terrible urgency to produce and achieve with little regard for other consequences. It is here that many of the critics of systems of athletics probe and attack.

The highest level in this hierarchy of demands placed on the coach revolves around the mode and degree of emphasis that he places on the educational purposes that his profession claims to represent. It is here that the other aspects of coaching ultimately rest for their support. The particular act and attitude shown in the coaching situation itself should have a rational source. The coach may act irrationally and without reference to any source of assumptions about educational or professional commitments that should guide his acts. In fact, he may not be aware that these ethical demands exist. Ignorance of ethical commitments is not a release from responsibility. When the coach acts as a leader of youth, he is making a value statement. If we are what we do, and if we are defined by our acts, then we are responsible for creating values. We need to be aware that by choosing to become a coach we have assumed and entered into an ethical project that only *we* are ultimately responsible for as individuals.

From the perspective of the educational role, at least three models for coaching seem to emerge. It is possible to create and explore many other coaching models. This effort is not meant to define the only ways to arrange and organize assumptions about educational tasks. This attempt is only an initial one to build a theoretical model for athletic coaching. As we separate and simplify the coaching task, we are trying to orient and clarify several basic stances or positions that seem to underlie the particular technical aspects of the profession. We should keep in mind that these models overlap and merge.

COMPETITION-ACHIEVEMENT MODEL

The competition-achievement model is probably the most widespread and traditional way that athletics are actually coached. The purpose of athletics is seen in terms of performance and production. The whole of the athletic program is usually judged on the number of games won and lost, the record-breaking performance, "All-American" and similar selections, filling the stadium, alumni support or financial contributions, profit and loss, and measurable results in general.

Coaching, by implication, concerns itself with developing an athlete who can "deliver the goods" or "bring home the bacon." The emphasis is on being able to stand a great deal of stress and to gain the ability to come through under pressure. The practice schedule is of necessity both grueling and arduous so that the athlete is ready to give his best effort at game time. The emphasis is also heavy on discipline and obedience, as little time can be afforded or lost to more democratic but inefficient means.

The competition-achievement coaching model has certain strong points. It can, by a process of either natural selection or reinforcement, produce people who have great psychological endurance, high achievement needs, and who are orderly and respect authority. Because of the Spartan and militaristic atmosphere that this model encourages on the field, the tasks of the coach are rather clearly defined. In order to be authentic the coach may simply rely on rule authority, make no exceptions, and let the ends justify the sometime harsh and exacting means.

The competition-achievement model has serious shortcomings. The need for efficiency and organization can lead to hostility and indifference to individual differences and uniqueness among team members. Any activity or project that places heavy emphasis on achievement and production seems to meet with similar difficulties. The leader in these situations must maintain and emphasize certain authority relationships that are accepted without question. The coach is interested only in maximizing improvement in performance in the shortest amount of time possible. This demand on task improvement may be solved simply by using an authoritarian approach. By assuming complete control of every aspect of practice and game situations that the coach considers significant, he also takes complete and full responsibility for eventual success or failure of the individual performance. This shift of responsibility from the individual to the coach can lead to a certain mindless dependency on any strong authority figure, and that seems to have unhealthy overtones in a democratic society. Even if the coach is greatly concerned with helping individuals develop in a broader sense, he is likely to be suspected of manipulation by the player because of the realization that his "problem" is only important to the coach insofar as it affects the next victory. As long as the emphasis is on production and not on people, the particular technique makes little difference.

The interest in sport psychology lately in coaching circles might be strongly influenced by coaches operating from the competition-achievement model. This coach is interested in "motivating" a player by using a psychological trick rather than the usual methods. The difference in approach might be likened to the contrast between the overly coercive atmosphere of George Orwell's *1984* and the more gentle but terrifying psychological manipulation of Huxley's *Brave New World*.

THERAPEUTIC MODEL

The therapeutic model offers a radically different approach. The purpose of athletics is perceived as individual or personal growth. The player is encouraged to find his own enjoyment and meaning in the sport experience that may have little or no reference to measurable outcomes. The following statement of the Educational Policies Commission on School Athletics illustrates the goal that can be called therapeutic:

> Athletic activities should foster, above all else, the growth and well-being of the individual student. It requires differentiations of experiences for different learners. It also means that welfare of the player in an athletic contest out-ranks in value the specious "glory of the school." (1954, p. 14)

The ideals of healing and serving are both implied in this statement. The young athlete is being given the opportunity to enter and use a community of peers to gain his own personal identity. Although each athlete in this model would be working to heal himself, to put himself together, he would be helping others to gain the same results in their own way. The purpose of this therapeutic community would be to have people come together in such a way that they can leave each other alone. The role of the coach in this situation would focus on the individual and his particular needs. The effort would be to develop each player's awareness of his own freedom for self-definition and self-determination.

The strong points of the therapeutic model are obvious. They put the emphasis on individual development in a personal sense. The relationship between player and coach would need to be both personal and deeply involved. The emphasis on personal freedom could develop a loose and unconfining atmosphere that could benefit some young people.

The weaknesses of the therapeutic model are the strengths of the competition-achievement model. The *laissez faire* attitude of the therapeutic community might lead to a complete disregard for excellence and all-out effort usually associated with great athletes. The coach would, of necessity, need to be continually open to change and be constantly aware of the need for communication between all of the people involved. This effort to keep a loosely knit organization together and growing would certainly make efficiency and achievement of secondary importance.

THE AESTHETIC MODEL

The coach who approaches athletics from an aesthetic viewpoint would be interested in helping the performers develop their expressive powers by use of a nonverbal medium. The well-proportioned and symmetrical performance would be the aim of both player and coach. The feats that both performed would be seen as means pointing toward an aesthetically perfect end. The emphasis on self-expression in athletics would encourage the sense of self-mobilization and self-utilization of one's complete powers much as the competition-achievement model would.

The aesthetic model of coaching would cast the coach in a role similar to that of a director in a theatrical production. The director is helping the actor as an individual and the cast as a whole to interpret the script so that the greatest artistic effect can result.

The coach would interpret his own particular athletic form in order to gain the maximum expressive aesthetic qualities for the performer or the team. The coach would help the individual players to learn to use athletics for their own self-expression and to appreciate other athletic forms from an aesthetic point of view.

The strong points of the aesthetic model involve the emphasis on excellence as the means for self-expressive ends. The athlete is totally involved in action. The action orientation demands the full use of the body. The body is at once an instrument of the athlete's self, an expression of that self, and a total engagement of the self in the body during all-out effort. During these periods of corporeal awareness the athlete is engaged in a stimulating and self-revealing dimension of experience that demands his attention. His will, his spirit, and his body drive the athlete to make sense out of his project. When the athlete is taught to see his performance as an artist views his project, and as he is encouraged to find his own meaning and interpretation about the whole or any part of his existence as an athlete, this experience can add new dimensions to athletic endeavor.

COACHING AS AN OPEN SYSTEM

Each model we have outlined for orienting the purposes the coach brings to his own separate athletic form has something important to offer. These models all exist in certain respects today. The therapeutic model is usually associated with elementary physical education activities or in programs for the emotionally disturbed where play is considered as therapy. The aesthetic model is most prevalent in dance, but also in the so-called "form" sports. The competition-achievement model has the most widespread acceptance in our culture.

Presently, the coaching profession is most concerned with competition-achievement, and the role of the coach is usually thought about from this viewpoint. As long as the prevailing value systems of the culture also emphasized the competition-achievement syndrome, athletics held a prominent position with reference to its contributions to "character" and "personality" formation, especially in the schools. Even so, however, there were always critics who suggested that the view of life as a competitive struggle was not an appropriate one for the school to purvey, and that athletics was a questionable "preparation for life" especially when "ends" were evaluated separately from means. Another significant question had to do with the athletic mode; for success in this setting depended upon both obedience to authority and external recognition. These motivations have been viewed as distinctly inappropriate when they were the pervasive personality expressions of adults. A view of sport and athletics, then, that transcends participation as an adolescent undertaking, must emphasize modes of experience that are more acceptable in light of enduring behavior. Furthermore, as our culture changes and value systems become diverse and varied within short time spans, all those involved with youth need to remain constantly open in their thinking.

In the field of athletics there is an urgent need to consider therapeutic, aesthetic, and any other coaching models that might allow us the freedom to reduce cultural lags. We need alternative categories that will provide a learning environment for students that allows them to experience the many important dimensions athletics have to offer.

DISCUSSION

Statements relative to the teacher and coach with emphasis on theoretical assumptions about the importance of the teacher's view of his roles and responsibilities and the demands of teaching in relation to students, school, society, and subject.

Teaching and Coaching

1. The basis of the teacher's role as a director of learning is his conception of the purposes of education and of his own subject matter area; this becomes the philosophical orientation and framework of commitments within which this role is defined and expressed.

2. The teacher has specific responsibility for (1) intelligent planning for learning both daily and over long periods of time; (2) selecting content and providing learning experiences; and (3) continually evaluating students, program, and himself in relation to the purposes of the program and the commitments he perceives for his role.

3. "Teacher" and "teaching" are words which imply a correlative "learner"; therefore, it may be more desirable to talk about a "teaching-learning process," which implies that teaching and teacher behavior are defined in relation to learning and the nature of the learner.

4. If learning environments and experiences are selected and structured by the teacher, they are done so on hypotheses about how pupils will best learn (as well as what learning is most desirable), and the validity of these hypotheses depends upon a great deal of knowledge about learning, growth and development, and related factors.

5. Everything the teacher does reflects his beliefs about the variables involved; *at least*, the teacher's behavior should be the result of conscious and examined choices based on intelligence and logic and as much knowledge and understanding as can be attained.

6. The assumptions that teachers make must be continually re-examined and refined in relation to their own behavior, student behavior, and the emotional climates and effects of the teaching-learning process.

7. Vague presentation of learning tasks is frequently the result of the grossness of the teacher's perception of the task, and refinement depends upon additional insight.

8. Because of his frameworks of beliefs about the teaching-learning process, the teacher is able to select knowledge and apply it in relation to the purposes that have been developed; only unknowledgeable teachers are guilty of theory-practice dichotomies at basic levels.

9. Insight into content and its demands permits innovation and experimentation with ways of learning; the inexperienced or non-insightful teacher is limited to teaching in ways which he himself has experienced—only as he understands the purpose and the content can he devise effective ways for learning to take place.

10. The physical educator is a member of a profession, and there are certain criteria implied by the concept of a "profession" which have ramifications for the knowledge and behavior of the teacher.

11. The physical educator is presumed to be an "expert" in his field; therefore, he is called upon not only to teach, but to answer questions and assume many other roles indicated by his presumed expertise.

12. Members of a profession are also members of a "community of scholars" in their areas, and the physical educator has some commitments to physical education as a profession beyond the specific requirements of his role as a teacher.

13. Professions are characterized by their body of knowledge and by their applied and occupational interests, but they also involve participation in the exchange and production of knowledge as well as the provision of service.

14. The teacher as a member of a profession is committed to his "community" and its ideals, to knowledge, and to service—professions are humanistic in their concerns, but depend heavily on the contributions of their members and on the maintenance of "standards" by the members of the profession themselves.

15. The physical educator has commitment both to the teaching profession as a whole and to physical education as a profession.

16. Each teacher must perceive his relationship to his profession; that is, his individual effort exists in relation to the growth and goals of the profession as a whole, and he is willing to participate in the activities that enhance growth for the profession as a whole.

17. The teacher is a member of a school staff (or other professional staff) as well, and has commitments to the teaching profession at large, and to a particular staff.

18. The commitment to one's own field must not interfere with staff and

institutional goals; that is, as a member of a staff, the teacher is committed to a total program, and as a representative of a particular field, his role is to clarify and enhance the contribution of that field to the generalized goals of the institution.

19. Members of professions and particular staffs must exemplify the characteristics of such groups as willing and able to oversee their own standards and committed to a humanitarian ethic; the moral imperatives implicit in the humanistic fields are expressed by the functioning of the representatives of such fields.

20. Every individual is somewhere in the process of knowing what he is and learning what he shall become, and in our responsibilities to youth, we must have a view which permits the most positive development of that process.

21. Insofar as people act within their own frameworks of beliefs, attitudes, values, needs, etc., then the teacher must not only understand his own perceptions, but must decide what perceptions of self and the world are most constructive for youth; for it is within social contexts that these perceptions develop, and teachers are frequently influential persons in such interactions.

22. The notion of a "self-fulfilling prophecy" indicates that best learning will take place when the pervasive view is one of opportunity and encouragement, and it is very dangerous to lend too much weight to restriction and limitation unless their certainty is clear.

23. "Experience" is always personal, but the immature person, especially, needs help in understanding his own experience, in examining it, and in using it to learn about himself and other people and the world.

24. The personal is the meaningful, and insofar as people act on the basis of personal meaning, then, as interpreters of an area of human experience, we must encounter individuals within their own meanings if the field we represent is to become important to them in their lives.

25. Physical education has all sorts of potential for meaning and enhancement to man; it is the responsibility of those who would represent that field to youth to seek the way in which that potential will be realized.

26. The "teacher" is considered a mature and responsible person; this implies that he has learned to cope with his own needs and perceptions and to extend his concern and understanding to his field and to the people with whom he works, and it is his responsibility to evaluate all the aspects of that growth and make viable plans and efforts toward his own excellence.

27. It is the teacher's role to mediate culture and community in ways which will be enhancing to the growth of the individual and contribute to the good of society.

28. The physical education teacher, sometimes, must make a conscious effort to develop his abilities so that he can fulfill his role in relation to the culture; an identity that is narrowly defined in interests and concerns purveys a less than fully relevant view.

29. Although it is the conventional wisdom to believe that youth derives its values from the peer group, "attractive and successful adults" are still viable models, but this definition rests on cultural participation and understanding.

30. Somehow, the teacher must develop conscious and examined values and attitudes about the world and the community and education and knowledge as well as about physical education so that he represents reasonable and constructive alternatives to youth.

SELECTED BIBLIOGRAPHY

Teaching and Coaching Physical Education

Berlin, Pearl (ed.) "The Physical Educator as Professor." *Quest VII.* December 1966.
Considers the roles of the professor in selections by various authors; includes a framework statement about "The Perplexed Professor," and the practicing physical educator as administrator, artist, author, coach, graduate adviser, evaluator, researcher, scholar and teacher.

Bruner, Jerome S. *The Process of Education.* Cambridge, Massachusetts: Harvard University Press, 1960.
The Report of the Woods Hole Conference that established the involvement of scholars in the process of curriculum development based on the academic disciplines.

————. *Toward A Theory of Instruction.* Cambridge, Massachusetts: Belknap Press of the Harvard University Press, 1966.
A collection of eight essays dealing with different facets of the instructional enterprise and directed toward the development of a cohesive theory of instruction.

Coleman, James S. *The Adolescent Society.* New York: The Free Press, 1961.
An analysis of adolescence in relation to social variables.

Cratty, Bryant T. "Coaching Decisions and Research in Sport Psychology." *Quest XIII.* January, 1970, 46-53.
Discusses the influence of psychological research in affecting decisions of coaches; categorizes types of decisions made by coaches and offers research findings.

Educational Policies Commission. *School Athletics Problems and Policies.* Washington, D.C.: National Education Association and the American Association of School Administrators, 1954.
A classic statement of the role of school athletics.

Frost, Reuben B. *Psychological Concepts Applied to Physical Education and Coaching.* Reading, Massachusetts: Addison-Wesley Publishing Company, 1971.
Presents psychological principles and applies them to teaching physical education and coaching sports.

Governali, Paul. "The Physical Educator as Coach." *Quest VII.* December, 1966, 30-37.
Deals with the physical educator in his role as a coach.

Kroll, Walter P. *Perspectives in Physical Education.* New York: Academic Press, 1971.
An interesting treatment of graduate study and research in relation to the field of study and profession of physical education in historical and contemporary perspective.

Lawther, John. *Sport Psychology.* Englewood Cliffs, New Jersey: Prentice-Hall, 1972.
Deals with sport and psychological variables with implications for coaching.

Moore, J. W. *The Psychology of Athletic Coaching.* Minneapolis, Minnesota: Burgess Publishing Company, 1970.
Discusses methods of improving the performance of athletes by utilizing psychological concepts in the coaching of sports.

Mordy, Margaret M. (ed.) "Educational Change in the Teaching of Physical Education." *Quest XV.* January, 1971.
Includes perspectives of innovation and methodology in teaching physical education, and represents a broad range of ideas and views of various authors.

Mosston, Muska. *Teaching Physical Education: From Command to Discovery.* Columbus, Ohio: Charles E. Merrill Books, 1966.
Analyzes teaching behavior and interactions between teacher and learner according to an evolutionary construct of a spectrum of styles of teaching.

Reich, Charles A. *The Greening of America.* New York: Random House, 1970.
Analyzes the shifts in consciousness of the changing American culture, and presents an idealized version of contemporary youth culture as Consciousness III.
Scott, Jack. *The Athletic Revolution.* New York: The Free Press, 1971.
Analyzes the changing scene in athletics related to various protest movements and the counter culture; includes contemporary statements and relevant data.
Tutko, Thomas A. "Some Clinical Aspects of Sport Psychology." *Quest XIII.* January, 1970, 12-17.
Discusses some problems the coach encounters in working with athletes.
————, and Richards, Jack W. *Psychology of Coaching.* Boston: Allyn and Bacon, 1971.
Explores psychological factors which are of concern to coaches. Concentrates on the emotional and attitudinal aspects of athletic performance.
Underwood, John. "The Desperate Coach." *Sports Illustrated.* August 25, 1969, 66-76; September 1, 1969, 21-27; September 8, 1969, 29-40.
A series of articles depicting the problems of the coach with reference to the values, attitudes, and behavior of athletes representing the counter culture and cultural change.
Vanek, Miroslav, and Cratty, Bryant J. *Psychology and the Superior Athlete.* New York: The Macmillan Company, 1970.
Discusses research related to superior sportsmen and sportswomen and application of these findings to improving the performance of top athletes in national and international competition.

Chapter VIII

PREPARING TO TEACH PHYSICAL EDUCATION

Concepts of teacher preparation are complex and depend upon a multitude of variables and considerations. Furthermore, there are several different frameworks within which professional education can be conceived; within each of these there are countless topical or problem-related concerns. Because physical education major programs in colleges and universities are still primarily, though not exclusively, teacher education programs, it is an important concern. Contemporary physical education is also characterized by diversity, and this is very true of major programs and graduate programs. The time has already come when a student cannot choose a school and expect the major program within it to be like a large majority of others. If that was once so, it is no longer, and institutional positions and programs not only vary, but often do not resemble many others.

Teacher preparation is treated here so that the actualization of the framework based on notions of a field of study can be demonstrated as it is applied to these concerns. Less than any other, this chapter is clearly not a definitive statement. The materials included are intended to demonstrate some theoretical and actual approaches to professional preparation curriculums. Like any educational program, a particular curriculum depends upon a specific institution and particular people.

APPROACHES TO PROFESSIONAL PHYSICAL EDUCATION
UP THE CURRICULUM!*

HISTORICAL APPROACHES TO THE PROFESSIONAL
PHYSICAL EDUCATION CURRICULUM (Ellen W. Gerber)

The preparation of physical education teachers through a formal course of instruction began in the United States in 1861. Dio Lewis's school, the Normal Institute for Physical Education located in Boston, offered a course for men and women of ten weeks' duration. By the end of the nineteenth and beginning of the twentieth centuries, there were more than a dozen teacher-training programs, the majority of which were two years in length and were sponsored by small, privately endowed, single-purpose institutions. The content of the curriculum at all of the institutions was remarkably similar. At Dio Lewis's Institute instruction was given in anatomy, physiology, hygiene, and gymnastics, and students were also taught the principles of the "Swedish movement cure." (Gerber, 1970, p. 265) The Normal College of the North American Gymnastic Union taught anatomy, first aid, aesthetic dancing, and later physiology, hygiene, and fencing, in addition, of course, to the history, aims, theory, practice, and teaching methods of German gymnastics or *turnen*. By 1895 the NAGU had also devoted a small amount of time to dietetics, orthopedic gymnastics, massage, anthropometry, pedagogy, and swimming, boxing, and wrestling. (Gerber, 1970, p. 269) The largest of the programs was carried out at the Sargent Normal School. Its curriculum circa 1900, which was fairly typical of the two-year course requirements during the decade, consisted almost entirely of theory courses in the natural and health sciences and practical courses related to exercise of various kinds. Sports instruction in basketball, field hockey, track and field, soccer, swimming, and so forth began to be added to the curriculum in significant amounts beginning in the early 1900s when aesthetic dancing and rhythmic gymnastics also began their rise to popularity. At approximately the same time some schools added practice teaching and courses in the history of education, psychology, and pedagogy, though the time devoted to these was minimal compared to that spent on science courses.

At William G. Anderson's New Haven Normal School of Gymnastics (now the Arnold College Division of the University of Bridgeport) an eclectic approach was taken to the subject of activities. Courses were given in American, Swedish, and German and Delsarte gymnastics, mili-

* A presentation by Jan Felshin, East Stroudsburg State College, and Ellen W. Gerber, University of Massachusetts, at the fall conference of the Eastern Association for Physical Education of College Women, Tamiment, Pennsylvania, October 23 to 25, 1970.

tary evolutions, voice training, games, track and field athletics, and fencing. A similar variety of courses was offered at the Chautauqua Summer School which Anderson also directed, but students were encouraged to select only one area for study. In what may have been the first written comment on the problem of specialization within physical education, Anderson commented to conferees attending the Seventh Annual Meeting of the AAPE in 1892:

> It requires a life study for a man or a woman, to thoroughly understand and teach medical gymnastics. It requires just as much time to properly comprehend and teach educational gymnastics. . . . We try to persuade our teachers to select one grade of work and make a specialty of that. It is well for the gymnastics teacher to "know everything about something, and something about everything"
> (Proceedings of the Seventh Annual Meeting, 1892, p. 199)

To summarize the early curriculums in professional physical education programs briefly, generally it can be said that the earliest teacher-training curriculums were two years long and consisted of theory courses in the natural sciences, particularly anatomy and physiology, and numerous health courses, such as diagnosis, orthopedics, or first aid, complemented by practical courses in the various gymnastic systems, usually predominantly the one system which was favored by the school's founder. In the early 1900s, both the theoretical and practical curriculums were expanded to include sports and dance activities and courses related to education, but the time devoted to these new areas was comparatively slight. By 1920 when Clark W. Hetherington, one of the earliest curriculum theorists in our field, proposed an ideal curriculum, these early approaches to study had been expanded, but kept roughly the same proportions of subject areas.

The curriculums as just described were a logical emanation from the purposes of the teacher-training programs. In the nineteenth century a number of educators began to be attentive to the health of the American people. When physical education was introduced into public schools and colleges, this concern was the uppermost reason. The Swedish and German gymnastics systems vied with each other and with American forms of exercise (e.g., Beecher's calisthenics, Dio Lewis's light gymnastics, Sargent's developing apparatus) for favor in the schools. The aim of each system was the correction of orthopedic defects and the maintenance of health. No matter which system was chosen by a school or college, it was necessary to have a gymnastics or exercise teacher trained to conduct the program. Therefore, the earliest training schools aimed to produce physical educators who could diagnose defects and prescribe individual exercise programs to correct them, and who could select and organize exercises for groups of students. Both duties (job roles) required a solid knowledge of the body, particularly its anatomy and physiological functioning, in order to understand the problems and the physical effects of each exercise chosen. Teaching also necessitated undertaking a detailed study of each exercise in order to be able to provide an appropriate teaching progression, and to ensure that each part of the body was being dealt with. Since teaching method at that time generally consisted of demonstration followed by the teacher leading the group in its exercise, the teacher's own skill and physical condition necessarily had to be high. The advent of games and sports in the curriculum did little to change this basic conception of the teacher's role. Sports as they were played at first, were nonserious, basically recreative endeavors. Little attempt was made to develop good skills for either teacher or the student.

CURRENT STATUS OF THE PROFESSIONAL EDUCATION PROGRAM (Ellen W. Gerber)

As the years have gone by, public school physical education has changed considerably. It has broadened its reach all the way to the primary grades. The goals for each school level, no matter what individual or group enunciates them, have been considerably expanded. Concomitantly, the course and teaching methods have been widened to encompass a broad span of activities and approaches to teaching. Furthermore, the concept of what constitutes physical education has undergone some important directional shifts.

The undergraduate professional preparation curriculum has, sadly, failed to undergo major changes. Although it has grown in length and added, therefore, more courses, these have largely been extensions and updates of the kind of courses offered in the nineteenth century. The bias towards the natural sciences has ensured that the predominance of theoretical courses within the professional preparation curriculum fall in this area. These courses are generally taught by physical educators and directed towards the needs of the physical education student. A smattering of courses in the social sciences is now required in most curriculums; these courses usually are taught in their "mother" departments, and the physical education student is left on his own to draw relationships to his interests as best he can. With the exception of a course in the history and philosophy of physical education, the humanities are still virtually ignored in the professional preparation program. Courses in education round out the theoretical side of the undergraduate professional curriculum. These may be taught by physical educators or in departments of education, and are meant to provide the student some understanding of teaching method and evaluation as well as provide a relationship with the "mother" discipline.

The activity curriculum has expanded in a much more varied way. As many activities as are likely to be found in the local secondary schools are incorporated into the undergraduate curriculum, usually in a required course. The expanse often includes sports, dance, exercise, and recreational games. Courses are offered in the teaching and officiating of these activities, as well as in learning the requisite skills.

From this brief historical and current perspective emerges a number of significant issues. For this presentation, we have, however, isolated two broad and, we think, crucial issues on which to focus our attention. First the identification of what has historically been considered to be *the* field of study for physical education, leads logically to the question of what should be the field of study today? In other words, what is the appropriate curricular content for a prospective secondary school physical educator to study? And secondly, is it necessary for that prospective teacher to take steps towards mastering the entire field of physical education or perhaps just some part of it? Or, shall there be specialization or generalization in the undergraduate curriculum?

Before proceeding to a discussion of these issues, it seems necessary to examine the underlying assumptions regarding the purposes and structure of professional preparation.

FRAMEWORK FOR PROFESSIONAL PREPARATION (Jan Felshin)

Professional preparation as it exists in institutions of higher learning has several sources of imperatives for its commitments and development of programs. Because it is related to an academic degree, the first commitment must be to the conception and role of the institution which grants that degree. Secondly, the discipline or field to which it is related is a source for defining its commitments, and, finally, it is committed to its ultimate purpose of serving the teaching profession in physical education.

As many institutions have learned, somehow these commitments must not be mutually exclusive; for if unwarranted priority is given any one, there is likely to be objection on behalf of the others. Obviously, the context within which professional preparation is conceived and understood does vary depending on the orientation of the degree-granting institution, the perception of physical education, and the related school or job demand which exists. But certain assumptions about each of these sources that provide the context for professional preparation can be made, and it is these which become the framework for understanding programs and their commitments.

The heterogeneity and dynamic aspects of higher education make it difficult to postulate imperatives. In general, however, there seems to be some contemporary agreement that programs which are solely vocational in nature, that is, conceived only in relation to job demand, are not acceptable. Certainly the responsibility to theory and the knowledge upon which it depends have been clarified in most colleges and universities.

This imperative means that credit for activity courses is somewhat limited; that a proliferation of "methods" or "how to" courses is not acceptable; that courses which "apply" the proper concerns of other disciplines
are frowned upon, and that academic credit is usually not given or given
most sparingly for experiences that utilize a great deal of practice and
rehearsal time with little or no theoretical attention.

The field of physical education has been an unclear source for determining the nature of professional preparation. As long as the field is
defined by its activities and the teaching-learning process, guidelines for
theoretical concerns are not clear. Obviously, the contemporary effort to
define a body of knowledge has been focused toward clarifying the theoretical nature of physical education. If physical education is conceived
only as it exists in schools, then even the theoretical concerns of professional preparation are seen as the *theory* of education or the profession,
i.e., the history of the profession, the administration of school programs,
the evaluation of learning, and so forth.

But the profession of physical education must be considered, and this
has provided the most clear source for professional preparation. Even
here, however, the assumptions of professional preparation programs
must be broader than simply "job demands"; somehow, we must clarify
the role of the physical education teacher and conceive of the professional
future of our students with reference to themselves and their students as
persons and to our field in its most exciting dimensions.

THE FIELD OF STUDY IN PHYSICAL EDUCATION (Ellen W. Gerber)

One may begin to consider the crucial question of what should be
the theoretical focus of the physical education major, as it is designed to
prepare secondary school teachers, by first surveying the immense variety
of courses now available within a college or university setting. The
breadth of society's interest and problems, coupled with a great knowledge explosion, has encouraged this variety and brought with it an attendant loosening of curricular restrictions. Students generally have more opportunities available and more freedom to make choices. However, the
physical education curriculum has remained narrowly construed and
lacking in area electives.

Physical education students today are asked to devote the major portion of their theoretical, professional learning to limited studies about
physical organisms; they develop a superficial knowledge of the body
and how it functions. Knowing the origin, insertion, and function of the
various muscle groups is expected to be of help to future teachers and
assumes that these rote facts will be retained in later years. But facing
the teacher is not an organism but a person. How do these studies assist
teachers in gaining insights and understanding about the people they
will be facing? *Within* the professional undergraduate curriculum there

is rarely even a single course with a humanistic orientation. Besides the courses devoted to anatomy and physiology, there are usually others designed to reveal salient facts about growth and development patterns, and others which purport to enhance student understanding of the processes of learning. These latter classes may be the closest students come to studying people qua people.

I am proposing a complete revamping of the undergraduate theoretical curriculum, deliberately building in a bias towards the social sciences and humanities. Physical education majors preparing to teach high school students should spend their greatest amount of professionally oriented time studying the adolescent age group and the American culture in which it functions. Adolescent individuals should be studied as a group and as normal individuals representative of an age. While sociological and psychological approaches come first to mind, anthropological, historical, philosophical, and literary insights are equally valid and important. Perusing the catalogue at my own university, I can find numerous courses more suited than biology, chemistry, zoology, anatomy, and physiology are in helping a future teacher understand and interact with students. Anthropology offers "The Individual and Society"; Sociology lists "Social Problems" and "Social Interaction"; while the English department has a course in "The Contemporary American Novel." (Parenthetically, how much more would you know about those before you if you had studied *Catcher in The Rye* instead of learning about how many bones Holden Caulfield had in his body? What could you learn of today's youth by studying Tom Wolfe?) Philosophy offers "Ethical Theory"; History provides a "History of American Thought and Culture" and a "Social History of the United States." And Psychology lists numerous relevant courses including the "Psychology of Adolescence," "Motivation," "Personality," and "Social Psychology."

It is important to note that I am not advocating increasing the number of required courses either inside or outside of the discipline. I am suggesting, instead, that we replace the numerous courses about the physical functioning of the organism with courses related to the functioning of people and their social groups. There is no particular evidence or even logic that dictates that greater value be placed upon understanding cardiovascular functioning than on understanding the sociology of small groups, e.g., teams. The culmination of courses such as biology and anatomy is kinesiology and physiology of exercise. In other words, courses that apply, in a particularly relevant way, the basic knowledges communicated in the prerequisite courses. A similar grouping of courses can be designed in the areas of the social sciences and humanities. Many institutions now offer classes in the psychology, sociology, philosophy, and history of sport and/or physical education. Courses in the art and literature of sport might well be added.

However, it is time to bring up still another issue relating to those courses which apply the knowledge of other disciplines. Today there has been much interest in viewing physical education itself as a discipline. While it is possible, from one viewpoint, to consider ourselves as an applied field, and our scholars as disciples of "mother" disciplines, it is also appropriate to recognize that we ourselves follow a discipline. Such a recognition would have great import for the undergraduate major curriculum. At the present, any relevant courses are organized in terms of applying the knowledge of another area of study. Hence the present interest in, for example, sociology of sport, or our more common courses in the history and philosophy of physical education. Furthermore, because of the time devoted to studying aspects of the "mother" discipline, the applied discipline approach is generally forced to leave out other important areas such as art, literature, anthropology, and ecology. We must move out of this pattern of discipleship and into a pattern appropriate to a discipline. We should be offering our undergraduate majors courses in "Theories of Play," "The Role of Sport in Adolescent Culture," "Girls and Women in Sport," "Physical Education and Value-Oriented Concerns," "The Meaning of the Sport Experience," "The Mind-Body Relationship," "Physical Education as a Function of Education," "Race and Sport," "The Nature of Play," "Sport and Athletics," "Motivation of the Sportsman or Sportswoman," and so on. In other words, we would be centering courses around the crucial problems and questions which relate to the subject we teach. The work of other disciplines should provide supportive evidence and theories to be used when relevant, but should not be the organizational framework around which we develop our programs. The undergraduate major should be introduced to the discipline, in and of itself.

So much for the theoretical side of the curriculum. I would like to raise one major point with regard to the activity emphases. The activities now offered in a local high school program are, by and large, traditional. They are the activities which generations of at least some youngsters have found enjoyable, modified by the availability of facilities, equipment, and time in an educational institution. Although we have formulated a rationale for the type of activities selected (e.g., team games teach social democracy), numerous activities have also been chosen independent from the rationale. Today's colleges offer a far more appealing array of activities than do high schools. This is not due to practical problems. College teachers have apparently been more open to change *and* have been fortunate in being able to secure the services of part-time instructors who could teach more specialized activities. It is interesting to note that in an institution such as my own, which offers to general students courses in Tai Chi, Yoga, and Karate (incidentally, all mass activities which require no particular equipment), majors continue to take heavy doses of field hockey, basketball, and volleyball, with other

7

traditional sports thrown in, but never do they have the opportunity to experience these newly popular and very interesting activities. We ourselves have moved with the times in our general programs but have failed to ensure that our students, the future teachers, will also be contemporary in their professional roles.

Competitive activities have been the foundation of physical education sports programs. Yet it is questionable that competitive sports programs meet interests and/or needs of today's youth. Many of them consider this facet of American society undesirable. On the other hand, the growth in participation in sports which can be pursued noncompetitively has, in this country, been phenomenal. It is time for our major programs to reflect this shift; we must begin to incorporate more of the self-knowledge types of activities such as Tai Chi, and outdoor activities such as skiing, climbing, surfing, spelunking, hiking, or whatever is appropriate to a given geographical locale. True, these activities may not be feasible within the bounds of a secondary school class period. But our secondary programs today extend far beyond the class hours. They encompass broad intramural and extramural sports competition. If more majors were exposed to activities such as previously named *within* their own curriculums, they might start recreational clubs within their secondary schools. They might pay more attention to the youngster who wants and needs noncompetitive sports. The professional curriculum today is narrow, tradition bound, and heavily dependent upon other fields. Its courses of study should be revised and geared more towards a study of people and society than of organisms. The courses relating to physical education should be regrouped and centered on the interests and questions of our own discipline. And the programmed activities should be refocused in more creative and contemporary directions.

IMPLICATIONS FOR SCHOOL PROGRAM (Jan Felshin)

The attention to physical education as a discipline is appropriate to conceptions of higher learning and the field itself as sources for professional preparation. It does not, however, have direct relationship to the role of physical education in school programs or to the demands of teaching. The question "What is physical education?" is still asked, and the teacher wants to know what he should be *doing* in school programs, and even, perhaps, why. Unfortunately, many of the outgrowths of disciplinary concern have simply been the use of school programs for teaching content of the body of knowledge, and not even in a very cohesive way. The unacceptability of seeing physical education simply as a medium for the achievement of nonrelated educational purposes is generally accepted, but it is just as unacceptable to use physical education as a means for teaching principles of physics.

The point that the teacher's conception of the essence of physical education should be more related to humanistic concerns is, of course, well taken. As long as the teacher perceives students as physiological systems or systems of levers, the uses to which he puts his program are questionable ones. Interestingly enough, except when we are acting out of some vague feelings of guilt, the secondary school curriculum is primarily humanistic. We use sport and games and social situations of all kinds as the basis of our programs. The problem is that we do feel some guilt, and mixed in with our own *feelings* about what the essence and worth of our field are, are vague allegiances to "fitness" and to "order" and to all of the other purposes we have embraced in our history.

Is the content of physical education worthy of time in the secondary school curriculum? If educational criteria include complexity of cognitive demand and potential for intellectual demand only, the answer is probably "no." But why else do we have things in the curriculum? Why Shakespeare, or symphonies, or art? It seems to me there are two reasons: (1) the school simply has an obligation to include "exposure" to those things which man has found meaningful—sort of a nonutilitarian and sometimes token nod in the direction of dimensions of sensibility, and (2) the school also has an obligation to the goal of cultural participation, and physical education cannot be denied. The school does have some responsibility with reference to the needs and welfare of youth as well, but frequently it finds ways to do this outside the curriculum, i.e., school lunch programs. If our field is humanistic in orientation and essence, and if one of the purposes of the secondary curriculum is to aid students to find experiences with potentials for providing meaning in their lives, the guidelines are fairly clear. There must be opportunities to pursue experience to the point of meaning, which implies that the struggle to master the basic elements is over. There must be ways to help individuals find those experiences which have the greatest potential for them. And, most importantly, the attitudes toward the field and its content must derive from an environment in which joy, and meaning, and self can flourish.

GENERALIZATION-SPECIALIZATION (Jan Felshin)

The concept of "curriculum" is pervasive and is used to refer to the design of programs themselves, the pattern of experiences that any individual pursues, and to both the processes and products implied by the term. The most basic choices confronting professional preparation institutions are those which are ultimately reflected in what is *offered*. In light of the preceding discussions, it seems apparent that somehow these offerings must reflect the body of knowledge, must be theoretical in orientation, and yet, must also reflect the needs of the profession. "Choice," when used in conjunction with curriculum planning, assumes rational and considered involvement, but the curriculum offerings themselves do then express the values and beliefs of those involved in choosing.

The second order of decision-making is probably the most crucial; that is, assuming that the offerings reflect possibilities for the student, how much choice among these should be allowed, and how should his choosing be structured? For a long time in physical education, we have believed that the teacher should be knowledgeable about all aspects of the field; be able to do or teach a wide range of activities and skills, and, therefore, be a "generalist" who could be presumed to be an "expert" in his field. For many reasons, this assumption is being challenged.

In the current vernacular, one gets "into" something when he both understands it and "grooves" on it. To me, the connotation of this process is the desirability of a notion of "mastery," without which both insight and excitement are difficult to achieve. The generalist in physical education as a "jack of all trades and a master of none" may not be the compelling teacher; for we know that of all the nebulous variables of teaching excellence, the one called "enthusiasm" is crucial. The implication of providing opportunities for the pursuit of mastery is obvious. Certainly, in sport and performance it is probably necessary. Perhaps, too, it is "mastery" as a process of developing excellence that generalizes insofar as it yields insight into its own meaning. Perhaps not, but then, we already *know* that the process of developing beginning skills does not generalize very well as we have approached it, or we would not have to spend so much time doing it.

And, what of insight? Is it ever gained while one is struggling with fundamental abilities, with reference to either intellectual or athletic tasks? It seems that it is not; rather, some mastery and some sophistication are prerequisite to the development of insight and to the experiencing of the essences of ideas or phenomena. The "meat and potatoes" man simply lacks the experience and insight that lead to discrimination and allow one more meaningful experience. We know, too, that the individual who is permitted and encouraged to consider and to choose is usually more committed to his own behavior. If the program offerings of an institution allow students to specialize and/or to chart their own professional preparation from several alternative pathways, we might have more committed students, and I suspect we would have a lot more excitement. Certainly, the curriculum must be structured in ways that enable students to choose wisely, and to know something about that which they do not choose. But is it not possible that films would be just as effective as six weeks for that purpose?

IMPLICATIONS FOR THE SCHOOL PROGRAM (Ellen W. Gerber)

The generalization-specialization problem is finally a question of whether the school program is a reflection of what the profession in a rational, considered way has decided upon, or if it is what the schools would like to have teachers do. Which is the tail and which the dog, and who is doing the wagging?

It is obvious that the undergraduate student must receive a broad, general preparation if he is to meet all the job demands created by school administrators—which include teaching all the activities for which the school has purchased equipment, plus exercise and dance, manning the health clinic, running recreational programs, advising cheerleaders, and so forth, not to mention participation as a knowledgeable professional in the affairs of the school. However, this kind of generalized preparation produces a young teacher who is largely incapable of handling any of these job roles well. In fact, it is my contention that one of the prime reasons for the six years of much-the-same-basketball-drills-syndrome is the fact that the teacher does not know enough to teach a progression through to its advanced stages. And if mastery generalizes, then so does nonmastery. Teachers, as a result of their undergraduate experiences, seem to have an idea of sport as a vague collection of odd skills performed in a mediocre manner. They have no idea of the sophisticated, complicated excellence that a satisfying game demands. Even physical fitness objectives are considered satisfied by five minutes of warmup exercises three times a week. This state of affairs is the direct result of the school system's dictation of professional programs by their specification of the job roles.

If those responsible for professional programs were to insist upon designing a program which prepares students to master a limited amount of content (parenthetically, perhaps it would have to be even more limited than we now imagine if true mastery is to be attained), then school administrators would have to revise their concepts of the job specifications of a physical education teacher. Resistance to this may be less than one would expect; school administrators want good programs. The profession can and should make an effort to educate administrators along these lines by presenting good academic rationale for hiring teachers trained as specialists. Finally, there is the undergraduate student himself. The term "physical education" is a collective noun. Under its umbrella is a field of diverse activities. We know that individuals have a propensity for one kind of activity as opposed to another. Dancers don't like field hockey; swimmers may not enjoy volleyball. It is fallacious to assume that an undergraduate can be interested in even attempting to master and subsequently teach in areas external to his sphere of interest. To press them to do so is to risk invoking a generalized state of apathy and/or insecurity on the student's part. To graduate a new teacher who has been forced to study activities he does not like, who does not do well in these activities, and who therefore will be uncomfortable in teaching them (again, a process which tends to generalize to all areas), is to assure disaster for the secondary school system.

Therefore, it seems appropriate to suggest that those of us who are responsible for the professional preparation of secondary school teachers should be sure that we are the dog who wags the tail. Let us not abdicate our responsibilities to the schools. We are the professionals who understand the nature of our discipline and know the capabilities of our programs. Let's let our programs reflect our convictions.

BIBLIOGRAPHY

American Association for the Advancement of Physical Education. *Proceedings of the Seventh Annual Meeting.* Philadelphia, Pennsylvania, 1892.

American Association for Health, Physical Education and Recreation. Report of a National Conference. *Professional Preparation in Health Education, Physical Education, Recreation Education.* Washington, D.C.: The Association, 1962.

Gerber, Ellen W. *Innovators and Institutions in Physical Education.* Philadelphia: Lea & Febiger, 1970.
Detailed histories of the early professional preparation curriculums.

Hetherington, Clark W. "University Professional Training Courses in Physical Education." *American Physical Education Review,* XXV (May, 1920), 185-197.

The National Conference on Undergraduate Professional Preparation in Physical Education, Health Education and Recreation. Jackson Mills, West Virginia, 1948.

Wacker, Hazel Marie. "The History of the Private Single-Purpose Institutions which Prepared Teachers of Physical Education in the United States of America from 1861 to 1958." Unpublished Ed.D. dissertation, New York University, 1959.

Zeigler, Earle Frederick. "A History of Professional Preparation for Physical Education in the United States." Unpublished Ph.D. dissertation, Yale University, 1950.

CURRICULUM OF THE DEPARTMENT OF PROFESSIONAL PHYSICAL EDUCATION AT EAST STROUDSBURG STATE COLLEGE*

CONTEXT AND RATIONALE

The goals of teacher education and programs of professional preparation are formulated in relation to several sources of knowledge and understanding. Because the programs themselves exist under the aegis of higher education and lead to some kind of academic degree, the college or university in which they are offered must be considered. The academic discipline or major that the degree represents is another variable that affects conceptions of the nature of professional preparation, and because it is "professional," the ultimate context in which abilities and knowledge will be used is another source for understanding. Finally, all curriculums are developed and modified in relation to the students within them, and in the case of teacher education, relevant ideas concern the student as he is and his future functioning in the roles of a teacher as well.

The task of identifying and refining purposes for programs of professional preparation is a complex one, but it is crucial if programs are to reflect cohesive theory and contain the potential for providing students with a meaningful pattern of experiences. Somehow the relevance of the diverse sources of commitment and purpose must be recognized and actualized in statements of purpose and programs. At the same time, a rationale for teacher education must express cognizance of the relatedness of the sources as a key focus for the design of the program itself as well as the curricular experiences and options of individual students.

* In 1968, under the leadership of a new director of the Department of Health and Physical Education at East Stroudsburg State College, Arne Olson, a committee was appointed to revise the curriculum. The existing curriculum had been in effect for almost a decade and was a prescribed program for all students. The Curriculum Committee (Lura Evans, Jan Felshin, Betty Lou Murphy, Arne Olson, Maryanne Schumm, K. O. Sisson, Robert Sweeney) accepted the primary assumptions of the desirability of providing a flexible program, opportunities for specialization, and a more cohesive approach to the field of study. The curriculum was developed and refined and ultimately accepted by faculty and students.

As part of the reorganization of the college, Arne Olson became Dean of the School of Health Sciences and Physical Education, and William J. Penny became Head of the Department of Professional Physical Education in 1970 and responsible for the professional program in physical education. The statement preceding the curriculum was developed in the fall of 1971 by a committee appointed specifically for that purpose (Jan Felshin, Betty Lou Murphy, Herb Weber). The chairman of the committee, Jan Felshin, invited any interested faculty to meet with the committee, and William J. Penny and Feno Volpe did.

It is obvious that this rationale and the curriculum itself are outgrowths of the framework presented in this text. At the same time, "perspectives" do not always reflect the same degrees of understanding and/or acceptance, and individuals, faculties, or departments committed to the kinds of tasks of concern here must be viewed as continually "in process" with reference to actual views or practices.

FIELD OF STUDY

Whereas many academic disciplines exist as clearly ordered and agreed-upon bodies of knowledge, those responsible for professional preparation in physical education must usually begin by identifying the field of study as a primary source for purposes of the program. Different institutions have approached this task from diverse perspectives and starting points. Generally, however, there is some agreement that the focus of physical education is on the study of man-in-motion. This focus may be expressed in the study of human movement, forms of movement, and experiences in movement and its forms. The academic focus of physical education is the knowledge related to these perspectives of the scope of study. Physical education is, of course, responsible for the identification and ordering of knowledge and for generating new knowledge as part of the theoretical development of the field. The diversity of the scope of knowledge with which it is concerned and the modes of inquiry appropriate to the generation of knowledge have usually meant that, although an individual may be conversant with the scope of the field, he is able actually to seek the production of new knowledge in limited aspects.

There are difficulties attendant to the process of identifying purposes on the basis of the field of study. In its long existence as educational programs, and in its close professional alliances with such fields as health education, recreation, and even safety education, physical education has been characterized by its essential concern with the welfare and development of children and youth. Furthermore, practitioners in physical education have been teachers, almost exclusively, and the student entering this field has pursued experiential answers to the question of how to become a good teacher.

The future of physical education in higher education depends upon the willingness and ability of those involved to use the field of study as a source of purposes without reference to its professional existence. This is not to suggest that all purposes derive from knowledge in the field of study, but it does presume that the ability to discriminate between the concerns of the field of study and those of educational demand is requisite to the development of the field.

The primary assumption of degree programs in physical education is that there is a distinct field of study underlying physical education. The purposes of the program in higher education must suggest that understanding the scope and the significance of the field of study is of primary importance. Students may not develop the ability to contribute to new knowledge and theoretical development during their undergraduate preparation, but it seems desirable that they should gain enough ability within at least some aspects of the field and its related modes of inquiry to make this a viable possibility for the future. There is, of course, a widely variable interpretation of the nature of what is "significant" in the field of study of physical education. Without clear commitments by the profession of physical education or imperatives from a structured academic discipline, the most acceptable position in relation to the value of various knowledge concerns would seem to be to include them as options for student consideration.

There is one other obvious aspect of the complexity of the field of study of physical education. Because human movement and sport, dance, and exercise exist as expressive and nonverbal form, understanding this field depends upon experiential dimensions. This means that acquaintance with the scope and any aspect of the significance of the study of man as he engages in movement or its forms implies both traditional approaches to knowledge and the experiencing of the sources of knowledge as well.

The rationale for physical education degree programs in higher education, without reference to the ultimate use of knowledge by the student, includes the following assumptions about the field of study:

1. There is a distinct and identifiable field of study underlying physical education; its focus is the body of knowledge concerning man as he pursues and engages in movement or its forms, either for their own sake or for his own enhancement.
2. The significance of the body of knowledge underlying physical education lies in the potential contribution of this field to human welfare as an outgrowth of knowledge that (a) seeks to explicate and describe movement as both a biomechanical or sociocultural phenomenon, (b) provides understanding of sport, dance, and exercise as forms that utilize movement in primary relationship of human and symbolic characteristics, and (c) concerns the experiencing of movement forms as personal, social, and aesthetic modes and meanings.
3. Knowledge in the field of study underlying physical education is developed and understood as a result of both cognition and nonverbal experiencing, and is subject to diverse theoretical approaches and modes of inquiry.
4. The field of study suggests obvious implications for use in contributing to the quality of human existence.

As an outgrowth of these assumptions, the following purposes for programs of physical education leading to degrees in higher education can be identified:

1. To be familiar with the scope of knowledge appropriate to the field of study underlying physical education, and to be able to discriminate among the various perspectives within which knowledge can be viewed and generated.
2. To be able to analyze the significance of knowledge in the field of study in at least one theoretical mode and relate that knowledge in logical ways to other aspects of the scope of concerns.
3. To experience both cognitive and nonverbal approaches to understanding human movement and its forms in ways that are meaningful enough to allow for expressive uses of knowledge.

4. To pursue the generation of new knowledge or theoretical understanding by applying modes of inquiry to ideas and data appropriate to the field of study underlying physical education.
5. To recognize the potential applications of the field of study in contributing to the welfare of man.

PROFESSION

Commitments about the nature and scope of professional preparation derive primarily from beliefs about appropriate roles and responsibilities of teachers within the context of education. Although individuals may utilize professional preparation in physical education as a basis for the pursuit of allied professions or may become practitioners in related fields, programs in general relate to educational conceptions. This does not mean that the program precludes the opportunity for individuals to major in physical education without meeting requirements for teacher certification. It does mean, however, that the curriculum in general is based on the demands of excellence in working with people, especially in the programming of movement experiences designed to fulfill the potential contributions of the field of study to the welfare of humanity.

Somehow, in the development of the vast system of education in the United States, schools have become vulnerable to contemporary indictments of them as joyless, dehumanized, and irrelevant institutions. If education is to be a viable institution, those concerned with the preparation of teachers must define their tasks in relation to goals that hold more promise for the individual in a complex and difficult social and human environment. This implies that the assumptions underlying teacher education programs must include perspectives of the field of study in relation to its applications in humanistic contexts.

The pervasive concept of "profession" is that of contributing to human welfare and serving humanity. It is this concept, rather than technical competence alone, that provides the basic commitment for professional preparation. The field of study of physical education contains an obvious potential contribution to the improvement of the individual and human condition. Knowledge contained in the field of study is focused on man as he pursues movement and its forms either for their own sake or for his own enhancement. The direct application of that knowledge is relevant to both self-realization and experiencing of joy and meaning and to functional development of the organism and its capacities.

It would seem that these potential uses of physical education are especially appropriate to a conception of education as a humanistic process, concerned with the concepts of meaning and relevance that enable individuals to develop and learn, and committed to the importance of capacity and ability as the central focus of education.

The program of teacher education must express rational and related views of both the field of study and its application within the roles of the teacher suggested by a view of education committed to individual and humane purposes. Such a program depends on the involvement of the student in the development of his own understanding, growth, and competence. Furthermore, it implies the responsibility of each individual to seek and refine his own commitments within the field of study and the educational context. The concepts of humanism, meaning and relevance, and capacity and ability are especially dependent upon experiential dimensions; that is to say, if these ideas are to serve the teacher in fulfilling his roles, then he must come to understand them in his own life and experience.

The rationale for physical education as professional preparation includes the following assumptions about the roles of the teacher:

1. The most pervasive source for understanding school programs and desirable roles of the teacher depends upon cognizance of the potential contributions of subject areas to the life of man and the humanistic and ethical context of education.
2. Any teacher behaves according to the beliefs and values he perceives about his role and responsibilities with reference to his field of study and youth; the behavior and methods of the teacher are crucial variables in the educational milieu.
3. Teachers formulate goals and purposes, select and structure experiences for students, and evaluate students and programs; this is done within particular educational settings and in relation to students who have been classified according to chronology or accomplishment.
4. The roles of the teacher in planning and carrying out program experiences are related to his knowledge and beliefs about the field of study, the individuals involved, how learning takes place, and what an appropriate image of the teacher is.
5. Excellence in teaching depends upon continual and rational refinement of understanding and commitment and abilities relevant to the roles of the teacher, and in physical education these include the use of movement as communication and expression.

As an outgrowth of these assumptions, the following purposes for professional preparation in physical education can be identified:

1. To perceive and value the importance of the contribution of physical education to the life of individuals and humanity, and to accept a moral imperative for improving the quality of individual and social existence.
2. To accept the responsibility for growth and understanding as a lifelong commitment to the application of rational and ethical processes to the development of increasing excellence in all aspects of teaching and educational and professional interaction.
3. To refine and improve understanding and ability within the field of study as it is applied in education as meaningful and relevant experience in the life of man and focused toward enhancing the opportunities of youth to develop abilities and pursue self-realization in movement experiences.
4. To be able to explicate a framework of understanding about physical education that expresses its potential contributions to humanity within the educational process, and to modify and enlarge the conceptual bases with changing insights about the field of study, education, the society, and the individual as a person and a learner.

DEPARTMENT

The commitments and beliefs of particular faculties are expressed in the programs that they plan and supervise, as well as in the myriad decisions that are made about curriculum, students, or any other contextual variable. Whether explicated or not, the perspectives within which programs exist are most clearly identified by analysis of the actual processes purveyed. Confusion and cognitive dissonance can characterize programs, and when they do, it remains for each individual member of a faculty to "make sense" out of his own environment by applying his rationale to the realities of the situation and simply ignoring the dissonant factors or coming into conflict with them and seeking resolution. Obviously, this is not desirable, nor is it ethical in relation to professional preparation; for both the field of study and the whole educational enterprise of our society depend upon the integrity and wisdom of those responsible for preparing teachers. Furthermore, there is every reason to believe that the student subject to nonintegrative experiences in his professional preparation simply "screens out" many of his experiences. Responsible departments must make an effort to subject their beliefs and knowledge to rational processes toward the goal of developing cohesive points of view and integrative curricular and personal experiences for students.

Since education is almost always an "ongoing concern," it is not untenable to begin to explicate a rationale for the program with the program that exists, especially if that program has been changed recently. That is to say one can gain insight into his beliefs and values by analyzing the ways in which he has expressed them. At the same time, every rational safeguard must be employed to prevent those involved from the human impulse to justify the past and protect against demands for too much change and adjustment.

The rationale for the curriculum in the Department of Professional Physical Education at East Stroudsburg State College includes the following assumptions:

1. The curriculum represents a wide range of knowledge and diverse approaches to both the field of study and conceptions of the roles of the teacher.
2. The curriculum is based on recognition of the individual differences of students and the diversity of the field of study insofar as these are dynamic concerns requiring flexible approaches.
3. There is an agreed-upon core of experiences requisite to a cohesive view of physical education and potential roles within it, but there is also opportunity for individuals to select options appropriate to their own goals and to seek the development of specialized abilities.
4. The program is carried on in relation to legal and institutional guidelines and provisions and is responsible to fulfill its purposes in relation to these as well as to the nature of experiences provided by other curricular areas.
5. The curriculum is designed primarily as teacher preparation, but there

is opportunity for those who do not wish to prepare to teach to pursue a course of study in relation to the field of study of physical education.

6. Professional excellence requires a commitment to knowledge and growth that transcends the curriculum; this perspective is fostered by affirmation of broad competence at the highest levels as the desired goal and evaluative standard.

7. The curriculum represents a cohesive view of its sources in the field of study and conceptions of the roles and demands of teaching.

PROGRAM

I. Scope of the Curriculum

A. This proposal is concerned only with courses offered by the Professional Physical Education Department for students pursuing a major within the department.

1. In addition to the major, students who wish to be certified to teach would take approximately 22 semester hours in Professional Education, including student teaching.

2. All students within the College must satisfy the requirements in General Education.

3. The total number of semester hours required for a degree is 128.

B. Because this represents a major in physical education (rather than health and physical education), *separate certification for physical education is assumed.*

C. Within this curriculum there is opportunity for those students who so desire to choose to specialize as follows: as an elementary school physical education teacher; as a secondary school physical education teacher; as a discipline-oriented physical education major; as an activity specialist in aquatics, dance, gymnastics, individual sports, or team sports; or as a generalist in physical education.

D. Within this proposal, there is a core of requirements which applies to all students pursuing a major; and, therefore all students who graduate in this curriculum will be professionally qualified physical educators, but they may develop a special strength as well.

II. Core of Requirements for All Physical Education Majors

A. Professional Theory Courses	Semester Hours
1. Introduction to Physical Education	3
2. Curriculum and Evaluation in Physical Education	3
3. Movement and the Learning Process	3
Total	9

B. Discipline Core Courses	
1. Kinesiology	3
2. Physiology of Exercise	3
3. Psycho-social Aspects of Activity	3
Total	9

C. Activity Courses (each course is one semester hour)   Semester Hours
   1. Courses representing each of the classifications of
      activity based upon body movement listed below.
   2. A selection representing both a team and an
      individual sport.
   3. Courses representing area of specialization,
      if chosen.
   4. Elective courses to a minimum total of 13
      semester hours

Total   13

BODY CONTROL	DIRECT CONTROL OF AN OBJECT	INDIRECT CONTROL OF AN OBJECT
Gymnastics	Basketball	Archery
Swimming	Bowling	Badminton
Diving	Football	Baseball
Dance	Handball	Field hockey
Wrestling	Soccer	Golf
Skiing	Volleyball	Lacrosse
Ice skating		Softball
		Squash
		Tennis

The above classification of activities is based upon the relationship of body movement to the objective of the activity: *body control* in some kind of environment or with a specific focus; the *direct control* of an object by the body; or the *indirect control* of an object with an intermediate object.

III. Specialization by Level (Each activity course is one semester hour and each theory course is three semester hours.)

Each area of specialization requires a minimum of 6 semester hours of specified activity courses and 6 semester hours of theory courses. Certification programs would include Methods and Student Teaching, which would be done at one level or at both elementary and secondary levels. Opportunities for combining specializations are available.

A. Generalist
   1. Activity: Aquatics, Dance, Gymnastics, Movement Experiences for Preschool Children, Movement Experiences for Primary Grade Children, Movement Experiences for Intermediate Grade Children
   2. Theory: Organization and Administration of Physical Education, Theory and Research in Elementary Physical Education, Care and Prevention of Athletic Injuries

B. Elementary
   1. Activity: Movement Experiences for Preschool Children, Movement Experiences for Primary Grade Children, Movement Experiences for Intermediate Grade Children, Rhythmics, Dance for Elementary Grade Children, Gymnastics and Tumbling for Elementary Grade Children
   2. Theory: Theory and Research in Elementary School Physical Education, Organization and Administration of Physical Education, First Aid Certification

C. Secondary
   1. Activity: Aquatics, Dance, Gymnastics, Individual or Dual Sport, Personal Development, Team Sport
   2. Theory: Organization and Administration of Physical Education, Care and Prevention of Athletic Injuries

IV. Activity Specialization (Specialization in Aquatics, Dance, Gymnastics, Individual Sports, or Team Sports)

  A. Activity: A minimum of 6 semester hours in the specific activity area. Experience in some organized extra-class form of the activity. Qualification in the area as certified by the faculty. Pursuit of two sports to the highest level offered if it is an Individual or Team Sport Specialization.
    1. Aquatics: Basic Aquatics, Survival Training and Life-saving Techniques, Water Safety Instructor, Aquatic Sports
      Plus 2 Electives: Skin and Scuba Diving, Competitive Aquatics, Small Crafts
    2. Dance: Rhythmics, Beginning Dance Techniques, Intermediate Dance Techniques, Advanced Dance Techniques, Social Dance Forms, Dance Composition
    3. Gymnastics: Basic Gymnastics, Intermediate Gymnastics, Theory of Gymnastics (2 credits), Gymnastic Coaching (2 credits)
    4. Individual Sports
      Note: 1. Number in ( ) indicates number of courses being offered. This represents Level I and Level II experiences.
           2. * indicates a coaching class will be offered in addition to the number of courses listed.
      Archery (2), Badminton (1), Bowling (1), Fencing (1), Golf (2), Ice Skating (1), Riflery (1), Skiing (2), Squash and Handball (1), Tennis (2), Track and Field (2)*, Wrestling (2)*
    5. Team Sports
      Baseball (2)*, Basketball (2)*, Field Hockey (2), Football (2)*, Ice Hockey (1), Lacrosse (2), Soccer (2), Softball (2), Volleyball (2)

  B. Theory: Two of the following depending upon the area (6 semester hours) Conditioning Theory (prerequisite: Physiology of Exercise), Analysis of Sport Skills (prerequisite: Kinesiology), Contemporary Sport, Psychology of Sport, Dance Theory (creative forms), Dance Theory (social forms)

V. Academic Specialization

  A. Activity: No specific activities required; 13 elective semester hours required
  B. Theory: Historical Concepts of Movement and Sport, Philosophical Concepts of Movement and Sport

VI. Suggested Electives for Majors in Physical Education

  A. Theory courses required in any specialization

  B. Safety Education, Health Education, Recreation Education, Outdoor Education, Athletic Training, Adapted Physical Education

VII. Certification Requirements

    The certification requirements in physical education will include 36 semester hours and/or competency as specified by the curriculum program defined previously. In addition, the person would need to satisfy the general education requirements of the institution as well as the professional education requirements and student teaching or the equivalent.

CONSIDERATIONS FOR A REVISED DANCE CURRICULUM

Edrie Ferdun*

What is really important is that students have *significant encounters* with *people, processes, structures,* and *perspectives* out of which each can build himself and use his powers and dance within the framework of his personal and social values.

The most important thing is the people, for they are living embodiments of process, structure, and perspective, but there is more than any set of unique individuals can embody or exemplify. The student must work through his own processes, command and build his own structures, and, most importantly, achieve his own perspective. This most often involves going to source data and experience. Commitment to a goal of this kind distinguishes "higher education" from most professional training.

DANCE

The question is what processes, structures, and perspectives can best bring students, in a period of approximately four years, to real understanding and competence to employ dance for the greater good of themselves and the society.

For me the fundamental dance *cycle*—forming dances, dancing, appreciating, and relating (synthesizing)—provides the first basis for curriculum planning in dance. Seen in process and structure terms, the following kinds of things come to mind:

Processes	Structures
Performing	
Moving—awareness, control, freedom, command	Body
	Movement patterns
Dancing—expressive quality; artistry	Techniques
	Dances
Choreographing	
Creating—acceptance, spontaneity	Image, idea
Forming—aesthetic quality, craft	Motion, media
	Forms, structures
	Dances

* This statement was prepared and distributed to the Dance Faculty, Temple University, in January, 1971, just prior to meetings for the purpose of revising the curriculum in dance.

Appreciating
    Perceiving—sensitivity, openness   Art-social content
    Grasping—insight, awareness   Forms, styles
                                          Dances

Relating
    Analyzing—knowledge, vocabulary,   Man
                tools   Art
    Synthesizing—understanding,   Culture
              perspective   Process

It seems to me that all dance majors must have experiences with these processes and structures in order to grasp the meaning and significance of dance. How competent they become as choreographers, dancers, audience members, scholars, or critics will depend on their unique talents and the depth and duration of their study in these and related areas. The curriculum should provide this opportunity to the limit of available resources.

EDUCATION

A commitment to the teaching of dance in public education provides the basis of another framework for curriculum planning. In a sense, there is a similar cycle for consideration involving planning, teaching, evaluating, and relating. These processes and structures and perspectives are similar for all kinds of teachers and demand appropriate experiences and opportunities.

But to teach a "subject," dance, one must know it in a special way; that is, understand and be able to program its processes and forms rather than just being able to use them personally.

The teacher of dance needs to understand children, learning, the school as a social structure and a phenomenon in relation to dance, what it is, how it works, and what it can do.

CURRICULUM SEQUENCE AND STRUCTURE

The curriculum we come up with will represent not only a concept of the nature of dance itself and dance in education, but our understanding of our students, how they can best learn and grow, and the potentials and limitations of our environment and resources.

It seems to me we learned or should have learned some important things about this over our short year of existence, and our resources and potentials have obviously changed. I know I have several suggestions which I would like considered.

First, beginnings are important, maybe even crucial, for students and faculty. I suggest a "First Course" with a full range of real experiences moving, improvising, composing, watching, reading, talking and being . . . involving all the dance faculty and all the dance major students on occasion. I would see this as a 4-credit course meeting two hours each day.

As far as the "Dance Forms" courses go, I suggest we work toward adding Jazz, Afro, and Mime to our current offerings of Modern, Ballet, and Ethnic; that we make no distinction between beginning, intermediate, and major courses but make them all 2-credit courses; that they be offered at two or three levels of accomplishment: beginning, intermediate, advanced. I suggest we consider Children's Dance and Social and Square Dance in terms of the needs of the prospective dance teacher in the schools.

I suggest we rethink the "composition" experiences. Instead of two 3-credit courses, perhaps it would be a good idea to have a number of 2-credit composition courses, each representing a different approach with different instructors: Improvisation and Game Forms, Group Constructions, Dance Drama, Preclassic Forms, and so forth. This might have the advantage of extending the growth experience, while allowing individuals to begin where they think best.

The Dance "appreciation" and perspectives courses still puzzle me. Perhaps, if they were in the junior and/or senior years following after two previous years of dance study, they might be perceived in their relevance. A 4-credit course in historical or anthropological studies meeting one hour and twenty minutes three days per week would seem wiser for the undergraduate.

The courses designed to help the teacher understand what is going on in movement and dance should be reshaped to meet our purposes better. Kinesiology should be a part of a course in Movement Analysis. I suggest we have a course which looks at the human body and movement in relation to structure and function; this course would aim at developing greater perceptual acuity and ability to articulate about what is or should be going on in movement. Notation might be included in this course as a symbolic system for manipulating movement. I see this as a 4-credit course.

I believe in the need for a Dance Processes course to deal with the phenomena of dancing, performing, creating, appreciating, and so forth. The teacher's grasp of these processes will determine the methodological and curricular decisions he makes. It is possible that this course should also be a 4-credit course with some studio and observation time built in.

Experiences with sound, media, and production are supporting the composition courses; they are part of creation and actualization in dance, but they are also technical problems for teachers. I believe they might be handled together in the latter context, assuming they would be integrated in the composition courses as well. I suggest we consider a 4-

credit production course which is team taught by qualified members of appropriate faculties.

As to the experiences for students to better understand children, learning, the school, why-what-and-how to teach, I think we must in part trust the College of Education in their requirements of Growth and Development and Learning, both of which have been changed to 4-credit courses with agency and/or tutorial experiences.

I think we need to do more, however, which is related specifically to dance and teaching. I propose that we consider setting up a regularly scheduled movement-dance program for community children, perhaps in six-week blocks during the middle of each semester with classes scheduled twice a week just after school. We, students and faculty, would direct and teach the program. Freshman and sophomores might be helpers with juniors, seniors, and graduate students having primary responsibilities. This might be handled in relationship with the Educational Psychology courses and a Dance Methodology course in our department.

Student teaching in the schools, a certification requirement, needs to be examined. I think it can provide good experience to grow on, but as to how to schedule it and make it most profitable, I am not sure. Finding schools with dance programs and making supervision helpful are problems. I do believe that the student teachers' effectiveness in the schools will make considerable difference in the future of dance in public education in the Philadelphia area. Perhaps we should acknowledge the "missionary" character of dance teaching and in some way prepare our students for that, if such is possible.

Perspective regarding education in today's world is something I think each student needs to work out. Up until now there has been a Foundations of Education requirement which, I presume, is intended to help students achieve this. Is there something we should do or ask the Foundations of Education Department to do for us in this regard? Should we offer a Perspectives on Dance in Education seminar or require the Aesthetic Foundations of Education course or presume it will happen without building in the intent in curricular structure?

WORKSHOPS AND PERFORMANCES

Should workshop and production activities be built into the curricular structure or remain extracurricular? It seems to me some could and should be within the context of the Temple curriculum, and some should be freer, open, and more flexible. I think we do have a role to play in the dance community that goes beyond our students, but I also think we have responsibilities to our students for their greatest growth and opportunity.

Perhaps a course in Dance Repertory could be a place for qualified students to learn and dance in choreographed works. Dances by outside artists, faculty, and students could be produced. Performances, whether lecture-demonstrations or concerts, would be billed accordingly—Temple University Dance Repertory-Spring 1971. I am presuming auditions, course credit, and scheduled time. I am also presuming a role for the dancers in selecting choreography, whenever possible, and the rights of a choreographer to say "no."

Workshops and productions small to grand could also exist in another context. Group work and individual student and faculty choreography should be going on and shared throughout the year. The beginnings of these rest with the idea group or individual. When selection of dancers needs to take place for specific works, open auditions should be held under the direction of an elected audition board, with the idea group or choreographer having primary authority in the selection. Nonstudent dancers should be welcome to audition.

REQUIREMENTS—POLICIES

Dance majors should begin their work the first semester of the freshman year, but sophomores should have a good chance of successfully completing the program in their three remaining years. Only rarely, when we are satisfied that previous work and accomplishment warrants it, should juniors be accepted into the dance major. If a student transfers to Temple for his junior and senior years and wishes to major in dance, he should be carefully evaluated. If he is not superior in background but moderately experienced and dedicated, he should have the opportunity to enter but with full knowledge that he will need to work an additional year. If we feel his background and experience are very limited, he should not be accepted into the program. All students should be evaluated toward the end of their first year for possible advisement out of the program or into special experiences within the program. Competency must be the dominant criterion for requirements and the ultimate graduation of each individual. There must be a means for individuals to work in ways that are most productive for them, and competency standards must be conceived in relation to an individual's goals and program focus.

DANCE CURRICULUM PROGRESS SUMMARY*

Purposes
    To serve Temple University students and the larger society by providing
        experiences and programs in the field of movement and dance.
    To provide opportunities to explore dance as a discipline and process of
        communication involving human movement.

* This was prepared by Edrie Ferdun to reflect the progress in curriculum revision, January 25, 1971.

To provide experiences to enable students to understand and use dance and movement as a potential means of meeting the challenges of a constantly changing society.

Program

Dance Forms (as movement experiences and technique):
Mime
Classical Ballet—Levels 1, 2, 3
Modern Dance—Levels 1, 2, 3, 4
Afro-American
Jazz
European Folk Dance
(Euro-) American Folk and Square Dance
Social Dance
    Note: Yoga, Aikido, Tai Chi, Gymnastics and acrobatics suggested to Health, Physical Education and Recreation majors are of interest to dancers

Composition (as process and form):
Improvisation
Small-group Forms
Large-group Forms
Dramatic Forms
Historical Forms (Preclassic Dance Forms)

Movement (as biophysical phenomenon):
Sources: anatomy, kinesiology, physiology, biomechanics, notation
Emphasis: perception, analysis, ability to use and apply
Form: one-year sequence—continuous interrelatedness of sources and processes with studio experiences

Cultural Perspectives (as anthropological-historical understanding)
Sources: history, anthropology, contemporary concerns
Emphasis: perspective, basic interrelationships (dance-man-culture)
Form: one-year sequence for breadth and direction regarding dance in culture; one-semester sequence devoted to twentieth century phenomena with studio experiences

Performance Environments:
Sources: lighting, sound, costuming, make-up, stage design
Emphasis: principles, bases for recognition and construction
Form: one semester with lab to be team taught with student required to assume a responsible role in a production as technical staff.

THE UNDERGRADUATE DANCE MAJOR AT TEMPLE UNIVERSITY*

The dance major program provides opportunities for students to explore and develop their abilities and understandings in dance for potential use as art and education. Students should consult with advisers in dance in order to discuss their competencies, needs, and future plans before enrollment in the dance major program. Although it is expected that students will begin their study in the freshman year, it is possible for sophomores and exceptional juniors to be accepted into the program.

As a framework to insure breadth of understanding and general education, the dance major is exposed to studies in the humanities, the social sciences, the natural sciences and mathematics, and human performance. The general education component of his program includes a total of 48 hours with a minimum of 24 hours distributed equally among the four areas.

CORE COMPETENCIES IN THE CONTENT AND PROCESSES OF DANCE

All dance majors are expected to understand the scope and sources of their field and to be able to relate themselves and their total experiences to the phenomenon of dance as manifested in the society.

To help the student achieve this understanding and to enhance his synthesis of related experience, an overall structure for study is provided in a continuous course involvement. A dance major begins his program with D-1 Movement and Meaning (4 semester hours) and continues in D-101 through 106 (1 semester hour) each subsequent semester until his final semester of D-201 (4 semester hours).

It is expected that the dance major will develop his ability and understanding in a wide range of techniques through daily movement experience in dance forms, achieving at minimum a mastery of the techniques and principles of modern dance and ballet. D-24 Advanced Modern Dance and D-32 Intermediate Classical Ballet represent appropriate levels of work in the respective dance forms.

The dance major is expected to understand the potentials of his medium with respect to content and form, including creative action and interaction in movement, achieving facility in the creative use of movement and music for choreography.

The student begins his developmental experience in choreography with D-70 Improvisation (2 semester hours) and then is asked to select two additional choreography courses from D-72 Small-Group Forms (2 semester hours), D-73 Large-Group Forms (2 semester hours), D-75

* This is the actual curriculum in the catalogue and in use at Temple University, Philadelphia, Pennsylvania, 1971.

Dramatic Forms (2 semester hours), and D-74 Pre-classic Dance Forms (2 semester hours). D-80 Music and Movement (2 semester hours) is also to be included in the early phases of dance major preparation.

The dance major is expected to understand dance in its historical and cultural aspects, including its roots and interrelationships, thereby achieving perspective for the present and future. D-310 Dance in Cultural Perspective (4 semester hours) and D-315 Forces and Figures in Twentieth-century Dance (3 semester hours) represent experiences considered essential to achieve this purpose.

DANCE PERFORMANCE CONCENTRATION

Those students whose primary goals relate to future participation in dance as a performing art are expected to extend their competencies in the above and related areas through additional courses in dance forms, choreography, and the related arts. They are expected to develop a range of artistic resources and skills applicable to the contemporary theater and actualize their abilities in performance and choreographic production D-380 Performance Environments (3 semester hours), D-374, 375 Dance Repertory (2-2 semester hours) and D-290 through 299 Independent Study in Dance (1-12 semester hours) represent appropriate avenues for this needed experimentation and achievement. All work is selected by the student and his adviser in relation to needed growth and development in dance as a performing art.

DANCE EDUCATION CONCENTRATION*

Students who desire to teach dance are expected to develop understanding and competencies in dance and education which will lead to effective and creative teaching.

The dance educator is expected to command a broad vocabulary of movement skills and dance forms and be able to use them imaginatively as content and method in the teaching situation. D-85 Children's Dance (2 semester hours) and selection of two from D-45 Afro-American Dance (2 semester hours), D-50 International Folk Dance (2 semester hours) and D-55 American Social Dance Forms (2 semester hours) should be included, in addition to Modern Dance and Classical Ballet as previously described.

It is necessary for the dance teacher to be able to analyze movement in its scientific and aesthetic aspects in order to communicate effectively in the learning process. PE 3 Analysis of Human Performance and Fitness (3 semester hours) is a course experience designed to develop this competency. Dance major students are grouped in a single section to enhance relevance and application.

* Dance is not at present an approved area for teacher certification in Pennsylvania, (1971).

In order to understand the learner, effectively manipulate processes, and design experiences of value for educational objectives, the dance educator is expected to study the processes of learning, growth and development, and the innerworkings of these phenomena in his own field. Educational Psychology 101 and 102 (4-4 semester hours) along with D-303 Dance Processes (3 semester hours) are considered valuable experiences in the development of this competency.

D-286 through 289 Field Experience in Dance (1-12 semester hours) are considered very helpful to the sequential development of the dance teacher. Each student is expected to begin teaching early in his program, increasing his responsibilities to an intensive experience in a school or agency. Courses in the Department of Health, Physical Education and Recreation, 250 through 255 represent an alternative course series designed for development preparation of the teacher.

Program Distribution		Semester Hours
General Education	48	
Dance Core Experiences	36-44	
Applications (Education)	28-32	
or (Performing Arts)	20-28	
Electives	4-25	
Total	128	

EVALUATION

Evaluation of student work is provided within the context of each course and culminates in a grade which is recorded on a permanent transcript. It is expected that a dance major maintain at least a 3.0 grade point average in his field.

In addition to this cumulative account of specific course work, the dance student is considered and evaluated with respect to his total integration of sensitivity, skill, and understanding. Periodically the student meets with the faculty with whom he has worked for purposes of guidance and, in some instances, judgment as to his continuance or successful completion of the program.

DANCE COURSES AT TEMPLE UNIVERSITY

DANCE 1. MOVEMENT AND MEANING: Introduction (4 s.h.) 6 hrs./ wk.
  Experience in movement and sensory perception as sources of art and communication. Movement processes and forms are explored in relation to motivation and environment as an introduction to the study of kinesics.

DANCE 20-21.   MODERN DANCE: Elementary (2 s.h.) 3 hrs./wk.
Movement experiences designed to develop aesthetic and movement
concepts, skills, and sensitivities as a basis for performance and appreciation of modern dance.

DANCE 22-23.   MODERN DANCE: Intermediate (2 s.h.) 4 hrs./wk.
Movement experiences designed to extend range and control with increasing demand for sensitive performance of more complex dance
sequences.

DANCE 24-25.   MODERN DANCE: Advanced I (2 s.h.) 4 hrs./wk.

DANCE 26-27.   MODERN DANCE: Advanced II (2 s.h.) 4 hrs./wk.
Movement experiences designed to develop defined, authoritative and
sensitive performance in a full range of design, dynamic, and rhythmic
qualities as demanded of professional dancers.

DANCE 30-31.   CLASSICAL BALLET: Elementary (2 s.h.) 3 hrs./wk.
Study of the discipline of classical ballet designed to develop understanding and skill in the basic vocabulary.

DANCE 32-33.   CLASSICAL BALLET: Intermediate (2 s.h.) 4 hrs./wk.
Designed to extend the classical ballet vocabulary with increasing demands for sensitive performance of more complex combinations and
sequences.

DANCE 34-35.   CLASSICAL BALLET: Advanced I (2 s.h.) 4 hrs./wk.

DANCE 36-37.   CLASSICAL BALLET: Advanced II (2 s.h.) 4 hrs./wk.
Designed to develop defined, authoritative, and sensitive performance
in the full range of classical vocabulary as demanded of professional
dancers.

DANCE 40.   JAZZ DANCE: (2 s.h.) 3 hrs./wk.
Movement experiences designed to develop skill, sensitivity, and understanding as demanded by the jazz idiom.

DANCE 45.   AFRO-AMERICAN DANCE: (2 s.h.) 3 hrs./wk.
Movement experiences emphasizing African rhythms and sensitivities
as developed in contemporary Afro-American dance.

DANCE 50.   INTERNATIONAL FOLK DANCE: Elementary (2 s.h.) 3
hrs./wk.
Dances and movement experiences to develop basic skills, sensitivities,
and knowledge in ethnic dance and cultural traditions for recreation
and/or performance.

DANCE 51.   INTERNATIONAL FOLK DANCE: Intermediate (2 s.h.) 3
hrs./wk.
Dances and movement experiences to extend range and mastery of
skills, styles, and concepts in ethnic dance and cultural traditions for
recreation and/or performance.

DANCE 55.   AMERICAN SOCIAL DANCE FORMS: (2 s.h.) 3 hrs./wk.
Study of folk, square, and social dances designed for students to learn
requisite skills for recreational dance participation.

DANCE 60.   PANTOMIME: (2 s.h.) 3 hrs./wk.
Observation and reproduction of behavior and appearances leading to
building scenes of dramatic interest using the techniques of mime.

DANCE 70-71.   IMPROVISATION: (2 s.h.) 3 hrs./wk.
Experiences in the spontaneous use of movement in given situations involving stimuli derived from movement concepts, imagery, related
media, and physical extensions.

DANCE 72.   CHOREOGRAPHY: Small-Group Forms (2 s.h.) 4 hrs./wk.
Study and creative use of the disciplines of solo, duet, and other small-
group forms for a specific number of dancers.

DANCE 73.   CHOREOGRAPHY: Large-Group Forms (2 s.h.) 4 hrs./wk.
Study of the distinguishing characteristics and potentials of a large-
group body and the development of original movement forms and
structures.

DANCE 74. CHOREOGRAPHY: Preclassic Dance Forms (2 s.h.) 4 hrs./wk.
Study and exploration of the major dance forms of the fifteenth and sixteenth centuries such as pavane, galliard, and minuet. Experiences in creating contemporary dance studies with emphasis on thematic development in relation to preclassic musical forms.

DANCE 75. CHOREOGRAPHY: Dramatic Forms (2 s.h.) 4 hrs./wk.
Study and exploration of the sources and dynamics of dramatic encounter leading to a synthesis of movement and dramatic concepts in dance form.

DANCE 80. MUSIC AND MOVEMENT: (2 s.h.) 3 hrs./wk.
Designed to provide understanding of fundamental relationships between music and dance. Students will explore basic qualities and ways of forming in both media.

DANCE 85. CHILDREN'S DANCE: (2 s.h.) 3 hrs./wk.
Dance experiences and materials appropriate for use with children. Designed for prospective teachers, recreation leaders, and parents interested in the creative and developmental use of movement and the related arts.

DANCE 101-102. MOVEMENT & MEANING: Explorations (1 s.h.) 2 hrs./wk.

DANCE 103-104. MOVEMENT & MEANING: Encounters (1 s.h.) 2 hrs./wk.

DANCE 105-106. MOVEMENT & MEANING: Integrations (1 s.h.) 2 hrs./wk.

DANCE 201. MOVEMENT AND MEANING: Seminar (4 s.h.) 5 hrs./wk.
A consideration of kinesics as it relates to current thought in art and education. Critical issues are identified, researched, and discussed as students work together to achieve professional perspective.

HPED 250. MICROTEACHING IN DANCE: (1 s.h.) 2 hrs./wk.

HPED 251. A TUTORIAL EXPERIENCE IN DANCE: (1 s.h.) 2 hrs./wk.

HPED 254. THE SCHOOL ENVIRONMENT: (2 s.h.) 4 hrs./wk.

HPED 255. STUDENT TEACHING IN DANCE: (4-12 s.h.)

DANCE 280 thru 289. FIELD EXPERIENCE IN DANCE EDUCATION: (1-4 s.h.)
Designed to provide opportunities for guided experience in teaching and administering dance.

DANCE 290 thru 299. INDEPENDENT STUDY IN DANCE: (2-4 s.h.)
Designed to provide opportunities for individual projects in areas such as choreography, production, and history.

DANCE 303. DANCE PROCESSES: (3 s.h.) 3 hrs./wk.
A study of significant processes operant in dance such as training, performing, creating, and watching. Variables which affect these processes are identified.

DANCE 310. DANCE IN CULTURAL PERSPECTIVE: (4 s.h.) 3 hrs./wk.
Introduction to means and materials for exploring and understanding dance in relation to life, thought, and culture. Investigation of historical and cultural forces affecting the function and development of dance as art and ritual, social activity, spectacle, and entertainment.

DANCE 315. FORCES AND FIGURES IN TWENTIETH-CENTURY DANCE: (3 s.h.) 3 hrs./wk.
Study of contemporary dance; its impulses and forms explored through concerts, films, theories, techniques, reading, and discussions.

DANCE 320. PRINCIPLES OF DANCE PERFORMANCE: (3 s.h.) 4 hrs./wk.
Study of the role of the performer in relation to the artistic demands of dance. Performance concepts are synthesized and principles developed.

DANCE 374. DANCE REPERTORY: (2-2 s.h.)
DANCE 375. DANCE REPERTORY: (2-2 s.h.)
   Dancers who have auditioned successfully serve as members of a dance
   company gaining experience in public dance performing.
DANCE 380. PERFORMANCE ENVIRONMENTS: (3 s.h.) 3 hrs./wk.
   Sound, light, and physical properties explored as means of environ-
   mental image-making in relation to movement. Participation in studies
   and demonstrations to discover interrelationships.

Chapter IX

UTILIZING THE CONTENT OF THIS BOOK

Maryanne M. Schumm

As one carefully examines the content of this text, it soon becomes obvious that to include it successfully in a college course requires extensive and careful preparation. Those of us in the area of teacher preparation, who are working with this information, recognize its importance in the future of physical education and in the lives of the students involved. We have, therefore, attempted to coordinate and refine our efforts with reference to the organization and presentation of material and have been guided by several underlying agreements.

We feel that it is desirable that students be confronted with the scope of this content during the freshman year in college. The material and the implied process suggest a framework for organizing and defining the knowledge within the field of physical education. If the student understands the intent and structure of the framework, all future knowledge has much more meaning, as it is seen in an organized perspective. The framework may change, but, hopefully, the practices of relating concepts and questioning purposes will have been accepted. Rather than attending to isolated courses for four years, the aware student should find his subjects more meaningful, as they merge in an all-pervasive concept of physical education. For this reason, we offer this course as an initial experience, but the possibility of students taking this course during the second semester of the freshman year should be considered. This would allow the student time for orientation to college life in general, and might help prepare him for the techniques used in the course. At the same time, recognizing methods of intelligence and developing rational approaches to knowledge are always desirable, and upperclassmen, graduate students, and faculty also find our approach interesting and meaningful.

Many of our students have conservative, small-town backgrounds, and some have never had the opportunity to participate in a discussion. There is no doubt that this material is challenging for college freshmen to grasp. Many spontaneously reject the new knowledge that causes familiar areas, such as sport, to become suddenly and unbearably complex. There is also no doubt that the field of physical education is becoming defined in a more scholarly way. To violate passively accepted and outdated traditions is precisely the responsibility of those working with this material. Today's professional student must be committed to understanding the theoretical framework of physical education, and must avoid being content with haphazardly wading through all the potential and practical applications of its parts. It should be the teacher's goal, through example and creation of the proper atmosphere, to foster that spirit of scholarly commitment on the part of the student. Hopefully, he will then be better able to examine before accepting, to interrelate new data, to analyze critically, to innovate, and to remain open to new and creative ideas and insights within his field.

A few years ago, we abandoned the self-contained class in favor of a large lecture/small discussion technique. The large lecture serves the purpose of providing a common core of material, while the small discussion groups help the students become personally involved in the material, with the guidance of the teacher. Some of the more successful small-group procedures now being utilized in our situation are described in the following pages. Hopefully, these will aid both teacher and student to work with the material in a variety of interesting ways. For those of us who have been involved in teaching a course under the present structure, it has been evident that the methods and processes used are crucial to the general comprehension and acceptance of the content by the students.

The experiences and assignments suggested here must, of course, be personalized and individualized for maximum effectiveness in each situation. Many of these ideas have been modified several times and are still being changed or updated. At times, it really is as exciting to work with new methods as it is with new content material. Creativity in adding to the suggestions presented can only enhance both the material and student experiences.

It is hoped that students reading this section will appreciate and gain a deeper insight into the attempts that are made to aid their comprehension of the course content. They may wish to suggest modifications or present new procedural ideas to the instructor in the situation. For the purposes of organization, the material is divided into four areas: Class Experiences, Assignments, Hand-outs/Circulating Material, Questions.

CLASS EXPERIENCES

Course Structure

After experimenting with several course structures, the one used as the basis for this chapter seems to be the most feasible. This consists of a one-hour lecture, attended by all students and discussion leaders, followed immediately by a one-hour small-group discussion. If a discussion leader has two sections, they combine for this discussion. No leader is ever assigned more than two sections, and each section has a maximum of fifteen students. Later in the week each group meets separately with its discussion leader. Generally, but not necessarily, the discussion after the lecture focuses on the lecture, while the second discussion deals with topics chosen by the group and/or discussion leader. The core content and framework are supplied in the lecture, while the discussion leader supplements this information and guides student discussion to aid understanding.

Atmosphere

Stimulating and thought-provoking discussion will occur only when the discussion leader works to create an atmosphere conducive to student participation. An informal, tension-free environment that focuses away from the leadership role of the teacher and places it on the students is, of course, the ideal one. This allows the teacher to assume a position of guidance, while students learn to gain respect for each other's opinions. Several techniques are suggested:

1. *Circular Discussions.* On the first day, ask students to arrange chairs in a circle. Although seemingly insignificant, it is important to consider several factors.
   a. Include everyone in one circle. A double circle creates an "in" and an "out" group, which is not desired at this time.
   b. All chairs in the circle should be occupied—empty chairs should be removed. The closeness created by the smallest possible circle adds to the informality. A large circle causes people to shout rather than talk, putting an unnecessary strain on communication.
   c. Remove empty chairs from the center of the circle. These at times can be barriers to discussion and are definite distractions.
   d. The circle should be "round" so everyone can see and be seen. Gestures and eye contact aid communication and should be visible to all.
   It often takes several days of reminders to "build a good circle." Students who have not participated in circle discussions feel very awkward at first, but in a short while feel uncomfortable with anything else. Simply explaining the reasoning behind such specific instructions usually results in complete cooperation.
2. *Introductions.* It is suggested that the entire first meeting period be spent on introductions. It helps to ask names, hometowns, summer jobs, travel and other experiences, and so forth, with the discussion leader volunteering the same information. Announce at the start that everyone is responsible for knowing classmate's first names as a first step toward interpersonal communication, and students will concentrate on each other. This will aid the discussion process tremendously. For several class periods it reinforces the responsibility if individuals are asked to name all classmates. Students begin

to recognize each other more quickly as individuals with thoughts and feelings, rather than as nameless faces.

a. Several forms of sensitizing experiences might be utilized the first day or so. One "gimmick" which works well is to have students get in groups of three or four and leave the classroom for about twenty minutes. Their object is to learn as much about each other as they can in that time. When they return, each in turn tells one interesting fact he learned about a specific person. It's fun and aids group cohesion.

Procedures

These are several organizational ideas that foster the discussion process:

1. Work toward a "no-hands" system of participating in discussions. Discourage students from raising hands before speaking or speaking only to the discussion leader. If students learn to talk to each other, the discussion leader becomes a group member and not an intermediary. Anytime a student raises a hand, he places the teacher in a leadership role. This tends to hinder spontaneous discussion, and students continue to rely on the teacher.

2. The manner in which class is started each day is important. School sports scores, news items of interest pertinent to the course, or the expression of any new idea or insight can be provided by students or the discussion leader at the beginning of the session. As the course proceeds, students should assume more responsibility for asking questions and choosing interesting discussion topics. The discussion leader, however, should always be prepared with alternative topics.

3. Try presenting a problem for examination, asking the class to reach some type of conclusion without teacher comment. Let the class find loopholes or strong points, or identify assumptions. This intellectual exercise, with little or no teacher interference, helps students gain confidence in themselves and their group, and affirms the usefulness of critical analysis.

4. A panel/group discussion can provide a unique learning opportunity. A successful example of this technique is as follows: Three discussion leaders met with all their students (about 100) in one room. The students formed small groups with both sexes and all sections represented in each group. The students assumed the roles of physical educators, while the discussion leaders portrayed a local board of education, composed of a farmer, an insurance salesman, and a clothing store owner. The board, after discussing physical education problems throughout the district, reached the conclusion that the physical education program should be dropped from the schools. Students were given forty minutes to discuss the problems (board

members left the room), and later presented their opinions to the board, which continued to react with conventional "lay" reasoning. Later a summation was offered by the discussion leaders, as professional physical educators, concerning the student responses in light of the course material. Students were extremely enthusiastic about this experience.

5. The use of "mini-groups" is effective at times. Three students per group seem to provide for maximum interaction. Groups can select their own topics, or discuss a preselected one. Always allow time for each group to share its ideas with the entire class.

6. If possible, occasionally change the class meeting place to student lounges, discussion leader's house, or another place to aid informality and group cohesion. One discussion leader's living room was cleared of furniture, students brought pillows, and the class enjoyed hearing a visiting recreational therapist. The examples and experiments during the session had a much greater impact due to the environmental change.

7. Call upon carefully chosen "qualified" personnel in different fields (administration, physiology, dance, sport) to join group discussions on different days. This serves to provide an opportunity for students to question various ideas presented in the framework and perhaps get a different point of view from that provided by either the discussion leader or the lecture.

8. One of the more successful and interesting techniques utilized by some discussion leaders is the "fishbowl" discussion group. The "fishbowl," used with the right group at the right time, works extremely well, and can be very exciting:

   a. Arrange chairs in the usual circle, but put four chairs facing each other, close together, in the center of the circle.

   b. Determine whether the discussion topic will be assigned or spontaneous, or suggested by the leader. A controversial suggestion by the leader is preferable for the first experience.

   c. Three members of the class fill three chairs in the center, leaving the fourth seat vacant. Students may be volunteers or part of an assigned group.

   d. Only the three members in the center may speak to each other. They may not communicate with the outside circle, or vice versa. Nor may the outside members communicate with each other.

   e. Any time an "out" circle person wishes to speak, he must occupy the empty chair. If the fourth chair is filled, any of the others may vacate his seat and return to the "out" circle. No more than one chair may be vacant at any time.

   f. If all chairs are filled and an "out" person wishes to speak, he may tap anyone he wishes on the shoulder, and that person must immediately give up his chair.

g. It seems to work best if the discussion leader remains in the "out" circle most of the time, or enters when all chairs are filled so that he can speak and leave.

Since students in the outer circle have no responsibility, they tend to relax and listen more carefully to what is being said. Once a lively discussion ensues, students are eager to get into the middle to be heard. The novelty of the situation is appealing, and it actually aids the normal circle discussion.

The discussion leader should be careful to present all rules, explain the purpose of the technique, and possibly expect to experience a difficult time during the first attempt. Again, the choice of a controversial topic can do much to assure success the first time around.

ASSIGNMENTS

The following are suggestions for the types of assignments that may be utilized during the course to acquaint students with the material more effectively:

1. *Readings.* These should be chosen carefully to supplement the ideas that are most important in the different areas. The Selected Bibliography appearing at the end of each chapter should prove useful. In our situation, we also found it helpful to prepare folders of reproduced articles for our students. These were placed on "reserve" in the library.

2. *Worksheets.* These might contain pertinent questions concerning comparisons of articles read, clarification of ideas brought up in lectures, and so forth. A sample worksheet can be found in the Appendix. Worksheets may be used as in-class "exercises" or assignments, and provide important feedback.

3. *Quizzes.* These usually test concepts or ideas discussed in class or heard in lectures. Ideas may be found in the "Questions" section of this chapter.

4. *Word Lists.* Students are advised to keep a running list of new words or words used in new ways throughout the course. Examples might be "academic discipline," "denotation," and "theory." Every effort should be made to accustom students to clarifying terminology, using a dictionary as a gross source for definitions, and continually refining semantic usage.

5. *Area Synthesis.* A paper may be assigned at the end of each area of study. A typical question would be: "Write a paper summarizing Area 1—Physical Education as the Field of Study. Tie together in a meaningful way all the material you have read, heard, or dis-

8

cussed." This causes students to select the major issues, and gives the discussion leader a chance to clarify misconceptions before entering another area of study.

6. *Group Project.* Students work together in coed groups of three or four. Each group selects a topic it wishes to pursue, and later gets the class involved using a fishbowl or circle discussion, or whatever technique it wishes. Projects are interspersed throughout the semester.

7. *Final Evaluation of Concepts.* Given in written or individual verbal form, and as either an "in-class" or "take-home" exercise. Students may also prefer to tape record the final. Test should deal with concepts and not factual information. Refer to section on "Questions" for ideas.

HAND-OUTS/CIRCULATING MATERIAL

Hand-Outs

Information sheets compiled by the discussion leader, supplementary articles, or particular items of interest can often stimulate additional ideas. Possible "hand-outs" are listed below:

1. *Personal Data Sheet.* Filled out by students the first day. A sample sheet can be found in the Appendix.
2. *Reading Lists.* Generally compiled by each individual discussion leader, and kept as current and pertinent as possible.
3. *Course Outline.* A sample can be found in the Appendix.
4. *Course Framework Sheet.* See Appendix.
5. *Class Name Lists.* Includes names, addresses, and phone numbers of all persons in class.
6. *Historical Overview of Physical Education Chart.* See Appendix.
7. *Worksheets.* See Appendix for examples.
8. *Process Tools.* See Appendix for examples.
9. *"The Teacher."* See Appendix.
10. *"ABC's of Physical Education."* See Appendix.
11. *Code of Ethics of the Education Profession.* See Appendix.
12. *Readings.* Any article or statement that is desirable for all to have. See Appendix for example.
13. *Institutional Materials.* Any forms or statements where acquaintanceship is desirable. See Appendix for advising materials used at East Stroudsburg State College in conjunction with curriculum.

Circulating Material

This method is useful when only one copy of something is available, or you simply wish to expose students to different books and magazines in the field. Attach a class name list to the top of the article. Students check their names off after they read the material, and pass it on to someone who has not. The last person returns the article to the teacher. Be sure to keep a record of any important circulating materials so that they are returned. This method has received enthusiastic student support. Some suggested materials are:

1. Professional Periodicals (JOHPER, *The Physical Educator,* State Journal, etc.)
2. Faculty newsletters or other institutionally related materials.
3. Specific articles from periodicals or newspapers.
4. Sports Magazines: *Archery World, Golf Digest, Tennis World, Sports Illustrated, Women's Sports Reporter,* etc.
5. *Outlook* (AAHPER)—programs for the handicapped.
6. *Update* (AAHPER)—current events newspaper.
7. New books.
8. Photocopies of pertinent articles.

By providing a variety of articles and items, all students are sure to find something that captures their interest.

QUESTIONS

The following are sample guideline questions or statements like the ones appearing at the end of each chapter, divided by areas, which can help clarify the course content, provide topics for discussion, or be used to obtain feedback on student progress.

Area 1: *Field of Study*

1. Physical education cannot yet be considered an academic discipline, but the potential for that development is clear.
2. Although the field of study of physical education is human movement, physical education is not concerned with all the movements of humans.
3. A focus of study on *movement* as such would yield different understanding than a focus on *movement within its forms.*
4. What does a "critical evaluation" of an idea mean? How does one go about it?
5. What can we assume to be true about ourselves, our class, and appropriate goals for our study?
6. What seem to be areas in which study and understanding should be developed?
7. Why should we, as professional students and prospective teachers, be considering theory?
8. How should theory relate to practice?
9. Discuss physical education as a field of study.
10. Discuss: The proper focus of our field is the study of sport, not human movement.
11. What are some of the subject fields from which we would draw

material in order to understand biomechanical aspects of movement more fully?

12. Identify the *assumptions* in the following statements:

   a. "It's time to get rid of the 'frills and fads' in the schools: there should be more time devoted to such things as science and math, and things like shop, home economics, and physical education should be eliminated."

   b. "Sports like archery and golf are a waste of time and have no place in a good physical education program. If games must be played, soccer and field hockey are appropriate."

13. How does man find meaning in movement?

14. How does the tradition of physical education influence our present-day thinking?

15. How is sport a "suspension of the ordinary"?

16. What is the difference between an academic discipline, a field of study, and a body of knowledge?

17. What is the scope of concern with man and his movement if the only purpose is to understand it?

Area 2: *School Program in Physical Education*

1. Explain: The term "physical education," when used to refer to the school program, implies different concerns than when it is used to indicate the field of study.

2. Explain: Purposes for the school program of physical education must be based upon the body of knowledge of physical education, and must also be consistent with the concerns and nature of education.

3. How can one identify the purpose of schools and the role of education?

4. How can one clarify the role of physical education in the school in today's society?

5. What assumptions underlie the creation of a public school system which is free, universal, and compulsory?

6. Comment on: Purposes for the school program are ultimately expressions of the teacher's understanding and values.

Area 3: *Profession: Physical Educator*

1. What qualifications are necessary for this profession?

2. What skill development is necessary?

3. How may we grow professionally?

4. What is AAHPER?

5. Discuss some values, beliefs, and/or attitudes that are important for teachers to possess, and support their importance by relating them to concerns for our study.

6. Discuss how the beliefs one holds about (a) the field of study, (b) the characteristics and potential of man (the student), and

(c) the teaching-learning process affect one's behavior as a teacher in his various roles.
7. What kinds of attitudes should teachers hold?
8. Define a "good teacher."

SUMMARY

We are personally committed to attempting to generate, within our students, the enthusiasm and excitement we feel for the framework of knowledge presented here. This involves being constantly aware of new and pertinent ideas in the field, becoming more knowledgeable in the area of teaching behavior, and finding new and accurate ways of obtaining feedback from our students.

Success in our endeavors can only result in more alert students; students who are attuned to the changes within the field of physical education and education in general, and who will be better prepared, as future educators, to accept the challenges that these changes imply.

EXEMPLIFYING MATERIALS

Personal Data Sheet

Course Outline

Course Framework

Historical Overview Chart

Worksheets

Process Tools

"The Teacher"

"ABC's" of Physical Education

Code of Ethics of the Education Profession

"In Search of Self"

Advising Forms

EAST STROUDSBURG STATE COLLEGE
Department of Professional Physical Education

J. Felshin

Name_____

Personal Data Sheet

College Class:_____ Hometown:_____ Date of Birth:_____

Local Address_____ Phone Number_____

Why did you choose to major in physical education?

Have you had any experiences in physical education or teaching that you feel were important to you?

What are your favorite activities or sports?

Indicate the highest level of achievement you reached in particular activities or sports; i.e., varsity teams, dance club, etc.:

What do you think is the most important thing a physical education teacher does?

If you had three wishes, what would they be?

1.
2.
3.

Is there anything you feel the instructor of this class should know about you?

EAST STROUDSBURG STATE COLLEGE
Department of Professional Physical Education

M. Schumm

Course Outline: Introduction to Physical Education

An introduction to physical education as a field of study, school program, and a profession; includes an overview of the foundations and content of the body of knowledge of physical education and the development of theoretical contexts for its role in schools and its professional trends and implications.

Text: Felshin, Jan. *MORE THAN MOVEMENT: An Introduction to Physical Education.* Philadelphia: Lea & Febiger, 1972.

Focus: The course is focused toward the development of ideas and insights and an emerging cohesive point of view about physical education and its related professional fields from the standpoint of knowledge about:

   I. The Nature of the Field of Study (includes movement perspectives and content relative to the phenomena of movement and movement forms)

  II. The Purposes for School Programs of Physical Education (includes assumptions about the context within which schools exist: i.e., society, the individual, learning, and the structure of education)

 III. The Profession of Physical Education (includes study of the ways in which physical education teachers function in relation to students, society, schools, and the profession)

Evaluation: A. Contribution to the group
             B. Papers, Worksheets
             C. Group Project
             D. Concept Evaluations

EAST STROUDSBURG STATE COLLEGE
Department of Professional Physical Education

Physical education exists as a FIELD OF STUDY, PROGRAMS IN SCHOOLS AND COLLEGES, and a PROFESSION. Knowledge within the field of study is centered around the study of man as he pursues and engages in movement or its forms, either for their own sake or for his own enhancement. Curricula in physical education are programs developed on the basis of the field of study but within the context of education; that is, programs designed in light of knowledge about how education functions in our society and how individuals develop and learn. Presently, the profession of physical education is most concerned with teaching and learning, and is focused on the teacher and coach in their relationships to the field and its contexts.

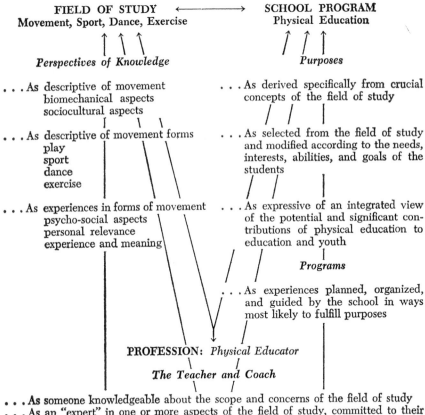

FIELD OF STUDY ←——————→ SCHOOL PROGRAM
Movement, Sport, Dance, Exercise   Physical Education

Perspectives of Knowledge   *Purposes*

. . . As descriptive of movement
        biomechanical aspects
        sociocultural aspects

. . . As descriptive of movement forms
        play
        sport
        dance
        exercise

. . . As experiences in forms of movement
        psycho-social aspects
        personal relevance
        experience and meaning

. . . As derived specifically from crucial
        concepts of the field of study

. . . As selected from the field of study
        and modified according to the needs,
        interests, abilities, and goals of the
        students

. . . As expressive of an integrated view
        of the potential and significant con-
        tributions of physical education to
        education and youth

Programs

. . . As experiences planned, organized,
        and guided by the school in ways
        most likely to fulfill purposes

PROFESSION: *Physical Educator*

The Teacher and Coach

. . . As someone knowledgeable about the scope and concerns of the field of study
. . . As an "expert" in one or more aspects of the field of study, committed to their importance, and a contributor (or interpreter) to them
. . . As someone committed to youth and education in our society and aware of what that involves as it exists and changes
. . . As a person who can be trusted to contribute to the lives of others, the good of society, and his own growth

IMPLICATIONS: *FIELD OF STUDY, SCHOOL PROGRAMS, PROFESSION*

EAST STROUDSBURG STATE COLLEGE
Department of Professional Physical Education

HISTORICAL OVERVIEW OF PHYSICAL EDUCATION IN SCHOOLS* IN THE UNITED STATES (1865-1970s)

The Nature of Education	As preparation for life, something "done to" the child, and training	As growth and development, something "done by" the whole child	As a social experience, something "done with others" in a group	As personal meaning in relation to knowledge
Implications	Formalized classroom Learning by listening 3 R's and repetition Mental discipline Transfer of training (wide turn of the nineteenth and twentieth centuries)	Learning by doing Understanding, process Objective evidence of mental development Education for complete living and Seven Cardinal Principles (1918)	Group-centered Learning by interaction EPC "Objectives of Education in a Democracy" (1938) Good citizenship Social behavior (1930s-1955)	Bodies of knowledge Academic disciplines Learning by insight and mastery Taxonomy of educational objectives (cognitive-affective) (1955-1970s)
The Nature of Physical Education	As remedial and corrective training, systematic exercise, and drill	As education; a medium for obtaining educational outcomes	As socialization; objectives derived from social concerns and focused on fitness for citizenship	As the art and science of human movement and the movement forms of sport, dance, and exercise

Implications	Formal drill Systems of gymnastics Remedial exercise Response to command	Natural programs Rejection of formal drill Games, sports, dance, developmental programs	Group processes Teams and team membership Lifetime sports Personal and social outcomes	Identification of concepts and knowledge Individual development Electives Movement as a source of meaning
Related Disciplines and Professional Preparation	Anatomy—Physiology Biological concerns Measurement Effects of exercise	Psychology—Education Teaching-learning process Tests and measurement	Sociology Total fitness Physical fitness Testing	Phenomenology—Self-theory—Cognition Movement and play All knowledge
Catch-phrases	Perspiration and peristalsis Physical training Middle third of the body Schoolroom stoop	Ontogeny recapitulates phylogeny Clean and manly athletics Education *through* PE Physically educated Better teaching through testing Individual differences	Education for citizenship in a democracy Life adjustment A sport for every player and a player for every sport	Individualizing instruction Education for meaning Relevance Sport as experience Excellence Realms of meaning

* Adapted from: Eleanor Metheny, "A Catch-Phrase Outline of Shifting Emphases in Physical Education in the United States, 1865-1955," mimeographed, 1955.

EAST STROUDSBURG STATE COLLEGE
Department of Professional Physical Education

J. Felshin

Worksheet # (sample)*

Name_____

Purpose: To develop understanding of a concept of the body of knowledge within the perspective of describing biomechanical aspects of movement:

Movement is related to human functioning and exists in a context of physical (mechanical) laws and principles.

IMPLICATIONS FOR STUDY (What we would have to know)	RELATED CONCEPTS (What we do know)	IMPLICATIONS FOR USE IN IMPROVING MOVEMENT (How an individual, on his own, would use this knowledge)

* This worksheet is an example of a way to approach both content and relationships; it could be used in class as a structure for discussion or as an assignment.

EAST STROUDSBURG STATE COLLEGE
Department of Professional Physical Education

J. Felshin

Worksheet #   (sample)*

Name_____

Identify the assumptions underlying the following statements. Do not argue or agree with the statement; simply identify the important beliefs that are implied by it and that you think must be related to it:

1. All these kids today need to "shape up." The school should see that they behave themselves properly and should insist on such things as proper dress and haircuts, and coaches, especially, must see that standards are maintained.

2. You can always tell whether or not a physical education teacher is any good by just looking at his class. If the students are in the proper uniform and well behaved, the teacher is doing a good job.

3. We need to bring our girls up to be ladies, and they should not wear pants and run around like boys. Girls should not be allowed to compete on teams, but all boys should have to.

4. The physical education teacher is the best counselor in the school; students look upon him as a friend and willingly confide in him.

5. It's time to get rid of the "frills and fads" in the schools; there should be more time devoted to such things as science and math and things like shop, home economics, and physical education should be eliminated.

6. It is much easier to "start with tight reins and then loosen them"; students have to learn that they "can't get away with anything."

7. Being a good performer has nothing to do with being a good teacher. In fact, the star athlete is very often a poor teacher.

* This worksheet is an example of the kinds of statements that might be given as an assignment to aid the clarification of ideas as well as logical processes; probably these statements and appropriate spaces would not appear on any one worksheet.

EAST STROUDSBURG STATE COLLEGE
Department of Professional Physical Education

J. Felshin

*Introduction to Physical Education**

Resume of content _____ (date)   Name _____

1. What were the important concepts illuminated in the discussion/presentation?

2. Questions or comments about today's class.

3. In your view, what would be the most logical focus for our next discussion?

EAST STROUDSBURG STATE COLLEGE
Department of Professional Physical Education

J. Felshin

Introduction to Physical Education

Resume of process _____ (date)   Name_____

1. How would you evaluate today's class in terms of our goals for individual growth and understanding?

2. Can you describe any occurrences that were particularly good or bad in their effects on individuals or the group?

3. Have you any comments or suggestions for the instructor as a result of today's class?

4. How would you evaluate your own feelings and understanding today?

* These may be used occasionally, or alternatively, and may be signed or anonymous.

EAST STROUDSBURG STATE COLLEGE
Department of Professional Physical Education

J. Felshin

Worksheet #   (sample)

Name_____

Purpose: To gather information for the purpose of setting up groups to work on the group project.

Opinions

1. If you had a choice, would you rather have groups assigned on the basis of selection of *people* or the selection of *content areas* of interest?

2. How many people do you think it would be desirable to have in each group? (Keep in mind the fact that each group will also make an oral presentation to the class.)

3. List specific questions that you think you would like to try to answer through your study; these must be appropriate to one of our three areas of focus.

4. Indicate the three people with whom you would most like to work if group assignments are made on this basis:

_____

_____

_____

5. Are there any people with whom you would prefer *not* to work?

_____ reason: _____

_____ reason: _____

6. Have you any additional comments?

EAST STROUDSBURG STATE COLLEGE
Department of Professional Physical Education

J. Felshin

DO NOT SIGN

Course evaluation:

Please evaluate this course in terms of the following items; consider their appropriateness and value, and indicate any personal reactions as well as suggestions for increased effectiveness in the future.

subject matter (material covered; theoretical framework; course focus)

Texts and materials

Class organization (meetings; assignments; evaluative procedures)

a. *Lecture*

b. *Discussion group*

Instruction (ability and personal effectiveness of instructor; individual guidance)

a. *Lecture*

b. *Discussion group*

Other comments (interpersonal factors; nature of the group)

Classes missed:_____ Lectures:_____ Discussion groups: _____

HAVE YOU RETURNED ALL MATERIALS TO THE INSTRUCTOR AND THE LIBRARY?

EAST STROUDSBURG STATE COLLEGE
Department of Professional Physical Education

J. Felshin

Focus: THE TEACHER

Framework: The consideration of this problem area shall be in terms of the roles, responsibilities, and competence of the teacher as a *person* who needs the knowledge and ability to function effectively:

(1) in relation to students
(2) in relation to society
(3) in relation to school
(4) in relation to subject

Problems: How can we understand the goals, demands, and diverse roles of the teacher in relation to their ideal effects, identify attendant responsibilities and implications, and then clarify and personalize goals as well as assess and evaluate ourselves and our progress in terms of them?

Assumptions:

1. Since behavior is a function of perception, teachers fulfill their roles as they perceive them. The beliefs and values that a teacher holds, especially those that relate to behavior, learning, personality goals and effects, and the area of knowledge concerned will determine the method and content of teaching, the image that is projected, the effects on all concerned, and the ultimate development of the field.

2. The understanding of an ideal teacher should be based on a valid consideration of purposes as derived from intelligent examination of the pertinent foundations; i.e., those which pertain to youth, society, schools, and physical education.

3. Once clarified, an understanding of the ideal teacher in any context must be developed to provide guidelines for action. This means that implications and responsibilities should be examined, but self-insight is the key to the process.

4. The meaningfulness of an examination of the goals and responsibilities of teachers depends finally upon the degree to which these are personalized and goals for individual growth established. The teacher's growth will occur to the degree to which the goal is clearly perceived, competence and self are evaluated in relation to it, and responsibility for the importance of personal development is accepted.

Conclusion: If we understood ourselves in relation to goals of becoming good teachers as these are ideally established in light of all relevant foundations, and accepted their importance, we could analyze the implications of these goals, identify attendant responsibilities and competency demands, and evaluate our own progress toward these goals. In a long-range sense, we could become self-directing in relation to the development of our own abilities, project goals, and insure our own continued growth.

EAST STROUDSBURG STATE COLLEGE
Department of Professional Physical Education

J. Felshin

The ABC's of Physical Education . . . . . .

		AAHPER			
NEA			NAIA		ASCD
	ACA	NCPEAM		USFHA	
NSCAA			USLTA		
		NHL			
	AAU		DGWS		
NFL	AACTE		PEA		ASA
	FIG		NAA		
NASPSPA		NATA	ASHA		
	YMCA				
	ERIC		CNCA		AIAW
		APHA			
APTA	HEW		AMA		
	ABA		YWCA		
AAPE					
WOCTP					
	NRA		ARFCW		
		SGORC			
	USGA	DMA	NASSP		
ICHPER		AASA			ABC
	ACSM		NAPECW	NIA	
YMHA		WIBC			
	USOC		LSEP		
LSF		IOC		NAA	
		USTFF			USWLA

. . . . AND *The Alpha, Beta, Chi's*

Phi Delta Pi   Pi Lambda Theta
Delta Psi Kappa   Phi Epsilon Kappa
                           Phi Kappa Phi

CODE OF ETHICS OF THE EDUCATION PROFESSION*

The educator believes in the worth and dignity of man. He recognizes the supreme importance of the pursuit of truth, devotion to excellence, and the nurture of democratic citizenship. He regards as essential to these goals the protection of freedom to learn and to teach and the guarantee of equal educational opportunity for all. The educator accepts his responsibility to practice his profession according to the highest ethical standards.

The educator recognizes the magnitude of the responsibility he has accepted in choosing a career in education, and engages himself, individually and collectively with other educators, to judge his colleagues, and to be judged by them, in accordance with the provisions of this code. (PREAMBLE)

PRINCIPLE I—COMMITMENT TO THE STUDENT

The educator measures his success by the progress of each student toward realization of his potential as a worthy and effective citizen. The educator therefore works to stimulate the spirit of inquiry, the acquisition of knowledge and understanding, and the thoughtful formulation of worthy goals.

In fulfilling his obligation to the student, the educator—

1. Shall not without just cause restrain the student from independent action in his pursuit of learning, and shall not without just cause deny the student access to varying points of view.
2. Shall not deliberately suppress or distort subject matter for which he bears responsibility.
3. Shall make reasonable effort to protect the student from conditions harmful to learning or to health and safety.
4. Shall conduct professional business in such a way that he does not expose the student to unnecessary embarrassment or disparagement.
5. Shall not on the ground of race, color, creed, or national origin exclude any student from participation in or deny him benefits under any program, nor grant any discriminatory consideration or advantage.
6. Shall not use professional relationships with students for private advantage.
7. Shall keep in confidence information that has been obtained in the course of professional service, unless disclosure serves professional purposes or is required by law.

* Adopted by the NEA Representative Assembly, July, 1968. Amended July, 1970. Reprinted with permission of the National Education Association.

231

8. Shall not tutor for remuneration students assigned to his classes, unless no other qualified teacher is reasonably available.

PRINCIPLE II—COMMITMENT TO THE PUBLIC

The educator believes that patriotism in its highest form requires dedication to the principles of our democratic heritage. He shares with all other citizens the responsibility for the development of sound public policy and assumes full political and citizenship responsibilities. The educator bears particular responsibility for the development of policy relating to the extension of educational opportunities for all and for interpreting educational programs and policies to the public.

In fulfilling his obligation to the public, the educator—

1. Shall not misrepresent an institution or organization with which he is affiliated, and shall take adequate precautions to distinguish between his personal and institutional or organizational views.
2. Shall not knowingly distort or misrepresent the facts concerning educational matters in direct and indirect public expressions.
3. Shall not interfere with a colleague's exercise of political and citizenship rights and responsibilities.
4. Shall not use institutional privileges for private gain or to promote political candidates or partisan political activities.
5. Shall accept no gratuities, gifts, or favors that might impair or appear to impair professional judgment, nor offer any favor, service, or thing of value to obtain special advantage.

PRINCIPLE III—COMMITMENT TO THE PROFESSION

The educator believes that the quality of the services of the education profession directly influences the nation and its citizens. He therefore exerts every effort to raise professional standards, to improve his service, to promote a climate in which the exercise of professional judgment is encouraged, and to achieve conditions which attract persons worthy of the trust to careers in education. Aware of the value of united effort, he contributes actively to the support, planning, and programs of professional organizations.

In fulfilling his obligation to the profession, the educator—

1. Shall not discriminate on the ground of race, color, creed, or national origin for membership in professional organizations, nor interfere with the free participation of colleagues in the affairs of their association.
2. Shall accord just and equitable treatment to all members of the profession in the exercise of their professional rights and responsibilities.
3. Shall not use coercive means or promise special treatment in order to influence professional decisions of colleagues.

4. Shall withhold and safeguard information acquired about colleagues in the course of employment, unless disclosure serves professional purposes.
5. Shall not refuse to participate in a professional inquiry when requested by an appropriate professional association.
6. Shall provide upon the request of the aggrieved party a written statement of specific reason for recommendations that lead to the denial of increments, significant changes in employment, or termination of employment.
7. Shall not misrepresent his professional qualifications.
8. Shall not knowingly distort evaluations of colleagues.

PRINCIPLE IV—COMMITMENT TO PROFESSIONAL EMPLOYMENT PRACTICES

The educator regards the employment agreement as a pledge to be executed both in spirit and in fact in a manner consistent with the highest ideals of professional service. He believes that sound professional personnel relationships with governing boards are built upon personal integrity, dignity, and mutual respect. The educator discourages the practice of his profession by unqualified persons.

In fulfilling his obligation to professional employment practices, the educator—

1. Shall apply for, accept, offer, or assign a position or responsibility on the basis of professional preparation and legal qualifications.
2. Shall apply for a specific position only when it is known to be vacant, and shall refrain from underbidding or commenting adversely about other candidates.
3. Shall not knowingly withhold information regarding a position from an applicant or misrepresent an assignment or conditions of employment.
4. Shall give prompt notice to the employing agency of any change in availability of service, and the employing agent shall give prompt notice of change in availability or nature of a position.
5. Shall adhere to the terms of a contract or appointment, unless these terms have been legally terminated, falsely represented, or substantially altered by unilateral action of the employing agency.
6. Shall conduct professional business through channels, when available, that have been jointly approved by the professional organization and the employing agency.
7. Shall not delegate assigned tasks to unqualified personnel.
8. Shall permit no commercial exploitation of his professional position.
9. Shall use time granted for the purpose for which it is intended.

BYLAWS, NATIONAL EDUCATION ASSOCIATION

Article I, Section 13. Adherence to the Code of Ethics adopted by the Association shall be a condition of membership. The Committee on Professional Ethics shall after due notice and hearing have power to censure, suspend, or expel any member for violation of the Code subject to review by the Executive Committee. A member may within sixty days after a decision by the Ethics Committee file an appeal of the decision with the Exceutive Secretary.

PROVISIONS FOR NATIONAL ENFORCEMENT

Code Development — It shall be the duty of the Committee to maintain a continuous review of the *Code of Ethics of the Education Profession.* Amendments or revision of the Code shall be presented for approval to the Representative Assembly.

Interpretations of the Code of Ethics of the Education Profession — A request for interpretation of the Code shall be in writing and shall describe the matter to be interpreted in sufficient detail to enable the members of the Committee on Professional Ethics to evaluate the request in all its aspects.

Disciplinary Action — In addition to the provisions of Article I, Section 13, the Committee on Professional Ethics will consider disciplinary action against a member when written charges are preferred by the official governing body of the NEA affiliated state or local education association or NEA Department of which the person in question is a member.

If charges are based on a hearing held by any of the groups authorized to prefer charges, a record of the hearing shall be submitted to the Committee on Professional Ethics. Disciplinary action will only be considered as resulting from a fair hearing or a proper hearing record. A member will have an opportunity to show cause why such action should not be taken.

NEA Committee on Professional Ethics

> Changes in the above text may not be made in reprints without permission of the Committee.

Maryanne M. Schumm

The Gymnastics Club is putting on a demonstration for the PTA. It is your turn to demonstrate two consecutive back flips in layout position on the trampoline. The gym is quiet and all eyes are upon you. You mount the trampoline, take five bounces, go up, turn gracefully through the air, land perfectly, go up again, turn, and break your bounce smoothly as you hit the mat. You dismount, and are greeted by spontaneous loud applause. . . .

Two things probably occurred during this short experience. First, you had a definite picture of your body in space. This is known as *body image.* Your body image was pleasing to you because you knew that you had performed gracefully, and that it was beautiful to watch. Secondly, your faith in your ability to perform in a demonstration situation is strengthened, and you leave with a general satisfied feeling. Your *self-concept* has been strengthened by your success.

Self-concept is simply a matter of how you see yourself. If someone conceives of himself as an athlete, then his actions are geared toward making others feel he is athletic, that he has an athletic appearance, and that he is at ease in any situation demanding physical skill.

When you think of the "self," it might help to think of it as being divided into three parts: the first is the *real self* or the self that actually *does* exist; the second is the *ideal self* . . . or the self that you would *like* to have exist! This self helps to maintain your goals, aspirations, and the best thoughts about you as an individual. And finally, the *social self*, the part of the self which works for your *acceptance by others.* These three selves remain integrated, then you become adjusted and satisfied with your total self.

We as teachers should be vitally concerned with the development of the self-concept in each student. As each person has more and more experience, he begins to react in an organized, changeable, but fairly consistent pattern. Every person begins with a unique body having unique characteristics. The result, therefore, is a unique personality.

Once we have started to form a self-concept, we are continually testing it, although we are not always aware that we are doing so. We interpret the reactions of others toward the things we choose to do. Their gestures and expressions may make us feel wanted, rejected, approved of, silly, and so forth. If you as the teacher covered your eyes just before a student did a Thief Vault over the horse, this could result in her losing a little of her self-confidence! *Part of our self-concept, then, is formed by checking what we feel against the thought of others.*

Now that you have had a quick review, let us see why physical educators should understand the implications of self-concept. I would like to quote a statement by Jersild from his book *In Search of Self:*

> The physical education program especially abounds in psychological possibilities. In it children can learn to discover and accept their bodies, to face up against false and prudish attitudes of shame and guilt which some of them have learned to associate with nakedness. Here they can discover, try, and test their capacity for acquiring enjoyable skills; here they can learn to recognize their competitive tendencies and the healthy as well as the morbid features of competition. Here they are introduced to a psychological laboratory in which they see, in raw form, acts of meanness, cruelty, and hostility which are symptomatic of emotional poverty or mental conflict; and they can observe behavior which reflects good sportsmanship, greatness in defeat, ability to "take it," and behavior which reveals a self rich in resources and inner assurance.*

We have a unique opportunity to view the hopes and strivings of each child. We can more easily spot the child who fears being tested, or being defeated, or making mistakes. We can usually pick out the ones who prefer to stand back and watch others perform. They conceive of themselves as inadequate to cope with the situation, and shy away from participating. The self is the most essential property of each adolescent's life. We know this, and we have so many opportunities to observe actions which reveal a child's concept of himself. Now, what can we do to apply this knowledge to our teaching?

Each child has a definite need to develop his *self-esteem,* to feel good about himself. We can offer the child situations in which he can experience pride in having achieved a level or degree of skill. Jimmy learned the one-hand push shot and soon after made a perfect score on a test. This is concrete evidence for him that he has done well, and will help to bolster his self-esteem. By being able to recognize the child's need in this area, you can better adapt a situation to coincide with the need. It may be vitally necessary for Jimmy to feel successful in physical education. Jane may be adept in some other area to a degree that does not necessitate her needing to prove herself quite as much as Jim. The tricky part is figuring out who needs what! You may not always be right, but you have a better chance if you are aware that a problem may exist.

Self-esteem is closely tied in with the child's *acceptance* of himself. *Self-acceptance* is the ability to realize and to accept your limitations and do the best you can with the resources you have. You realize you are good in some things, but will never be quite as good in others. Also, just because you are good, does not mean you will always be *best.* The statement "I usually beat her in the jumps, but she sure can run faster . . .," is an example of self-acceptance and good integration of the *real* self with

---

* Arthur T. Jersild, *In Search of Self,* New York: Teachers College, Columbia University, 1952, 103-104.

the *ideal* self. On the other hand, Mary the golfer knows that she is very good, but she is afraid to have her image shattered, so she shies away from any testing situation. Perhaps calling attention to Mary's form, rather than score, would take emphasis off the evaluative aspect for her.

If you think about it a little, you will see that there are many opportunities to guide and direct the formation of certain aspects of self-concept. And you do not always have to use some big spectacular innovation. Sometimes it is of much greater importance to try to *anticipate* the little details in a class experience that may have terrific impact. . . .

. . . And in this lies the key to a successful experience for both student and teacher.

I: 4/70

EAST STROUDSBURG STATE COLLEGE
Department of Professional Physical Education

ADVISER-STUDENT RECORD

Name _____   Address _____   Date of Entry _____

Phone _____   Projected Date of Graduation _____

Required Core:		Semester Hours	Grade
Introduction to Physical Education		3	
Movement and the Learning Process		3	
Curriculum and Evaluation in Physical Education		3	
Kinesiology		3	
Physiology of Exercise		3	
Psycho-social Aspects of Activity		3	
Activities: Representing categories	A.	1	
A, B, and C, and a Team and an	B.	1	
Individual Sport:	C.	1	
	Team		
	Ind.		
	Other Activities		
	TOTAL		

Specialization: Professional Education and Certification:

___Elementary   ___Aquatics   Methods of Physical Education _____ _____
___Secondary   ___Dance   Student Teaching   _____ _____
___Generalist   ___Gymnastics   Practicum   _____ _____
___Academic   ___Individual Sports   _____   _____ _____
                 ___Team Sports   _____   _____ _____
                                        _____   _____ _____

        TOTAL S.H. in Theory___   TOTAL _____

General Education:	S.H.	Grade	Electives:	S.H.	Grade
_____	___	___	_____	___	___
_____	___	___	_____	___	___
_____	___	___	_____	___	___
_____	___	___	_____	___	___
_____	___	___	_____	___	___
_____	___	___	_____	___	___
_____	___	___	TOTAL	___	
_____	___	___			
_____	___	___	Summary:		
_____	___	___	General Education	___	
_____	___	___	Professional Education___		
_____	___	___	Physical Education	___	
_____	___	___	TOTAL ___GPA___		
_____	___	___			
_____	___	___	Comments:		
_____	___	___			

EAST STROUDSBURG STATE COLLEGE
Department of Professional Physical Education

Specialization at a Level
Adviser-Student Record

Name _____

Date of Entry _____

Projected Date of Graduation _____

GENERALIST

Activity:

_____Aquatics _____
_____Dance _____
_____Gymnastics _____
_____Level I Movement
_____Level II Movement
_____Level III Movement

Theory:

_____Theory & Research in Elm. P.E.
_____Organization & Administration of P.E.
_____Care & Prevention of Athletic Injuries

ELEMENTARY

Activity:

_____Level I Movement
_____Level II Movement
_____Level III Movement
_____Rythmics
_____Dance for Elementary
_____Gymnastics & Tumbling for Elementary

Theory:

_____Theory & Research in Elem. P.E.
_____Organization and Administration of P.E.
_____First Aid Card

Certification Requirements for Elementary Level
_____The Teaching of Reading
_____Growth and Development

SECONDARY

Activity:

_____Aquatics _____
_____Dance _____
_____Gymnastics _____
_____Individual Sport _____
_____Personal Development
_____Team Sport _____

Theory:

_____Care and Prevention of Athletic Injuries
_____Organization & Administration of P.E.

Other Departmental Requirements and Electives

Activity (7 s.h.)

_____ _____
_____ _____
_____ _____
_____ _____
_____ _____
_____ _____

Departmental Certification Requirements

Pre-Student Teaching Experiences:

_____ _____
_____ _____
_____ _____
_____ _____

_____Methods of Teaching Physical Education
_____Student Teaching

Theory:

_____ _____
_____ _____
_____ _____

Professional Education Requirements:
_____Foundations of Education
_____Audio-Visual Education
_____Educational Psychology
_____Practicum

III: 4/70

EAST STROUDSBURG STATE COLLEGE
Department of Professional Physical Education

Activity Specialization
Adviser-Student Record

_____
Name

_____
Date of Entry

Activity Requirements in Specialization:

Aquatics   *Gymnastics*

_____ ____   _____ ____
_____ ____   _____ ____
_____ ____   _____ ____
_____ ____   _____ ____
_____ ____   _____ ____

Dance   Individual Sports___ or Team Sports___

_____ ____   2 Sports to Highest Level_____
_____ ____
_____ ____   Sport _____ ____
_____ ____
                               Sport _____ ____

                                        ____ _____ ____
                                              _____ ____

_____6 s.h. in Activity area.   ____
_____Experience in Extra Class Form of Activity:
_____Certification by Faculty   _____
                                       Faculty Approval
_____Care and Prevention of Athletic
     Injuries   _____
_____Theory (6 s.h.)   Date

     _____ ____
     _____ ____

Other Departmental Requirements and Electives: Departmental Certification
   Requirements:

Activity (7 s.h.)   Pre-Student Teaching Experiences:

_____ ____   ____ _____
_____ ____   ____ _____
_____ ____   ____ Methods of Teaching Physical
_____ ____   Education
_____ ____   ____ Student Teaching
_____ ____   Professional Education Requirements:

Theory: ____ Foundations of Education
                                      ____ Audio-Visual Education
_____ ____   ____ Educational Psychology
_____ ____   ____ Practicum
_____ ____

IV: 4/70

EAST STROUDSBURG STATE COLLEGE
Department of Professional Physical Education

Academic Specialization
Adviser-Student Record

Name _____

Departmental Requirements:	Departmental Electives:		
Activity:		S.H.	Grade

Theory:

Historical Concepts of M & S _____

Philosophical Concepts of M & S _____

Total S.H. in Major Field _____   TOTAL_____

Area of Special Interest:_____

Supporting Electives from Other Fields:

Social Science and/or Philosophy		Psychology		Natural Science	
S.H.	Grade	S.H.	Grade	S.H.	Grade

TOTAL_____   TOTAL_____   TOTAL_____

Total S.H. in Other Fields _____

V: 4/70

EAST STROUDSBURG STATE COLLEGE
Department of Professional Physical Education

Theory Requirements of All Majors and Specialists

	Freshman	Sophomore	Junior	Senior
All Majors	Introduction to Physical Education	Kinesiology Movement and the Learning Process	Physiology of Exercise Psycho-social Aspects	Curriculum and Evaluation in Physical Education
Generalist			Care and Prevention of Athletic Injuries Theory and Research in Elementary Physical Education	Organization and Administration of Physical Education
Elementary			Theory and Research in Elementary Physical Education	Organization and Administration of Physical Education
Secondary			Care and Prevention of Athletic Injuries	Organization and Administration of Physical Education
Activity			Care and Prevention Theory	Theory
Academic		Historical Concepts of Movement and Sport	Philosophical Concepts of Movement and Sport	

VI: 4/70

EAST STROUDSBURG STATE COLLEGE
Department of Professional Physical Education

Classification of Activities for Basic Activity Requirement

The basic activity requirement for all students is an individual and team sport and representation of each of the categories indicated below. This represents a minimum of 3 semester hours of activity.

This classification of activities is based upon the relationship of body movement to the objective of the activity: *body control* in some kind of environment or with a specific focus; the *direct control* of an object by the body; or the *indirect control* of an object with an intermediate object.

Category A: *BODY CONTROL*

Gymnastics
Swimming
Diving
Dance
Wrestling
Skiing
Ice Skating

Category B: *DIRECT CONTROL OF AN OBJECT*

Basketball
Bowling
Football
Handball
Soccer
Volleyball

Category C: *INDIRECT CONTROL OF AN OBJECT*

Archery
Badminton
Baseball
Field Hockey
Golf
Lacrosse
Softball
Squash
Tennis

VII: 4/70

EAST STROUDSBURG STATE COLLEGE
Department of Professional Physical Education

Activity Specialization

Activity: Specialization in *Aquatics, Dance, Gymnastics, Individual Sports* or *Team Sports.*

ACTIVITY: A minimum of 6 semester hours in the activity area.
Experience in some organized extraclass form of the activity.
Qualification in the area as certified by the faculty.
Pursuit of two sports to the highest level offered.**

** Pertains to Individual or Team Sport Specialization.

Individual Sports	*Team Sports*
Archery (2)	Baseball (2)*
Badminton (2)	Basketball (2)*
Bowling (1)	Field Hockey (2)
Fencing (1)	Football (2)*
Golf (2)	Ice Hockey (1)
Ice Skating (1)	Lacrosse (2)
Skiing (2)	Soccer (2)
Squash and Handball (1)	Softball (2)
Tennis (2)	Volleyball (2)
Track and Field (2)*	
Wrestling (2)*	

* Indicates a coaching class will be offered in addition to the number of courses listed.

THEORY: (6 semester hours required); Each course is 3 semester hours.

Conditioning Theory (prerequisite: Physiology of Exercise)
Analysis of Sport Skills (prerequisite: Kinesiology)
Contemporary Sport
Psychology of Sport
Dance Theory (creative forms)
Dance Theory (social forms)

VIII: 4/70

EAST STROUDSBURG STATE COLLEGE
Department of Professional Physical Education

PROJECTED PLAN OF STUDY

Name _____

First Semester	S.H.	*Second Semester*	S.H.
Activity _____ _____		Activity _____ _____	
Introduction to Physical Education _____		General Education _____ _____	
General Education _____ _____		_____ _____	
		_____ _____	
TOTAL _____		TOTAL _____	

Third Semester		*Fourth Semester*	
Activity _____ _____		Activity _____ _____	
Kinesiology _____		Movement and the Learning Process _____	
Foundations of Education _____		Audio-Visual Education _____	
General Education _____ _____		General Education _____ _____	
		_____ _____	
TOTAL _____		TOTAL _____	

Fifth Semester		*Sixth Semester*	
Activity _____ _____		Activity _____ _____	
Physiology of Exercise _____		Psycho-social Aspects of Activity _____	
Educational Psychology _____		General Education _____ _____	
General Education _____ _____		_____ _____	
		_____ _____	
TOTAL _____		TOTAL _____	

Seventh Semester		*Eighth Semester*	
Activity _____ _____		Methods of Physical Education _____	
Curriculum & Evaluation in P.E. _____		Student Teaching _____	
_____ _____		Practicum _____	
_____ _____			
_____ _____			
TOTAL _____		TOTAL _____	

AMPLIFYING READINGS

Concept of Fitness

Concept of Cultural Participation in Movement

Concept of Meaning and Significance of Movement Experience

"Dance Concentration in Elementary Education"

"A Personal Philosophy of Physical Education"

CONCEPT: THE DEVELOPMENT OF FITNESS IS A VALID CONCERN OF PHYSICAL EDUCATION, AND THERE ARE ATTENDANT PRINCIPLES THAT CAN BE IDENTIFIED

Arne L. Olson

The efficiency of a motor performance, as well as the quality and level of physical movement, is related to the motor fitness of an individual. Such aspects as strength, endurance, and cardiorespiratory efficiency are components which are commonly considered to be "physical fitness." Such skills as running speed, balance, coordination, agility, and arm and leg power are added to evaluate an individual's present status estimates for motor performance. Individuals in play, exercise, dance, or sport frequently wish to improve their status in order to improve specific or general aspects of their performance.

Most aspects of fitness performance are specific characteristics, and improvement in one aspect of fitness allows increased performance as it relates to other aspects of fitness only when the elements are identical or supportive. Such related characteristics of fitness as flexibility or range of movement possible without strain are frequently important in dance, sport, or exercise movements. Although one individual may be "generally more flexible" than another individual, studies have made it clear that attempts to improve flexibility in one area will not affect the flexibility in another area of the body unless the individual is required to increase his flexibility in the second area with the first exercise. For example, exercises designed to increase the range of motion in one ankle have little or no effect on the range of motion in the opposite ankle or in other joints of the body. Increased flexibility, however, might make it possible for a dancer to apply his strength motion in a more efficient manner.

Most improvements of motor or physical fitness require specific exercise programs designed for specific purposes. Of all the factors involved, perhaps the one that comes closest to being a general factor is that of endurance and, in particular, the cardiorespiratory aspects of endurance. It has been hypothesized that cardiorespiratory endurance may be a general factor in that one of the best ways to improve cardiorespiratory endurance is to involve most of the large muscles of the body in an extended intense training program. This program would project greater efficiency of most of the large muscles of the body as well as result in the expected increase in cardiorespiratory endurance. Reactions of the oxygen-carrying capacity of the red blood cells, for example, frequently would affect muscular endurance in other portions of the body in addition to the area being specifically stressed because of the fact that blood circulates throughout the body and not just within a particular region. Similar parallels could be made for the heart and lungs as well. With improved functioning of these or other organs or systems, the potential for improving the quantity as well as the quality of human movement comes within the capacity of an individual.

GENERAL PRINCIPLES OF IMPROVING PHYSICAL FITNESS

There are general principles which apply to a conditioning experience whether the conditioning program is designed to improve strength, endurance, flexibility, or some other specific aspect of fitness. Indirect factors such as body type, fitness level, age, maturation, and motivation also are involved in predicting success considering individual differences, but the following principles should be directly considered:

Use-Disuse

Use affects function; lack of use results in deterioration. If you require part of your body to perform a certain task, it will either improve its efficiency in doing the task or stay nearly the same. In other words, if a part of the body is stressed regularly its function may improve, while the function will decrease if it is not used occasionally for maintenance.

Overload

It is necessary to overload the organism in order to improve fitness. In order to make improvements in the physical condition of the human organism, it is necessary that the parts of the body being developed do more work than they would normally be called upon to perform. This overload can be accomplished in two general ways: (1) increase the total work, i.e., lift heavier weights in weight training; or (2) do more work in less time, i.e., do 30 sit-ups in one minute rather than 30 sit-ups in one minute and thirty seconds. This increased stress is called overload. You must continue to overload the body parts involved by increasing the effort as your strength or endurance increases.

Progression

Since the body may adjust (adapt) to the stress put upon it, it is necessary that the work be continually increased if improvement is desired. For example, consider a person who runs the 7-minute mile each day; for most, this would be an overload considering their present condition. They would, therefore, probably improve their general physiological functions if they ran a 7-minute mile each day for several weeks. However, after a period of time, they would no longer have a physiological stress as a result of the 7-minute mile. As an example of how to use the progression principle, we should progressively increase the stress by running the mile in a little less than 7-minutes or by the addition of a half-mile run after a short rest if continued improvement is desired. This progression would put more stress on our body, and it would continue to adjust to the increased load.

Specificity

Improvements in fitness are specific to the type of training undertaken. Although the various attributes of fitness are related, as are the various parts of the systems of the body, specific types of training result in the development of certain attributes just as exercising specific parts of the body generally results in the greatest change in these parts. A strength routine, for example, will not generally improve endurance although strength may be an underlying factor in endurance performance. A body-building program will not ordinarily improve coordination. Improved skill in one sport does not usually result in improvements in other sports except insofar as the elements involved are identical.

Retrogression

Fitness performance may temporarily retrogress before it improves. When a conditioning program is undertaken, one may experience a period of time after the first day when performance diminishes rather than increases. During this period it is hypothesized that the body is mobilizing its resources to meet the demands of the overload. Once this has taken place, improvements in performance are usually found, although plateaus are also frequently experienced during later periods of training.

Warm-up

Few of us would undertake participation in a vigorous physical activity without engaging in some type of a "warm-up." The benefits of warm-up seem to differ depending upon the activity involved and the type of warm-up. There are two different types of warm-up currently practiced: (1) Related or specific warm-up involves practicing the specific event to be performed. Examples of this type of warm-up are practicing shooting baskets or hitting a tennis ball prior to playing a game. This type usually improves performance in events requiring skill and accuracy. (2) General warm-up consists of completing a series of general exercises prior to participation. This type of warm-up is believed to aid performance by improving the immediate function of the circulatory and respiratory systems thus helping these systems "pre-adjust" to the pending activity; and by raising the muscle temperature so that the chemical reactions that occur during contraction can take place more readily. Part of the pre-adjustment phenomenon occurs because the capillaries in the muscles to be used become perfused with blood, thus increasing their oxygen supply. Another part of the adjustment occurs when the connective tissue and tendons at the end of the muscles are stretched. This is related to the fact that the muscles that are injured during strenuous activity are the antagonists to the strong contracting muscles. This phenomenon has been described by Morehouse and Miller as follows:

These cold antagonistic muscles relax slowly and incompletely when the agonists contract and thus retard free movement and accurate coordination. At the same time the force of contraction of the agonists and the momentum of the moving part exert a terrific strain on the unyielding antagonists, with consequent tearing of the muscle fibers or their tendinous attachments.*

Taper-off

The period for tapering-off should include slow movements, similar to those in the warm-up phase, which allow for a gradual decrease in heart rate, respiration, and body heat and recovery from the more strenuous activities of the exercise phase. If a person stops too quickly after a long bout of strenuous activity, the need to dissipate body heat may cause pooling of blood in his arms and legs. For a man who possibly has a compromised circulatory system, this reduction in central blood volume might result in fainting or circulatory collapse if he continues to stand still. Walking and other forms of mild exercise assist the return of blood to the heart and allow the person to recover more gradually.

* Morehouse, Lawrence E., and August T. Miller, *Physiology of Exercise*, St. Louis: C. V. Mosby Company, 1963.

CONCEPT: PHYSICAL EDUCATION PROVIDES OPPORTUNITIES FOR EXPERIENCING PERSONAL MEANING IN MOVEMENT*

Man's major differentiation from the animal kingdom is based on his ability to rationalize, to think, and to communicate his thoughts to others. What, then, motivates this rational being to hit a ball, follow it, get it into a small cup, and then repeat the process 17 more times? What possesses a person to drive himself to exhaustion by running up and down a 50' × 94' wooden floor trying to get possession of an orange ball to put it in a basket as many times as possible within 40 minutes? Why does a sane human being go into a 40' × 20' × 20' cement-walled box and continually hit a small black ball against the sides of the box time after time after time? Why does he defy gravity by using a pole to thrust his body into the air, over a bar, only to have gravital reality bring him down to earth again? Why *does* man participate in a host of movement activities that tax his every capacity for no apparent logical reason?

The scope of this concept is an endeavor to provide the major answer to this paradoxical phenomenon. In order to pursue this paradox, the writers have found it necessary first to define the scope of movement in physical education and then to discuss the physiological and psychological aspects of man that predispose him to participate in a taxing host of movement activities.

It has generally been agreed that the focus of physical education is human movement. According to Kenyon:

> Few have disputed that *man in motion* is the central phenomenon about which knowledge is sought. The scope varies sometimes, but nevertheless, for most writers human movement is taken to include the full range of organized gross physical activities, whether manifested in active games, dance, aquatics, gymnastics, or developmental exercises. (Kenyon, 1970, p. 291)

Therefore, movement in physical education is defined as the full range of forms of physical activities in which man participates, either structured or unstructured.

In order for man to participate in these gross physical activities, he must have neurophysiological integration or body awareness. Body awareness, an integration of feedback mechanisms, is indispensable to the performance of movement. The movement feedback mechanism is primarily supplied by the kinesthetic sense. According to Margaret H'Doubler:

* This paper was prepared for use in the AAHPER-sponsored Physical Education Public Information Project (PEPI Project), March, 1971, by Virginia Caruso, Suzanne Hoffman, and Henry Kearns as part of the requirements for the graduate course Professional Perspectives for Physical Education at East Stroudsburg State College.

> The kinesthetic sense is a sense of body movement by which one can judge the timing, force, and extent of his movements and adjusts himself consciously or automatically to information received from sensory nerve fibers in the muscles, tendons, and joints throughout his entire body. To this group of sensory receptors also belong the organs of static and equilibratory sensations, which serve to maintain body balance and posture. (H'Doubler, 1940, p. 72)

The kinesthetic stimuli are carried by afferent axons into various segments of the spinal cord, transmitted into "the basal regions of the brain, including the medulla and pons," and finally relayed "into the higher regions of the brain, including the thalamus and the cerebral cortex." (Guyton, 1969, p. 259) Once in the thalamus, the quality of these sensory impulses is determined and then is channeled to the appropriate circumscribed area of the cerebral cortex. The kinesthetic stimuli are directed to the portion of the cerebral cortex known as the somesthetic cortex. (Guyton, 1969, pp. 278-299) "The function of the somesthetic cortex is to localize very exactly the points in the body from which the sensations originate." (Guyton, 1969, p. 279)

Adjacent to the somesthetic cortex is the somesthetic association area which is responsible for interpretation of the sensations and which constantly records the exact position of each body segment. In this area memories of past sensory experiences are stored, and new sensations are compared to them and interpreted and accumulated. (Guyton, 1969, p. 283)

Once the impulse has been interpreted and compared with similar sensory experiences, it is relayed to the common integrative area in the angular gyrus of the brain. It is in the common integrative area, or gnostic area, where signals from the somesthetic, auditory, and visual association areas join and become integrated to form a common meaning. (Guyton, 1969, p. 284)

This common meaning is made up of sensory perceptions that have been integrated in the individual's brain. Smith, in discussing kinesthetic perception, states:

> Kinesthetic perception is more than the reception of afferent impulses from joint receptors to the sensorimotor cortex. Perception includes the complex process through which the individual receives, extracts, organizes, and interprets sensory information. The extraction of the sensory information may be selective, as Ittleson and Cantril explain: "perceiving is always done by a particular person from his own unique position in space and time and with his own combination of experiences and needs." (Smith, 1969, pp. 36-37)

Sartain et al. fortified the psychological importance of perception when they stated:

> In 1690 John Locke laid the foundation of modern empirical science with the famous dictum that there is nothing in the mind that was not first in the senses. Since all knowledge of the world comes through the senses, no aspect of human behavior is more important than that of sensing and perceiving. (Sartain et al., 1967, p. 232)

The basic assumption for the concept of this paper is that once an individual has these sensory perceptual experiences he then is able to formulate a meaningful conceptualization of the experience. Metheny enhances the scope of meaning by saying:

> The concept of meaning implies some form of conceptualization derived from experience, because what men call "meanings," are abstractions of the mind. (Metheny, 1960)

Because it is based on one's own concept of experience, meaning is then highly personalized. In order for meaning to exist, there must be a conscious experience. The word "conscious" refers to the intrinsic or inner life of the person, an individual's sense of reflectiveness or self-awareness. An experience results in a response in which the responding is a conscious thing, not mechanical. (Phenix, 1964, pp. 21-22) According to Phenix, "As the psychologists say, thought is a 'mediating process' intervening between stimulus and response. Reflective mediation is the basis of meaning." (Phenix, 1964, p. 22)

The modes of personal meaning are infinite. However, there are two major categories under which meaning can be placed—extrinsic meaning and intrinsic meaning. Coutts discussed extrinsic meaning by saying:

> When sport is used as a means to ends outside the realm of sport, then individual initiative and freedom are denied, and through this denial the true existence of sport is lost. (Coutts, 1968, p. 71)

Consequently, the intrinsic meanings derived from sport (a factor of human movement) must be the major focus; for it is only within this realm that true meaning in movement can exist.

Intrinsic meaning is based on fulfilling inner needs.

> Perceptual motor performance is treated within Lewin's Field Theory as the vehicle through which the individual communicates between his inner needs and environment. Therefore, as the person moves and attempts to aquire skill, it is assumed that he is not only learning the game, but also expressing his inner nature and is in turn changing his environment. (Cratty, 1964, p. 31)

Fulfilling inner needs is the foundation for self-expression. Combs and Snygg referred to the self as "the individual's basic frame of reference, the central core, around which the remainder of the perceptual field is organized." (Combs and Snygg, 1959, p. 132)

Since intrinsic meaning is based on fulfilling inner needs and the fulfillment of inner needs is the foundation of self-expression, then movement is a mode of self-expression. Phenix explains the self-expressive role of meaning in movement: "No other instrument is as elaborate, sensitive, and immediately responsive as the human body. This is why the arts of movement are so important for the expression and perception of human meaning." (Phenix, 1964, p. 165) Consequently, movement, as a mode of self-expression, provides the individual with a total integration of all his physiological and psychological capacities. Phenix said:

> This union of thought, feeling, sense, and act is the particular aim of the arts of movement . . . Nowhere else is the coordination of all components of the living person so directly fostered nor the resulting activity so deeply rooted in the unitary existence of the person. (Phenix, 1964, p. 166)

The answer to the question posed in the introductory phase of this paper, "Why *does* man participate in a host of movement activities that tax his every capacity for no apparent logical reason?" can now be answered.

Movement is a mode of man's self-expression in which his total being is integrated and involved. Movement is derived from body awareness and sensory perception and is conceptualized in thought. Consequently, man does have a logical reason for participating in movement activities— the most logical reason of all—man experiences personal meaning in movement.

Since the focus of physical education is human movement, then physical education truly does provide opportunities for experiencing personal meaning in movement by opening the avenues of a unique totality of self-expression to all who participate in it.

Bibliography

Combs, Arthur W., and Snygg, Donald. *Individual Behavior.* New York: Harper Brothers, 1959.

Coutts, Curtis A. "Freedom in Sport." *Quest,* X, May, 1968, pp. 68-71.

Cratty, Bryant J. *Movement Behavior and Motor Learning.* Philadelphia: Lea & Febiger, 1964.

Guyton, Arthur C. *Function of the Human Body.* 3rd ed., Philadelphia: W. B. Saunders Company, 1969.

H'Doubler, Margaret N. *Dance: A Creative Art Experience.* New York: F. S. Crofts, 1940.

Kenyon, Gerald S. "On the Conceptualization of Sub-Disciplines Within an Academic Discipline Dealing With Human Movement." *Anthology of Contemporary Readings: An Introduction to Physical Education.* 2nd ed. Edited by Howard S. Slusher and Aileene Lockhart. Dubuque, Iowa: Wm. C. Brown Company, 1970.

Metheny, Eleanor, and Ellfeldt, Lois. "An Inquiry into the Nature of Movement as a Significant Form of Human Experience." Paper presented at the World Seminar on Health and Fitness, Rome, Italy, August 28, 1960.

Phenix, Philip H. *Realms of Meaning.* New York: McGraw-Hill Book Company, 1964.

Sartain, Aaron Q., North, Alvin J., Strange, Jack R., and Chapman, Harold M. *Psychology: Understanding Human Behavior.* New York: McGraw-Hill Book Company, 1967.

Smith, Judith L. "Kinesthesis: A Model for Movement Feedback." *Perspectives of Man in Action.* Edited by Roscoe C. Brown and Bryant J. Cratty. Englewood Cliffs, New Jersey: Prentice-Hall, 1969.

CONCEPT: PHYSICAL EDUCATION PROVIDES A SIGNIFICANT MODE OF CULTURAL PARTICIPATION*

American society is you and me! It's Ron and Nick and Sue and all of our friends. Although we, as individuals, make up our society, the term "society" usually refers to groups of individuals who interact and cooperate with one another in order to achieve a particular purpose. (Kluckhohn, 1949, p. 24) In such a diverse and discontinuous society as ours, there are a variety of groups with a variety of purposes. For instance, we have the youth culture, the Black Panthers, and the Republicans. Despite the diversity, the groups and subgroups are bound together by those things that they share and understand—the culture. Lüschen, attributing the concept to Kluckhohn and others, stated that culture

> deals with those patterns and abstractions that underlie behavior or are a result of it. Thus, culture exists of cognitive elements which grow out of everyday or scientific experience. It consists of beliefs, values, norms, and of signs that include symbols of verbal as well as non-verbal communication. (Lüschen, 1970, p. 86)

Since culture is "shared *learned* behavior" (Levy, 1952, p. 39), the particular aspects of the culture that are learned differ from individual to individual. It has been suggested that

> not everyone participates equally in that which we consider our culture. . . . Certain segments of our society are not able to participate in the "good life" as culturally defined in the United States, which means owning a television and driving cars and all those kinds of things, but we can still talk about our culture as though we all participated in it, and you and I will mostly understand because we do, in part, participate in it. (Felshin, 1968)

Human movement reflects culture. It is *shared, learned behavior* that is determined in part by individual personality but, to a great extent, by social and cultural systems active in the society. Günther Lüschen illustrated this point by describing the walk of the Yemenitic Israelite:

> Since in their former society in the Yemen, the Jews were the outcasts, and every Yemenite could feel free to hit a Jew (whenever he could get hold of one), the Yemenitic Jew would always run in order to escape this oppression. This way of walking finally became an integrated pattern of his culture. And though the environment in Israel is no longer hostile to them, the Yemenitic Israelite still carries this pattern with him as a part of his culture and walks in a shy and hasty way. (Lüschen, 1970, p. 85)

* This paper was prepared for use in the AAHPER-sponsored Physical Education Public Information Project (PEPI Project), March, 1971, by Lynne Fitzgerald, Claudia Geyer, and Lorraine Schwinger as part of the requirements for the graduate course Professional Perspectives for Physical Education at East Stroudsburg State College.

Even in the United States the acceptability of movement skills connotes cultural values; for example, desirable male and female roles and traits. Females are to be graceful and nonaggressive. Eleanor Metheny, in her paper, "Symbolic Forms of Movement: The Feminine Image in Sports," discusses the appropriate sport roles for women. Very generally she suggested that it is appropriate

> for women identified with the more favored levels of socioeconomic status to engage in contests in which the resistance of a *light object* is overcome with a *light implement;* the body is projected into or through space in aesthetically pleasing patterns; the velocity and maneuverability of the body is increased by the use of some manufactured device; a spatial barrier prevents bodily contact with the opponent in face-to-face forms of competition. (Metheny, 1970, p. 229)

For its young ladies, American society sanctions sports like diving, skiing, golf, tennis, swimming, and gymnastics. The muscular Russian Olympic shot and discus champion, Tamara Press, does not exemplify social desirability because of the effects of her sports participation as viewed by Americans. (Higdon, 1970, p. 327) Not only does sport reflect the cultural traits of males and females, but also the very basic American values of "achievement, asceticism in individual sports, obedience (collectivity) in team sports, and exertion of power." (Lüschen, 1970, p. 93)

Human movement, particularly physical activity and sport, are extremely important in our culture, Cozens and Stumpf state:

> Sports and physical recreation activities belong with the arts of humanity. Such activities have formed a basic part of all cultures, including all racial groups and all historical ages, because they are as fundamental a form of human expression as music, poetry, and painting. (Cozens and Stumpf, 1953, p. 15)

As evidence of the powerful position of physical activity and sport in American society, Beisser asks us to examine a newspaper or the World Almanac as follows:

> In many American newspapers, the sports pages constitute the largest specialized daily section. One-tenth of the World Almanac is devoted to sports. In both newspapers and the Almanac the sports sections are greater in volume than the sections about politics, business, entertainment or science. (Beisser, 1967, p. 2)

Sports starts recruiting believers at an early age. A boy's dream is to become a professional athlete. Although very few boys can achieve that, Beisser suggests that

> the preparation is continuous throughout childhood to adult life. Unlike other models, which eventually are discarded as impossible or impractical, the role of sportsman, in some form, is continually and firmly reinforced by society. (Beisser, 1967, p. 12)

In fact, Cozens and Stumpf suggested that the term "good sport" has become a cultural ideal that has practically replaced "lady" and "gentleman" and stated further:

> The ideal of sportsmanship is continually reinforced in the culture by citations in the press, on the radio, and in the television. It is an ideal which imposes a type of self-control which in many instances is more effective in preserving and promoting satisfactory human relationships than the invocation of the written law. (Cozens and Stumpf, 1953, p. 20)

The importance of physical activity and sport in our culture becomes even more evident when we cite the numbers of persons attending games or watching athletic events on television during the weekend. When Muhammad Ali fought Joe Frazier for the World Heavyweight Boxing Title, every acculturated American knew of the outcome. Felshin has said:

> There are just a lot of ways in which we know that sport is important. And if you would participate fully in our culture then you had better be aware of sport. You have to know what it *means*. When you see a headline that says, "Tigers Slaughter Cardinals," you should know that it isn't about "big cats" and "little birds." And we do. (Felshin, 1968)

Traditionally, schools have had a major responsibility to society for transmitting the culture. They are one way in which a society preserves what is considered important by the group.

Special institutions that preserve and continue the culture are known as *social institutions*. Some major social institutions in our society are the educational system, religious organizations, the family, the political structure, and the economic structure. The idea that sport is also a social institution was alluded to in the discussion of the cultural values reflected through human movement and the importance of physical activity and sport in our society. Loy and Kenyon have said:

> To declare that sport, during the present century, has become a cultural phenomenon of great magnitude and complexity is an affirmation of the obvious. Sport is fast becoming a social institution, permeating education, economics, art, politics, law, mass communication and international diplomacy. (Kenyon and Loy, 1969, p. 36)

As was previously mentioned, the educational system has a major responsibility to society for transmitting the culture. Physical education is a definite part of the American educational system not only because it is compulsory, but also because:

> Physical education programs are also based on a concept of the commitment of education to help youth learn those skills that will enable him to participate in his culture. In a simple analysis these abilities are necessary in order for the individual to feel adequate in his world. They are requisite

means in the pursuit of the good life. The advantage of the movement activities is that they represent important areas of cultural emphasis while contributing to the participating individual's health and well-being. (Felshin,
1967, p. 161)

The pervasiveness of physical activity and sport in our society emphasizes the importance of physical education in providing opportunities for
acculturation. "Games valued by a culture and accepted as part of physical education should describe (1) the philosophical values the culture
wishes of its citizenry, and (2) the movement skills needed to perform
in the culture." (Brown and Cassidy, 1963, p. 159) As part of education,
physical education not only concerns itself with the perpetuation of culture, but also evaluates the culture and influences social change. (Felshin,
1967, p. 51) Celeste Ulrich has even said:

> Physical education has a very real responsibility to enrich the cultural heri-
> tage, to provide innovative techniques for cultural change, and to assist
> with cultural transmission. (Ulrich, 1968, p. 25)

One cannot fully participate in the American culture without adequate
knowledge and understanding of movement and sport. Physical education provides a significant mode of cultural participation because:

1. Much of the social interaction in our culture revolves around movement forms. Therefore, being able to participate is important. One
   cannot imagine the successful business executive unable to participate with his associates or clients on the golf course.
2. Aesthetic aspects of culture are expressed in dance and sport. Students in physical education gain an appreciation and understanding of movement forms that enable them to participate more fully
   in our culture. Developing an appreciation of movement forms is
   just as important in our culture as developing an appreciation for
   art and music.
3. Physical activity provides opportunity for active participation in
   the culture. Physical activity is the most significant recreational pattern in the United States. Those Americans who attend Saturday
   football games, dance, or bowl on Wednesday nights are actively
   participating in their culture.
4. Movement forms, because they reflect the culture, tend to reinforce
   social roles. For example, society sanctions particular sports as
   being appropriate for women. The woman who hopes to enhance
   her feminine image participates only in those movement activities
   that are approved for her by society. On the other hand, women's participation in movement activities may contribute to changed perceptions of "appropriateness" and enhance the movement toward liberation from rigid role expectations.

Bibliography

Beisser, Arnold. *The Madness in Sports: Psycho-Social Observations on Sport.* New York: Meredith Publishing Company, 1967.

Brown, Camille, and Cassidy, Rosalind. *Theory in Physical Education.* Philadelphia: Lea & Febiger, 1963.

Cozens, Frederich W., and Stumpf, Florence. *Sports in American Life.* Chicago: Chicago University Press, 1953.

Daniels, A. S. "The Study of Sport As An Element of the Culture." *Sport, Culture, and Society.* Edited by John W. Loy, Jr., and Gerald S. Kenyon. New York: The Macmillan Company, 1970.

Felshin, Janet. *Perspectives and Principles for Physical Education.* New York: John Wiley and Sons, 1967.

Felshin, Janet. "Sport and Culture." Speech given at the Eastern Regional Conference of the ARFCW, October, 1968.

Higdon, Rose and Hal. "What Sports for Girls?" *Sport and American Society.* Edited by George H. Sage. Reading, Massachusetts: Addison-Wesley Publishing Company, 1970.

Kenyon, Gerald S., and Loy, John W. "Toward a Sociology of Sport." *Sport, Culture, and Society.* Edited by John W. Loy, Jr., and Gerald Kenyon. New York: The Macmillan Company, 1969.

Kluckhohn, Clyde. *Mirror for Man.* New York: McGraw-Hill Book Company, 1949.

Levy, Marion. *The Structure of Society.* Princeton, New Jersey: Princeton University Press, 1952.

Lüschen, Günther. "The Interdependence of Sport and Culture." *The Cross-Cultural Analysis of Sport and Games.* Edited by Günther Lüschen. Champaign, Illinois: Stipes Publishing Company, 1970.

Metheny, Eleanor. "Symbolic Forms of Movement: The Feminine Image in Sports." *Sport and American Society.* Edited by George H. Sage. Reading, Massachusetts: Addison-Wesley Publishing Company, 1970.

Ulrich, Celeste. *The Social Matrix of Physical Education.* Englewood Cliffs, New Jersey: Prentice-Hall, 1968.

DANCE CONCENTRATION IN ELEMENTARY EDUCATION*

Edrie Ferdun

DANCE IN EDUCATION

Man has created and used dance in every time and culture. The need for dance is rooted deeply in the psychological, biological, and social nature of man. Dance has evolved into several different forms, each serving different aspects of his need. The social, folk, and theatrical forms emphasize factors of personal and cultural maintenance and stability, while the art forms emphasize factors of personal and cultural growth and change. All dance forms reflect and express the meanings of their time.

In recent history, dance has suffered from a lack of verbal explanation which could adequately define its nature and, therefore, its usefulness. This has been especially evident within the context of formal education where the potentials of movement and dance have gone relatively unused, with commensurate reduction in total and effective education.

Recent advancements in our understanding of the role of movement and the arts in personal and cultural growth and well-being, along with the stresses and symptoms of our times, have provided a basis for curricular imperatives with regard to dance. The potentials inherent in dance must be tapped and used.

An identification of objectives should help to clarify the potential relationships of the child to dance and to point out the necessity for finding ways to extend the use of dance in the schools.

Dance can be studied in several ways depending upon the objectives to be served. Immersion in dance in the manner of a dancer has special values in the areas of body and movement awareness, understanding and skill, as well as its effective use in creative expression and communication. Studying dance as a reflection of man and culture provides for important humanistic learnings as well as forming a basis for appreciation of all art. There are special potentials for studying dance as a dancer, a choreographer, a member of an audience, or a scholar. All are important.

The following objectives are explained in general terms with the hope of providing a sense of the directions which dance should take in the educational process.

* Although originally prepared as a proposal for a curriculum Dance Concentration in Elementary Education at Temple University (October, 1969), it is presented here is an amplification of the related concepts.

To Develop Personal Identity and a Sense of Worth and Effectiveness

Personal identity and the sense of being "centered" in space and time are dependent upon movement experience. This experience helps in the definition of one's body image which is so important to the developing self-concept. The need for definition continues through life, but is strongest in the growth years. In dancing there is constant attention paid to defining and articulating the body in motion.

Two important attitudes leading to personal development can be described as "I am worthy" and "I am able." These feelings about oneself get started very early in life and are dependent in large part on the child's bodily being, his motor behavior, and the responses he gets from others in relation to it. The dancing experience focuses on the "I," the total being, and its power to feel and move. The teacher of dance has the opportunity not only to help the child clarify himself but also to enhance his capacities and attitudes toward himself.

To Extend Range, Control, and Sensitivity in Movement

Movement represents an important dimension of human sensibility. Its capacity for extension and refinement is nearly limitless, but as with all human potentials it needs cultivation. Refined and articulated movement is as much associated with the civilized man as are vocabulary and grammar.

Extending range and control in movement demands the experiencing of motion above and beyond that encountered in day-to-day action. Strength, flexibility, and endurance grow with the stress of movement mastery. An extension of movement experiences and their patterns of organization and performance brings with it new forms of feeling and meaning. This provides a basis for greater empathy and openness in oneself and in relation to those of different personal and cultural style.

To Develop Sensitivity to the Expression of Feeling in Oneself and Others

Dance is always expressive of the personal realities of those engaged in its performance. Feeling finds its objective form in movement and anyone who desires effective and satisfying human relationships must be sensitive to this medium. Reliance on the formalized and abstracted verbal symbol has time and again led to inappropriate or incomplete understanding.

The medium of dance is movement, bodily gestures, and postures through space and time. Sensitivity to the nuances of movement pattern and meaning is part of the cultivation which dance demands.

To Develop the Powers and Technology to Create and Communicate in Dance

To communicate one's most significant awareness is an aspiration shared by all, but the means to do so effectively are not always found or developed. Along with the other arts, dance is a method, but it has the advantage of initial availability and directness. All one needs to have is oneself, and moving expressively is natural. Even when this process is subdued, as is one of the unfortunate problems of our style of education, it is never obliterated or unavailable.

To be effective, communication of any complexity requires tools and understanding which must be learned. Dance in education should provide for this learning so that dance can serve the individual in his search for understanding.

To Develop Aesthetic Responsiveness and the Bases for Participation and Appreciation of the Dance Arts

Aesthetic awareness and values can be promoted in dance, beginning with the integrity and beauty of human form and function through the complex aesthetic logic of a major dance work. Dance in education should lead the student to the understanding and attitudes which will help him in his grasp and appreciation of all art.

Access to the meanings and joys of art depends upon a background which has fostered appropriate approaches and perspectives. There is a great need for every individual to become aware and to value the aesthetic dimensions of men and the environment so that he can create the best environment for himself and others. There is also a need for significant participation in the arts as a means of understanding the feelings, tempos, and ideas of men.

The Potential Roles and Needs of Dance-Qualified Teachers in Elementary School

Movement and dance need to be an integral part of the elementary school curriculum, but until such time as there are teachers who know how to go about using it thereby providing models for its effective implementation, neither its need nor its usefulness will be understood sufficiently to provoke change or progress.

Without a ready-made curricular tradition in dance, it is expected that qualified personnel in dance would, at this time, primarily play facilitating roles in contributing to existing programs and extending their range of method and content. At the same time they would be working toward developmental programming in dance education.

In his own classes, a teacher with special preparation in dance would be expected to have at his command a medium other than words alone to use for the child's experiencing, communicating, and learning. His movement sensitivity should open new channels for feedback from the child and provide data for insight into the child.

A teacher with special preparation in dance would be expected to provide leadership for movement education, dance, and aesthetic education in the schools as well as for recreational uses of dance. Cooperation among qualified personnel in music, art, and dance should yield a stronger aesthetic dimension to elementary education and provide resources for other teachers. The competent teacher of dance would also enhance the physical education program, strengthening its breadth and availability.

In order to use dance effectively as a means to learning about self, others, movement, dance, art, and concepts important to other fields of study, it is necessary for the teacher to know the nature of dance and its potentials. The teacher must feel free and confident in the medium of movement to be his own resource for its creative use with children. He must have insight into the movement base of dance and the relationship of this base to other movement forms.

Objectives of Area of Specialization Program in Dance

The proposed area of specialization in dance for the elementary school major is based on the following objectives:

1. To develop awareness, sensitivity, and insight into movement and its relationship to growth and behavior.
2. To develop powers of movement analysis and performance especially within the context of dance.
3. To develop insight and personal freedom relative to the creative aspects of movement and dance.
4. To develop a vocabulary of movement material appropriate to various dance forms.
5. To develop perspective with regard to dance as a cultural and aesthetic phenomenon.
6. To develop understandings and skills necessary for designing and conducting movement and dance experiences for the elementary school child.

A PERSONAL PHILOSOPHY
OF PHYSICAL EDUCATION*

Some physical education teachers are content to teach each day's lessons—passing on to a new generation the knowledge of movement, the ability in specific sports, the awareness of body and self which they sense intuitively is important and worthwhile. Others ponder the why—the "what is it all about?"—the "is it worth it all?" of physical education.

Here are the thoughts of some of these physical educators. They approach the question of a personal philosophy differently—their answers are different and indeed contradictory. But they are all worthy of our attention—and may lead one more physical education teacher to the dedication and conviction which will make his teaching make a difference for young people.

* Reprinted with permission from JOHPER, June, 1970.

THE FIVE TRADITIONAL OBJECTIVES OF PHYSICAL EDUCATION

*Anthony A. Annarino**

The perennial state of fermentation and flux existing in physical education is not only obliterating the directional goals of our discipline but is having a deleterious effect upon the effectiveness and morale of the physical education teacher. The time has come for us to review the basics and fundamentals of our discipline. The basic design for a well-balanced and effective program in physical education should be dependent upon the following factors: a philosophy based on sound principles and objectives which are clearly stated, interpreted and weighted.

Although this is an over-simplification of the problem, it merits serious discussion.

PHILOSOPHY

New social trends and forces are causing turbulence in American education today. As a result, changes need to be made. In light of these changes, considerable soul-searching and philosophizing need to be done. In seeking an answer to the "meaning of physical education it is the function of a philosophy of physical education to provide us with this answer.

The meaning and worth, the relation of the facts of everyday living should be of vital concern to everyone of us. Science may provide the intellectual tools for our use; how we use them will depend upon our respective philosophies. Science determines means but philosophy determines ends.

Pragmatism, idealism, realism, existentialism, naturalism—which? The choice is a difficult one. Is it more feasible to adopt a specific school of thought as the philosophy of physical education or is it to our advantage

* Anthony Annarino is associate professor of physical education, Purdue University, Lafayette, Indiana.

to structure a composite system of thought from all the systems? Whichever is selected, the soundness of our philosophy should be determined by the validity of the principles that are selected and incorporated into our system.

OBJECTIVES

Objectives change because they are directly related to changing cultural patterns. Nevertheless, a study of the history of physical education and an evaluation of accumulated evidence tends to indicate the retention of our five traditional objectives—organic, neuromuscular, interpretive, social, and emotional development. Substitute words have been proposed, but for the purposes of standardized conceptualization, let these serve as a working base.

The interpretation of objectives is determined by the available results of sound research. Credence must be given to the nature of our society, the nature of the individual, and the nature of the learning process. It is from the relationships among these phenomena that our interpretation of objectives must be derived. It becomes necessary to define these general terms into more specific understandings.

The weighting of objectives is determined by a number of factors, namely, the growth and developmental stages of the students, teaching styles, teacher competencies, and teacher values. Other criteria for weighting value would be the uniqueness of the objective to the physical education discipline and the degree of objective measureability.

Based on these criteria, the uniqueness of the organic, neuromuscular, and interpretive objectives would be allotted more weighting value and the social and emotional objectives, less value. Too often objectives, their interpretations, and relative value are overstated in relationship to operational programs.

To show these factors in graphic form may help to point up their significance. The chart places physical education content and experiences under the five traditional objectives and gives clues for the selection of curriculum and for the techniques of measurement.

DEVELOPMENTAL OBJECTIVES OF PHYSICAL EDUCATION

ORGANIC

Proper functioning of the body systems so that the individual may adequately meet the demands placed upon him by his environment. A foundation for skill development.

Muscle Strength

The maximum amount of force exerted by a muscle or muscle group.

Muscle Endurance

The ability of a muscle or muscle group to sustain effort for a prolonged period of time.

Cardiovascular Endurance

The capacity of an individual to persist in strenuous activity for periods of some duration. This is dependent upon the combined efficiency of the blood vessels, heart, and lungs.

Flexibility

The range of motion in joints needed to produce efficient movement and minimize injury.

NEUROMUSCULAR

A harmonious functioning of the nervous and muscular systems to produce desired movements.

Locomotor Skills

Walking Skipping Sliding Leaping
Pushing Running Galloping Hopping
Rolling Pulling

Nonlocomotor Skills

Swaying Twisting Shaking Stretching
Bending Handing Stooping

Game Type Fundamental Skills

Striking Catching Kicking Stopping
Throwing Batting Starting Changing
direction

Motor Factors

Accuracy Rhythm Kinesthetic awareness
Power Balance Reaction time Agility

Sport Skills

Soccer Softball Volleyball Wrestling
Track and Field Football Baseball
Basketball Archery Speedball Hockey
Fencing Golf Bowling Tennis

Recreational Skills

Shuffleboard Croquet Deck tennis
Hiking Table tennis Swimming
Horseshoes Boating

INTERPRETIVE

The ability to explore, to discover, to understand, to acquire knowledge, and to make value judgments.

A knowledge of game rules, safety measures, and etiquette.

The use of strategies and techniques involved in organized activities.

A knowledge of how the body functions and its relationship to physical activity.

A development of appreciation for personal performance. The use of judgment related to distance, time, space, force, speed, and direction in the use of activity implements, balls, and self.

An understanding of growth and developmental factors affected by movement.

The ability to solve developmental problems through movement.

SOCIAL

An adjustment to both self and others by an integration of the individual to society and his environment.

The ability to make judgments in a group situation.

Learning to communicate with others.

The ability to exchange and evaluate ideas within a group.

The development of the social phases of personality, attitudes, and values in order to become a functioning member of society.

The development of a sense of belonging and acceptance by society.

The development of positive personality traits.

Learnings for constructive use of leisure time.

A development of attitude that reflects good moral character.

EMOTIONAL

A healthy response to physical activity through a fulfillment of basic needs.

The development of positive reactions in spectatorship and participation through either success or failure.

The release of tension through suitable physical activities.

An outlet for self-expression and creativity.

An appreciation of the aesthetic experiences derived from correlated activities.

The ability to have fun.

10

PHYSICAL EDUCATION SHOULD HELP THE CHILD TO ENHANCE HIS "PHYSICAL ME" CONCEPT—IT SHOULD PREPARE THE HIGH SCHOOL STUDENT FOR HIS PHYSICAL AND RECREATIONAL ADULT LIFE

*Paul R. Varnes**

We need to take a new look at our objectives and procedures in devising and implementing our programs of physical education. The time is long since past that we can legitimately claim the socialization of children as the major objective of instructional time. Children no longer come to us from predominantly rural areas where social contacts with their age group are limited due to distance. Our society is predominantly urban and children are socialized long before the physical education teacher is able to affect them.

We need to point our efforts toward those goals which our programs best accomplish. We need to relegate to secondary consideration those goals which are general goals of the total educational endeavor contributed to, in part, by all curricular areas. We have too much work which needs to be done, too much to contribute as a profession, to be concerned in a major way with incidental results. Socialization goals should properly be left to the interpersonal relationships developed in intramurals and athletics. This is where the personal relations, the sportsmanship objectives, and strong emotional ties should be developed. Intramural and athletic participation, over a long period of time, can develop the strong personal attachments, the sense of cooperation, the esprit de corps which we often refer to as the socialization objectives of physical education. Class time is too short and instructional needs are too great to devote adequate time to team sports competition within the class period to accomplish these goals other than at some shallow level. What then are the proper and foremost goals for physical education instructional classes in our public schools?

At the elementary level, we should seek to remove existing deficiencies in physical fitness and body development through a program of vigorous activity. We should seek to develop the capacity of each child to use his full range of movement and give basic motor experience for use in all learning situations whether they be motor or cognitive. We should provide special motor training to those students who show serious perceptual deprivation. We should develop basic motor skill in the physical activities which are a part of our culture and with which the child will subsequently be involved in his adult life. We should instill concepts related to

* Paul Varnes is chairman, Department of Intramural Athletics and Recreation, University of Florida, Gainesville.

the maintenance of physical health and understanding the physical requirements of the human body. We should constantly look for new ways by which we can help the child to enhance his "physical me" concept.

Physical education is, to a large extent, perceptual motor development for all elementary students at all levels of development. We have come to look at perceptual motor development as development only for deprived children. This is in effect, simply a remedial program and when we have helped a child achieve to a certain level, we consider the job done, but in reality it has only begun. The development of this ability should be a continuous goal.

At the junior high school level, we should continue the program of fitness and body development. We should continue the program of basic skill development. We should provide an extensive exploratory program so that a student becomes familiar with enough activities to choose those with which he wishes to be associated the rest of his life. The activities selected should be dictated, in part at least, by the society in which we exist. The curriculum should be a practical one, one which is useful now and one which will be useful when he is no longer a student.

At the senior high school level we should provide an opportunity for the student to develop a high degree of competence in an activity, or many activities, of his own choice. We should allow for a study in depth of one or more activities of lifetime value as chosen by the student. We cannot justify continuing the short unit approach and the resulting shotgun effect of activity involvement. Exposure is not the desired end product. Competence should be the goal, and it is only too obvious that not all students can gain competence in the same period of time. In such a complicated activity as golf, it is doubtful that any student can gain competence in a six-week unit of instruction and some perhaps cannot gain competence in a year; but a student should be allowed to try for as long as it takes, if this is his choice and if he is highly motivated toward this goal.

If we do not develop competence in our students by the time they graduate from high school, then what can we claim as our objectives? If the development of competence is left to the college program then we have lost over half of our population as far as the effectiveness of our program is concerned. It is the function of the high school program to prepare a student for life. It should be the function of the high school physical education program to prepare students for their physical and recreational life.

THE PROPER FOCUS OF OUR FIELD IS THE STUDY OF SPORT

Betty Lou Murphy*

There has been a great deal of discussion in the profession concerning the nature of the body of knowledge of physical education and whether this body of knowledge can be so structured as to be acceptable as an academic discipline. Some scholars have formulated concepts of physical education based upon the study of human movement. In my opinion, the proper focus of our field is not human movement but rather the study of sport. With sport as the focus, there may be possibilities for disciplinary development acceptance.

There are two characteristics of sport, as opposed to human movement, which provide the basis for considering it worthy of study at any educational level. First, sport provides potential sources of meaning for the individual which are unique and significant and allow for true realization of self. Second, sport is an enduring and important social phenomenon of man.

One of the pervasive meanings inherent in sport appears to be the element of freedom. It is both a freedom "from" and a freedom "for" that one experiences in his participation in sport.

In considering sport as a potential source of meaning, several conditions must be operative if meaning is to be derived from the sport experience. First, the participant must be sufficiently skilled in the fundamentals of the game so that he can experience the game as it is, and use his cognitive abilities relative to the situations that arise, rather than having to master his body movements in the game. An answer to the question, "Just how skilled must the participant be?" is very likely highly dependent upon the individual, and it is doubtful that objective measurement is possible. It would seem that there is more potential for meaning as the level of play increases past this initial point of experiencing the game, and that this is a mandate for the continued pursuit of excellence in sport.

A second condition is that participation must be intrinsically motivated in order that the meaning many be *positively* significant. External motivation or participating in sport as a means to an end removes the authenticity of the experience. Motives directed to other than sport produce significance outside the realm of sport. For example, if one plays tennis for socializing motives, significance is in the socializing, rather than in the playing of tennis. Meaning is inherent in the structure of the sport, but it is only a potential and is dependent upon the individual and his motivation in playing.

* Betty Murphy is assistant professor, East Stroudsburg State College, East Stroudsburg, Pennsylvania.

If this discussion has been sufficiently developed to indicate the potentiality of sport to be truly significant for the individual and allow for realization of self, then it is apparent that curriculum and learning experiences must not only be so conceived and structured as to maintain the integrity of the body of knowledge but must also provide the requisite conditions which make meaning possible.

Historically, physical education found its way into the schools as a medical-remedial program aimed at correcting defects and providing better bodily function. Sports became important as the notion of "education through the physical" was developed, and sports were seen as functional in the physical, social, and psychological development of the individual. As long as physical education is viewed functionally in serving individual developmental needs, it is not likely to establish a discrete body of knowledge nor justify an academically viable position.

I firmly believe that sport is the proper focus and content of the body of knowledge of physical education and that there must be commitment to that body of knowledge.

It seems that physical educators are guilty of perpetuating a "lie" when they say that they are teaching football, basketball, swimming, gymnastics, etc., for physical fitness, social interaction, physiological, or psychological development, when "deep down" they know that they are in physical education because they have found something very meaningful in sport. However, because they have not consciously accepted this realization, they are taking sport out of context in their teaching and, in using sport to serve other ends, are corrupting sport and thus preventing their students from finding significant meaning in it.

When physical education is viewed as sport with potential for significant meaning, then directions for development or for changes in current curricular and teaching practices are somewhat clarified. Common teaching practices of warm-up and fitness exercises in the beginning of the period, followed by review of past skills, and, if there is time, playing the game are irrelevant and detrimental to educational purposes when physical education has a clear focus in sport. Fitness is relevant to participation in the game and can usually be accomplished in relation to the demand of the skills. New skills are taught only as the level of play dictates the need for their introduction, not as a matter of course.

The focus of teaching must be on developing the ability to *play the game* at ever-increasing levels of complexity and skill. The key is found in the playing of the game—not just the development of skills. The stress from the beginning of each sports unit should include the realization by the students of what the game requires and then providing direction toward developing those skills and abilities so that they can better play the game.

The curriculum must provide opportunity for the game to be experienced in a holistic manner; i.e., with scoring, equitable or at least similar time segments, and all the other requirements which make the game the game and which are so often deleted in class play. There should be provision for the formation of stable teams to allow students to develop a feeling of team membership. This feeling is not developed when team composition is changed each time the game is played; the player has to have the opportunity to develop the sense that his "stake" is in his team and that the team depends on him. And all students must be given an opportunity to pursue the game to the highest level at which they can participate in it.

Some implications for curriculum derived from the above might include grouping of students by ability, more flexible scheduling within the school and within the physical education program, and more extensive instructional, intramural, and varsity programs.

The knowledge that sport is meaningful and can be more or less so depending upon the individual implies that students be given the opportunity to make choices. Following an introductory period in which students are exposed to numerous sports, provision should be made for students to pursue in depth those sports which are most meaningful to them. The introductory period might be concluded at some point in junior high school or following ninth grade; much depends upon the nature of the students' previous experiences. When the choice is open to students, the possibility for "no choice" is also one which must be considered, for some students may not find any activity meaningful.

An additional implication of physical education based upon sport is the specialization of teachers in a limited number of sports. One cannot be a master of all the possible sports that might appear in a school program, and teaching in this type of program requires not only mastery by the teacher but also intense interest. How can students become enthusiastic about anything which is presented by someone who has minimal knowledge, insight, and consequently little excitement? The more important question about the unknowledgeable teacher is how material or experiences are selected, at all; that is, the intelligent planning of learning depends on sophisticated knowledge of the whole. Thus specialization and the possibility of team teaching or other systems to make wisest use of available faculty must be another factor to consider.

A summary of current physical education programs across the United States would reveal that sport already composes the major portion of our programs. However, in few cases is sport viewed by physical educators in the manner suggested, and most often graduates of our instructional programs have not found any significant meaning in their experience. Is it not time to focus our teaching on the content of our program and accept its great potential contribution to human life instead of focusing on disparate individual needs and *using* our field in haphazard and largely unsuccessful attempts to meet these needs? Each physical educator holds the answer within his experience and choice of profession.

PHYSICAL EDUCATION IS A FOUNDATION FOR THE DEVELOPMENT OF DEMOCRATIC LIVING IN AMERICAN LIFE. IT DEVELOPS COMPETENCIES OF FUTURE CITIZENS

Edward H. Kozloff*

Physical education has evolved from strict disciplinary drill situations to a pupil involvement, problem-solving, discovery approach and has claimed to be a vital part of the American educational system. Perhaps today more than ever before, physical education can claim added respectability as a foundation for the development of democracy and democratic living in American life. Although all subjects should contribute in one way or another to the American "ideal," perhaps no other field has as inherent an opportunity for instilling democratic principles as does physical education.

The list of the objectives of a democratic society varies with each writer. Although there are differences, the lists all rest on a deep conviction of the uniqueness, dignity, and worth of the individual person; responsibility for one's own actions; concern for the welfare of others; belief in cooperative action; and belief that government is controlled by the citizens for the good of all and is not a value or end in itself. Let us elaborate on physical education's specific contributions to these tenets of democracy.

First, there is the belief that physical education lends itself to the supreme importance of the individual. All physical education programs should allow each participant an opportunity to succeed or fail on his own ability. While the team may carry a nonachiever for a while, the individual worth of the participant will make or break him in physical education. When a pass is thrown to a teammate, all members of the team will work to complete it. In physical education and athletics, one does not give the wealthiest boy the advantage. The race goes to the swiftest, not the richest. Status levels soon become valueless in the realm of physical education.

Moral responsibility, a second value, is an outgrowth of the first. Since each participant represents the most important part of the physical education program, he also has an obligation for the responsibility of his own actions. Physical education contributes to this attribute by progressively increasing the delegation of responsibility both in making and accepting the consequences of decisions. The successful physical education program will allow the student to gradually increase in the decision-making process as he progresses upward through the school system. As

* Edward Kozloff is head, Health and Physical Education Department at Beer Junior High School in Warren, Michigan.

the pupil participates in activities he realizes that his decisions often affect the outcome of the game. Thus, there is a striving to make the correct decision, and this leads to the development of moral responsibility.

A third factor in a successful democratic situation involves the necessity of cooperation for the common good. One often observes teammates contributing to each other's success. The rare individual who does not participate in a team effort is soon overshadowed by others who are willing to "pass the ball off," despite having a clear shot themselves, if a teammate is in a better scoring position. In athletics, the "superstar" will often forego his favorite event in order to participate in two or three events for the good of the team. The unselfishness inherent in a good physical education program develops this much-needed trait of cooperation for the common good in our highly materialistic society.

A high regard for excellence is a necessity in a democracy. Physical education offers its participants many avenues through which success can be achieved. There is an activity available for all somatotypes. The joy expressed by a student who has improved his best effort in a particular event supports the essence of excellence. In a world of uncertainties, the measurable aspects of physical education allow the individual a special area in which he may improve and strive for superiority.

A final value to be considered is the pursuit of happiness. The truly "happy" life is not founded upon the gratification of immediate pleasures. At times, sacrifice is necessary immediately for happiness in the future. Success in many avenues of physical education necessitates disciplining oneself and adapting to a training schedule which, at times, may be unpleasant. However, the long-range goals and future happiness make the struggle worthwhile. Physical education promotes the acquisition of happiness through which the more profound goals of life will be achieved.

In a sophisticated society, it is often easy to lose sight of the true meaning of life and neglect the Socratic contention that "the unexamined life is not worth living." During the late 1940s, the literature concerning democracy was voluminous. Let us hope the lack of recent writings in this area does not reflect the actual state of the American democratic ideal. The field of physical education can do much to develop the future competency of our citizens. By looking in retrospect at the ideals of democracy, let us step forward into the 1970s with renewed vigor for ourselves, for physical education, and for the nation.

FANTASTICALLY EXCITING AND WORTHWHILE EDUCATIONAL EXPERIENCE

*Charles Schmidt**

To establish any personal philosophy of physical education, one must first consider all the meaningful experiences of a lifetime that constitute his purpose of existence. One cannot separate his personal philosophical position from how he views his profession. No matter how one teaches physical education, viewpoints and attitudes will be communicated to his students. Basically we never get that far outside ourselves (even with much training) and what we communicate to students are basically our own attitudes on life.

A second point is how much should one say if some of his thoughts are radical enough to be actually offensive to the established profession. The view I take is that the popular cliché, "tell it like it is," is acceptable. Therefore, what follows are thoughts, fragmented ones to be sure, on a topic I am much concerned with and now am finally getting a chance to put down on paper. This paper is at best only a framework of a flexible personal philosophy of physical education.

As I see it, physical education could be a fantastically exciting, worthwhile educational experience instead of what it is—for the most part, a dull meaningless collection of sports skills. Instead of functioning as an educational guide to the attainment of one's realized physical self, it is nothing more than a tool used for maintaining the status quo of society as most education is. I am an advocate of the idealist life philosophy and believe that education should exist to help man in the development of his objective reason as a means of returning to his once pure state as a reflection of the absolute.

History is the defense of my position. Throughout history man is marked by his sense of striving toward some goal. Years ago learning sports skills was a goal considered important in physical education, this goal does not meet modern needs. There are some progressive thinkers in the field who are looking at physical education in terms of the social and psychological implications as well as the health benefits derived from the subject area. The problem I find even for the progressive thinkers is that they have lost the true perspective of the term "physical education" in a hodge-podge of meaningless research, testing, shooting baskets, and sweatsocks. It seems that no matter what one expects out of physical education the approach is always the same—basic learning of sports skills.

* Charles Schmidt is a senior in physical education at New York University. (Since the time of this article, Charles Schmidt has graduated and is teaching in Suffolk County, New York.)

This failure to reevaluate the approach to physical education in terms of the needs of the times is my main criticism of the field.

While I believe modern physical education should be rooted in the idealist thought, it should be flexible enough to appreciate the values in the other philosophies. It is one's duty to enjoy nature as the naturalists say; one should know how to survive well as the realist points out; and a person without social intelligence is a sham person as maintained by the pragmatist; but of main concern to all should be the striving toward the absolute through the facilities of the mind. Obviously by my philosophical position I place physical education lower on the education ladder, but I do see its great importance in the picture of what the total man should be through learning through his body. Physical education does not even come close to this.

While learning sports skills does have some importance, consider the greater sphere of the words "physical education" and you come up with topics such as conditioning, grooming, sex information, aesthetics, movement, recreational activities, first aid, social sports knowledge, and self-discipline. All these activities should be used as guides to a revised program of physical education that would be truly education of the physical for the ultimate purpose of physical self-knowledge. A "total" learning of physical experience is, as I see it, clearly necessary for developing the mind's self-awareness.

How does one go about guiding toward physical self-awareness? A theory without a method of practice is meaningless. The key to mastery of any subject is the importance or concern we place on a subject area. How important can a subject area be in which the subject and the teachers of that subject cannot relate to the students? Why should a student want to be guided toward optimum physical self-awareness if his guide only knows how to teach sports, has a pot belly, wears a crew cut, and basically has such a misconception of what a male role is that he considers dancing and art only for sissies.

Of course, in my stereotype I exaggerate what a physical educator should not be, but if one looks hard enough an occasional "dull jock" can be found. To offset this image the profession first has to make itself desirable to the student through its instructors. If the late Bobby Kennedy, Bishop F. J. Scheen, Joe Namath, or Richard Harris were physical education teachers, students would easily identify with their masculine image and guide themselves toward what is desirable in the way of their own physical being. Realizing that not every one is a Namath and that he probably could not teach very well, the point I am making is that all physical education teachers have as their first obligation the presentation of themselves as examples of what a desirable modern physical person should be.

The second obligation of a physical education teacher is to develop a fine sensitivity to the human needs of people. Basically the sensitivity has to already be there or a person has no business being in education, but I feel that it can be developed further through study of the social sciences and the humanities. These studies should replace the majority of the present skill courses found in the required physical education training curriculum for teachers.

As far as the physical education programs on the school levels go, this field has a great advantage over every other form of study. People are made to move. Movement provides a release for stored up psychic energy which leads to bodily discomfort if not displaced. I find it strange that a subject that caters to our bodily functioning is soon learned to be disliked by a vast majority of students. As I see it, the only way for physical education to survive is by first ridding itself of the trivia in the field and then returning to educating the physical as the subject maintains it does.

PHYSICAL EDUCATION'S PRINCIPAL EMPHASIS IS UPON BUILDING A FIT AMERICA

M. Evelyn Triplett*

A question receiving great scrutiny in the past few years has been that of the proper role of physical education—and other so-called "frill" subjects—in the overall educational curriculum. Some of the problem has stemmed from the confusing array of opinions expressed. Educators from other disciplines as well as school administrators have raised penetrating questions. Criticisms have been leveled and accusations made by well-known scientists, by specialists in other fields, and by the lay public as well. Physical fitness, on the other hand, has been considered of sufficient importance that it has been an issue in every White House Conference.

One factor involved in the problem seems to be some confusion in terminology. The very term *physical education* itself probably needs clarification, since erroneous definitions of physical education range from calisthenics and muscle building on the one hand to athletics on the other. Physical education cannot properly be considered an ornamental frill tacked on to the school program but is rather a vital part of education as a whole. The term *fitness* is more commonly applied to the physical development areas alone, but we in physical education accept a concept of total fitness, implying the mental, emotional, social, and spiritual as well as the physical well-being of the individual. Underlying this view is the basic educational concern for the development of the whole child. We believe that the long overdue and greatly needed concern for more challenging and more effective academic experiences for our youth need not and should not lessen the importance of educational experiences in other areas as well.

In evaluating the plethora of facts, opinions, and suggestions concerning the importance of physical education as well as the place it should hold in education as a whole, certain current challenges and conditions come into focus. These should be apparent not only to those in physical education but also to all those involved in the re-examination and the revitalization of our entire educational pattern.

For example, we are aware that American knowhow and technological advancement have made this largely a pushbutton era. Our many labor-saving devices are causing us to lead an increasingly sedentary life. In these times life in the United States characteristically lacks the physical expenditures so necessary to our earlier frontier existence. In our large

* M. Evelyn Triplett is associate professor of health, physical education, and recreation, Kansas State College, Pittsburg. (Since the time of this article M. Evelyn Triplett has been promoted to Professor.)

cities, lack of space makes free play of children almost impossible. Readily available transportation makes even walking almost a lost art, something we seem to avoid at all costs. The mechanical devices we have developed in most job areas have reduced to a minimum the output of physical energy. In their after-school play hours children are very often found in front of the television set instead of engaging in the vigorous physical activities which their young bodies need. Paradoxically enough, as we view these changes, we realize that the physical needs of the human body at the various ages have *not* changed.

In these times, more people have more leisure than they have ever had before. The eighty-hour work week has given way to the forty-hour work week; there is now talk about a three-day work week. The age of retirement has been lowered from that age when the individual could no longer do the work to the age of 60 or 65 regardless of ability to do the work and there is now talk of enforced retirement at age 55. Leisure activities have not only become big business in America but also a source of some status. It should be noted that the skills basic to leisure activities of all types do not develop in and of themselves but are the result of constructive guidance in the use of leisure time. Sometimes it is discouraging and frustrating for those of us in physical education to realize that some of the most vociferous doubters of the value of physical education are the first to be on the golf course.

As industrialization and urbanization tend to make emotional stability more difficult to maintain, we find mental illness definitely on the increase. Our technological world is full of noise and confusion and distraction. We are in constant competition not only for salary and status but also for what is variously described as "the good life." For many of us, relaxation and the time to enjoy life seem increasingly hard to achieve. Tension and anxiety seem to be rather constant companions. Yet we recognize that to get the most out of life we must all find means of freeing ourselves from hate and worry and fear, of learning to get along with others, of finding appropriate outlets for self-expression.

In these times there is mounting awareness on the part of Americans that in the Cold War we are often compared negatively with Russia and Communist China in our concern for, our expenditures for, and our success in various sports activities. At a time when many persons in the United States are looking at physical education as an expendable frill or an unnecessary expense, Russia has developed a special organization to involve all Russians of all ages in regular sports activities. Particular emphasis is given to youth.

It is an accepted fact that individual physical vigor and strength are basic to national welfare. If this fact is true in so-called normal times, it is doubly so in this space age of ours. It is awesome to realize that the children of today will be the astronauts of tomorrow. According to the schedule of space events, within the next decade or so many of today's children will be manning space stations and traveling to other planets. These predicted experiences place great responsibility on those of us who are concerned with the education of children. Will they be adequately and appropriately trained for the mental and physical demands made upon them? We as adults must be aware that in these rapidly changing times the security and leadership status of the United States will be affected by the accumulated mental and physical skills which we represent. Furthermore, we cannot forget that youth characteristically looks to the adult for leadership and example.

The question then, it seems to me, which we as educators should be raising is how best to improve the overall fitness of our people, to develop the necessary competencies in all areas. Those in the field of physical education believe that physical education activities are not only an important part of the total educational program but are *essential* to it.

Under what basic principles does the discipline of physical education believe it can function most effectively in building and maintaining fitness?

1. To meet the fitness needs of our youth, physical education should begin in the elementary school and such instruction should be conducted by personnel trained to understand and appreciate the physical and maturation characteristics and needs of young children at various ages.

2. To meet the fitness needs of our youth, there should be no cutoff time, no early terminal point, for the program of physical education activities. Continuity of training should function until the student has reached his terminal education, whether this is graduation from high school or college.

3. To meet the fitness needs of our youth, more attention should be given to the development of social and emotional skills through educational experiences.

4. To meet the fitness needs of our youth, physical education should be broad enough to serve all skill levels. The program should provide an instructional aspect, an intramural aspect, and an interscholastic aspect, and the contribution of all three approaches should be recognized.

5. To meet the fitness needs of our youth, the physical education program should contain a broad variety of activity experiences.

6. To meet the fitness needs of our youth, the program must be viewed with a long-range perspective. To be effective, the program must instill in youth an appreciation of the importance of physical fitness, it must create in youth a desire to maintain physical fitness, and it must teach them the skills necessary for the continuation of physical activities throughout their adult years.

It has been said that the purpose of education is to develop the potentiality of each individual in all phases of life. Primarily and characteristically we have in the past concerned ourselves more with the responsibility of promoting intellectual growth. This has been reflected in our curricular requirements among the various disciplines. We must not lose sight of the fact, however, that the mind and body cannot properly be separated. The body may be said to furnish the climate in which the intellect grows and flourishes. Within this context, it is apparent that physical education plays an important role in the total educational experiences of today. Our principal emphasis is upon building a fit America—socially, emotionally, mentally, morally, and physically.

The immensity of education's task is apparent. Obviously no one discipline can or should be expected to shoulder the responsibility alone. Neither should any discipline be excluded or educational lopsidedness may be the result. To achieve the ultimate in education for the atomic and space age will necessitate the combined efforts of all disciplines. Truly then, as we in physical education view our responsibilities to the youth of America, it may be said, " 'tis neither this nor that but both and more."

INDEX

(Page numbers followed by n, e.g. 109n, indicate references in footnotes)